·Final Gig·

Also by George Eells

THE LIFE THAT LATE HE LED:
A Biography of Cole Porter (1967)

HEDDA AND LOUELLA (1972)

GINGER, LORETTA, AND IRENE WHO? (1976)

MERMAN (1978)
by Ethel Merman with George Eells

HIGH TIMES, HARD TIMES (1981)
by Anita O'Day with George Eells

MAE WEST: *A Biography* (1982)
by George Eells with Stanley Musgrove

ROBERT MITCHUM (1985)

·Final Gig·
The Man Behind the Murder
George Eells

Harcourt Brace Jovanovich, Publishers

San Diego · New York · London

Requests for permission to make copies of any part of
the work should be mailed to: Permissions Department,
Harcourt Brace Jovanovich, Publishers, 8th Floor, Orlando, Florida 32887.

Library of Congress Cataloging-in-Publication Data
Eells, George.
Final Gig: the man behind the murder/George Eells.
p.   cm.
Includes index.
ISBN 0-15-130986-8
1. Young, Gig, 1913–1978. 2. Motion picture actors and actresses—
United States—Biography. I. Title.
PN2287.Y58E36   1991
791.43′028′092—dc20   91-455 [B]

Designed by Camilla Filancia
Printed in the United States of America
First edition   A B C D E

IN

MEMORY OF

GLORIA SAFIER:

MY AGENT,

MY FRIEND

Contents

PART TWO

"You don't know what hell there is in life, do you?"

Acknowledgments

I wish to express my gratitude to the following people who assisted me in creating this book—as well as to a few who for their own reasons wish to remain anonymous.

First and foremost, I want to thank Gig's sister, Genevieve Barr Merry; Kim's mother, Rosemary Schmidt; and Kim's sister, Irmi Schmidt Tatter, without whose reminiscences, letters, and memorabilia much important material would have been lost.

I am also indebted to Beverly Linet for urging me to undertake this project and to persevere; to Leonore Silvian for buoying up my sometimes flagging spirits; and to Patrick Pacheco, not only for his incisive interviews with Kim's Hong Kong cohorts (Russell and Hai-Tien Jones, Ted

Thomas, Harry Rolnick, Geoffrey and Sonia Archer, Jacques Schmidt, Sol Lockhart, Andrew Simpson, Peter Bennett, and Russell Cawthorne) but also for investing endless hours in helping refocus this book.

For their help in gaining access to New York police files and/or for personal interviews I thank Police Lieutenant Richard Gallagher (ret.), Detective Richard Chartrand, Sergeant Peter Sweeney, attorney Tom Doepfner, Eneeta McCalister, and Herbert Jaffe.

Thanks are also due journalists Jim Meyer, Liz Smith, Radie Harris, Dominick Dunne, David Ehrenstein, Elaine Daspin, George Rush, Bill Reed, Jim Bacon, Rona Barrett, Kevin Thomas, Robin Little, Richard Lamparski, Doug McClelland, Lee Israel, Michael Buckley, and Bob Thomas.

I want to express my gratitude to staff members of the St. Cloud *Daily Journal* and the St. Cloud *Daily Times;* S. Owen Linblad of *Escape* magazine; Richard Coe, drama critic emeritus of the *Washington Post;* W. E. Pretzer, Technical High School, St. Cloud, and Barbara Williams, McKinley High School, Washington, D.C.; John Decker of the Stearns County Historical Society, St. Cloud; Katherine Y. Armitage of the Haywood County Public Library, St. Cloud; Sara Magee of the Great River Regional Library, St. Cloud; Charles G. Howell, registrar of deeds, Haywood County Courthouse, St. Cloud; the staffs of the Billy Rose Theatre Collection, Lincoln Center, Manhattan, and the Library of the Academy of Motion Picture Arts and Sciences; the Waynesville, N.C., Chamber of Commerce; Leith Adams of USC's Doheny Library, Special Collections; attorneys Harvey Bagg, Jr., and Edward Fogel of New York and Irving Apple of Los Angeles.

The account of Gig and Kim's final days is made much richer through the cooperation of Panda Hoffman, Ronald Alexander, Constas Matsoukas, John Clark, Muriel Fleits, Bert Knapp, Roz Starr, Anita Starr, Sy Presten, David Meyer,

Robert Whitehead, Arthur Miller, and Patrick Shields. In addition to help from Kim's mother and sister, valuable insights were provided by Judy Washington Powell, Sanae Yamazaki, Jovi Couldrey, and Elliot Bass.

For medical background I owe thanks to Dr. Stanley J. Wittenberg, Dr. Eugene Landy, and Dr. Eugene Vickery. Firsthand information on LSD therapy at the Hollywood Hospital in Vancouver, B.C., was given by Mrs. Al Hubbard and Bill Darling, to supplement secondhand accounts from Gig's intimates.

Among those who contributed recollections of the early Hollywood years, I am grateful to William Orr; Henry Brandon; Rex Everhart; Russell Gold; Rose Freeman; John Alvin; Loretta Bowman (County Clerk, Las Vegas, Nevada); Susan Naulty, curator of the Pasadena Playhouse Archives at the Huntington Library, Pasadena, California; and Diane Alexander, author of *Playhouse,* a history of the Pasadena Playhouse.

Subsequent Hollywood memories were generously provided by Frank Liberman, Viveca Lindfors, Elizabeth Fraser, Bob William, Benson Fong, Peter Brook, Jayne Meadows, Mae Einfeld, William Bakewell, Irving Rapper, Jean Sullivan, Audrey Baer Ourette, Robert and Sue Douglas, Dania Forest, Phyllis Thaxter, and Ivan Goff. Also by Martin Baum, Tom Korman, Wilt Melnick, Helena Sterling, Robert Webber, Zetta Castle, Meg Young, Gary Stevens, Jim Dunsford, Robert Wise, Sally Kellerman, Robert and Marilynn Horton, Michael Hertzberg, Lenny Dunne, Colleen Camp, Rupert Allen, Cy Howard, James Gallagher, Kirk Crivello, Rose Freeman, Skye Aubrey, Jay Bernstein, Elaine Young, Harriette Vine Douglas, Peggy Demein, Sue Hann, Robert Stephens, and Tom McDermott.

Among those who shared recollections of Gig's New York years were Elaine Stritch, Sherry Britton, Betsy von Furstenberg, Howard Erskine, William Harbach, Charles Forsythe,

Lawrence Roman, Sharman Douglas, Guy Vincent, Archer King, Bert Knapp, Joanne Jacobson, Patrick Shields, Arnold Saint-Subber, Sandra Church, Mike Hall, Leslie Cutler, Jack Eddleman, T. Edward Hambleton, Dong Kingman, Robert Whitehead, Leon Quain, and Marilyn Miller.

Major sources for the account of Gig's attempt to play James Tyrone in *Long Day's Journey into Night* were Joanna Helming and David Feigelson.

I am especially grateful to Eddie Jaffe for getting this project rolling and for his continued support; to the original editor, Daphne Merkin, the eventual editor, Claire Wachtel, and their assistant, Ruth Greenstein, as well as to agent Connie Clausen.

Finally, I want to thank friends who contributed in various ways. These include John Mitchell, Lowell and Nancy Swortzell, Harriette Van Horne, Natalie Schafer, Nellie McCaslin, Daty Healy, Jean White, Aurand Harris, Louis Scott, Carol Britton, Robert Slatzer, Millie Vickery, Hugh White, Robert Ullman, Earl Clark, Stan West, Noble "Kid" Chissell, Alvista Perkins, Allison Gold, Samuel Stark, and Richard Segel.

Author's Note

I was only one of many who were stunned and who continued to be mystified by the murder at the Osborne. Whispers about what really happened in apartment 1BB, as opposed to the official version, continue to circulate to this day. There were rumors of a double murder. Of a suicide pact. Word that the Young folders were in the CUPPI (Circumstances Undetermined Pending Police Investigation) File fed speculation. As columnist James Bacon, among others, wrote, the case seemed destined to take its place as "a Sunday supplement perennial," along with the cases of Thelma Todd, William Desmond Taylor, Jean Harlow–Paul Bern, and Sal Mineo.

Yet almost a decade elapsed between the time I first

became intrigued by the mystery of Gig and Kim Young's violent deaths and the time I actually began this book. The reason for the delay was that cursory investigation indicated little material to draw upon. The tragedy of Gig's death had left his grief-stricken sister (and chief heir) too distraught to travel from her Minneapolis home to New York—much less to oversee the emotional task of sorting out his effects. She designated others to take charge of the disposal of his possessions. Those that had not been sold or donated to the Salvation Army had unfortunately been set out to be hauled away as trash. Boxes and boxes of letters, personal papers, press clippings, photos, and audiotape cassettes—the minutiae of a lived life—were consigned to oblivion.

Most frustrating was the loss of the audiocassettes. As tape recorders had become smaller and more sophisticated—and Gig more paranoid—he took to taping everything from his fourth wife's personal phone calls to grocery orders. And during the final year of his life, he undertook a bastardized form of analysis under the direction of his voice teacher–guru, in which, it was rumored, Gig dwelt on a lifetime of traumas and triumphs—social, sexual, and professional. For a biographer, locating them would have been comparable to a treasure hunter's finding markers leading to the Flying Dutchman mine.

One friend of Gig's insisted these tapes were being held by the New York City Police Department. I secured a letter from Gig's sister, requesting that they grant me access to evidence in their possession. No tapes surfaced.

Then, during an interview I conducted with an acquaintance of Kim and Gig's, I was casually asked if I'd be interested in listening to some of Gig's tapes. I masked my excitement and nonchalantly accepted the offer. It was suggested that I play them at home. Only a few—a painful recital of Gig's many health problems and an equally painful and much more devastating description of his firing from Mel Brooks's *Blazing Saddles*—proved pertinent. But these tapes gave me hope that the analytical tapes had survived.

Time proved my hunch correct. After a couple of squibs about my project appeared in New York tabloids, I received a phone call from someone who offered to turn over some of Gig's tapes. He wanted no money. His only stipulation was a guarantee of anonymity. We made an appointment for lunch. He showed up—without the tapes. He had misplaced them, he said. I suspected I'd hear no more from him, but about ten days later he called back. Again we met, and this time he handed over several cassettes.

Two or three tapes confirmed my fears: they recorded voice lessons, as had several in the first batch. Then I put in another tape, and the hairs on the back of my neck stood up as I heard Gig's velvety voice ruminating over his past—delivering prepared material, free associating, skipping back and forth over the troubled periods of his life. Occasionally the voice of his vocal coach would interrupt to flatter, browbeat, or cajole. Even as I empathized with Gig, I confess I felt elation at having in my possession something better than an interview. Here was Gig's self-search—an attempt to reach an understanding of himself that he hoped would lead to a settlement of the war that raged within him.

I could now write the book.

·Part One·

*"You can't tell about people
from the outside. . . ."*

Prologue: The End

On October 19, 1978, between 2:30 and 3:30 P.M., Constas Matsoukas, the manager of the Osborne, was enjoying his lunch break in his second-floor apartment when he heard two sharp reports. Since the Osborne—a stately Victorian building—is located on the busy corner of Fifty-seventh Street and Seventh Avenue in New York, noise is not unusual. Even so, the short, chubby Greek prided himself on having become so familiar with the premises that he could identify almost any sound emanating from the site.

The two reports puzzled him, though. For a moment he thought they were gunshots. Then he recalled he had instructed the handyman to break up some windows that were to be discarded. Matsoukas concluded that those were the sounds he had heard.

Returning to duty around 3:30, the manager passed through the lobby on his way to his office in the basement. As he approached apartment 1BB, he was irritated to see that a brown-bagged delivery from the Grenoble market had been left outside the door. It struck Matsoukas as odd, since the occupants—the sixty-four-year-old Academy Award–winning actor Gig Young and his bride of three weeks, thirty-one-year-old Kim—had recently been spending most of their time at home. Also, it was unlike Young, a meticulous tenant, to order perishables—milk and lettuce—when he was not going to be home to refrigerate them.

Matsoukas checked with doormen Brendan DeLaney and John Fornos, neither of whom had seen either of the Youngs that day. He rang the apartment on the house phone. No response. Concerned, he instructed the doormen to continue to knock and phone.

By 5:30 P.M., Matsoukas was beginning to suspect that the sharp reports he had heard were neither windows being demolished nor an automobile backfiring, but indeed gunshots, which came from 1BB. When Mike Stemen, the president of the Osborne's cooperative association, arrived home, Matsoukas told him about the two bags of unclaimed groceries. He also reported that so far as he could determine, neither Gig nor Kim had left the apartment, and no one had visited them. In fact, the only communication from them seemed to have come midmorning, when Gig called the doorman to inquire about weather conditions, and around noon, when Kim had phoned in her grocery order.

Stemen suggested that Matsoukas use his passkey to investigate the Young apartment. Matsoukas declined. When the president urged that they take a chance on invading the

Youngs' privacy, Matsoukas handed him the key. Reluctant to use it, the president decided that perhaps it would be wiser to go on to his apartment to plan their next move.

On the way, Matsoukas volunteered, "Maybe all these things are my fantasy, but if those noises I heard were shots, then it's possible there's someone in there with a gun. I'm not going to take a chance."

At that point, Stemen said, "Let's call the police."

At 7:25 P.M., police officers converged outside the Osborne, at 205 West 57th Street, and the agitated manager began repeating his suspicions. As the group hurried through the lobby to the door of 1BB, Matsoukas told the officers that the only other access points were two heavily barred windows that opened onto a light well. Two men were immediately sent to check the windows.

Meanwhile, two more policemen politely cleared the lobby of curious residents. Another group rang the bell and pounded on the door of 1BB. Guns drawn, they demanded that anyone inside come out with hands over his head. There was no response.

The uniformed officers were aware of their limited options. This was the apartment of a man of fame and, presumably, of wealth. No kicking in the door here. The policemen requested a key.

Matsoukas handed over the passkey. Then he stepped back.

An officer again shouted the demand to open up. No answer. He quietly inserted the key in the lock. Pushing the door open, he stepped out of the range of fire.

The air smelled faintly acrid from recently applied paint; a check made out to the painter Efriodinas Polyritis stood on a table near the entrance. The apartment, with its tasteful mixture of bamboo, antique, and Oriental furnishings, looked undisturbed.

Guns drawn, the policemen moved cautiously around the five-room apartment, scanning the dimly lit interior for any sign of movement. The first four rooms—kitchen, sitting room, den, and loft (the latter overlooking the sitting room)—were clean and neat. But as they moved toward the bedroom, the police were confronted with a grisly sight. Light, spilling in from the adjacent bathroom, caught two fully clothed bodies lying on the floor. They were facing in opposite directions.

The blond woman lay on her back. The dim light hit her made-up face, grotesquely exaggerating her features. She wore a long-sleeved green velour blouse, gray slacks, and expensive brown leather boots. There was jewelry: a gold chain around her neck, rings on her fingers, and a clip earring on her left ear. Its mate lay hidden beneath her body. Around her head, almost like a red halo, was a pool of blood. It had drained from the single bullet hole at the base of her skull. She was Kim Young, Gig Young's recent bride.

Lying close by was Young himself. In life, his familiar crooked smile and laugh-crinkled yet sad eyes would have been recognizable to millions of film and television viewers. But his face was now buried in the blood-soaked carpeting. Blood also stained his red-white-and-blue-checked shirt and pearl-gray trousers. Around his neck was a tie he never got around to knotting. His right hand clenched a .38-caliber snub-nosed Smith & Wesson pistol. The bullet had entered through his mouth.

In quick succession, Detectives Richard Chartrand and Louis Monaco, Lieutenant Richard Gallagher, and Chief Duffy of the Third Homicide Zone arrived at the death scene. Obviously Gig's drawing power was still strong.

Chief Duffy planted himself on the couch in the sitting room. The investigation swirled around him, but Duffy had his own priorities. "Make sure you lock up that silk screen—that's expensive," he called out. The men, busy taking fingerprints, photographing the premises, and conducting their search, interrupted their routine to satisfy the chief.

Chartrand, who had just opened a closet door, was startled to see a fleece-lined gun case on an upper shelf. Inside it was a box of .38-caliber shells—three hundred fifty hollow-nosed bullets, or forty-five rounds.

"Voucher and lock up the jade," Duffy called, still concerned about the valuables.

Chartrand concentrated on looking for liquor and drugs. He was surprised to find only two bottles—one of sherry, the other a California red. No hard liquor. Drugs? Nothing except seven Oxazepam pills and approximately one hundred bottles of vitamins of every description. Despite the grim circumstances, he smiled. A sixty-four-year-old man trying to keep up with his thirty-one-year-old bride.

"Secure that Academy Award," Duffy warned. "Don't want that missing."

The men wanted to ask the chief to move so they could search the area where he was sitting—but no one had the nerve. They worked around him. Lying on the desk in the sitting room was an appointment diary. Although this was October 19, the diary was open to September 27. On that page, Gig had recorded: "We were married today." It was the final entry, almost as if Gig was implying that on that day the world had stopped.

Screenwriter Panda Hoffman was sitting on the bed in a grim motel room in Sedona, Arizona, concerned about her daughter's unhappiness with the private school she was attending. Suddenly the phone rang. Panda was startled to hear Robert Stack's voice.

"Panda, are you sitting down?" he asked.

She assured him she was.

Stack said, "This call . . . I wanted to reach you before you heard it on television." Then he told her Gig Young had shot himself and his wife. Both were dead. Panda was shocked. She had met Kim only a few weeks before, in Edmonton, Canada, where Gig had been appearing in a play. He and Kim had seemed so much in love, so happy.

Panda sat stunned, recalling the last time she had seen her old friend Gig. In a restaurant in Edmonton, Gig and Panda had detached themselves from the group they were with to catch up on what had been happening since they had last been together. When Panda mentioned that during one bleak period she had felt suicidal, Gig had quickly cautioned she must never think like that. Life, he said, was too sweet ever to consider ending it.

"Oh, come on, Gig," Panda interrupted. "You've been there."

He responded as if she had slapped him. "How did you know that? Who told you?"

"Nobody told me. When you've been there, you recognize it in somebody else."

He grabbed her arm so hard that it brought tears to her eyes. He dried up, couldn't speak.

As she sat in the Sedona motel, all Panda could think of was that Gig couldn't have done it. "I was so in shock then because I believed he could kill himself, but I just knew there was no way he could have killed that girl," she said years later. Mulling it over, she decided that no matter how strongly the facts might point to another conclusion, she would always believe it was an accident. Gig was probably playing around with one of the pistols, with Kim begging him to put it away. He laughed. Said it was unloaded. "I know guns," he probably said, pulling the trigger. The bullet hit her as she was walking away.

Panda wondered whether it had been a few seconds or an hour before he did away with himself. She hoped and prayed that it was seconds, because of the anguish Gig would have suffered at taking anyone's life, let alone that of the woman he loved. She wondered whether she should call anyone and pass on the awful news. Whom would she call? She decided to remain silent.

Twelve years later, she still believes her scenario. It still obsesses her.

On the day after the bodies had been discovered at the Osborne, the telephone rang in Detective Chartrand's office. On the wire was a woman with a fluty voice who identified herself as Harriette Vine Douglas.

"I was the lady in Gig Young's life for the past thirteen years," she announced.

She went on to say that she was calling from Beverly Hills and was a former dancer and actress. "I've been in show business all my life," she told Chartrand. "I've known the top, I've known the dregs. I've known them all, but this man was special. And I loved every rotten corpuscle in his body." She burst into tears.

Chartrand waited patiently for her to pull herself together. Once composed, Harriette said that she planned to fly to New York in the next day or two to represent Gig's sister, Genevieve Merry. Harriette volunteered to meet with him and fill him in on Gig's life. She was, she said, Gig's closest friend. But before she got there, she thought the detective ought to know that there were probably three more guns in Gig's apartment, in addition to the one the police had found.

Chartrand expressed surprise.

Harriette insisted she had shipped four guns to Gig at the Osborne, along with his other belongings from California. The way he usually hid things, they were probably in drawers among his shirts and underwear. They would be unloaded, and the bullets would be stashed somewhere else.

Chartrand inquired what use Gig would have for that many firearms.

Harriette couldn't answer that. "That's the funny part," she confided. "He didn't really like guns."

The detective kept her on the phone, probing to find out whether she knew anything else that might be useful. She tearfully concentrated on the mistakes she felt she'd made in their relationship that had contributed to Gig's tragic death. Then, just before hanging up, she asked, "Have you talked to that SOB Bert Knapp?"

"Who?"

"Bert Knapp," she said, her voice filled with sarcasm. "He claims he was Gig's best friend." Beginning to weep again, she abruptly hung up.

Early the next morning, Chartrand visited Bert Knapp in his vocal studio–living quarters on the eleventh floor of a big ugly corner building at Seventh Avenue and Fifty-fourth Street. In his seventies, Knapp had thinning gray hair, darting nervous movements, and a hacking speech pattern that was suggestive of a monkey. Despite this, he earned his living as a vocal coach and was a man obviously accustomed to being in command.

Chartrand identified himself, and Knapp immediately said he had no idea what could have caused Gig to do what he did. He told the detective that for the first time since he'd known Gig, the actor had been truly in love.

Although Chartrand surmised from Harriette Douglas's sarcastic tone that there had been trouble between Gig and this man, Knapp made no reference to it in discussing the two deceased. He spoke of his former pupil, whom he had known for a quarter of a century, in affectionate terms.

Chartrand inquired whether Knapp was aware of any enemies Gig might have had.

Knapp was not.

"Was double suicide a possibility?"

"Out of the question."

"Despondency over health?"

Knapp said there had been rumors that Gig was depressed over possible skin cancer, but they were lies. His friend had had some spots on his skin that came from being out in the sun too long, but they had been easily removed.

"Gig never looked better in his life, in my opinion," Knapp stated. "And my doctor, who did Gig's premarital medical exam, told me he was in great shape."

Chartrand listened sympathetically, if somewhat skeptically, to the too-rosy picture Knapp was painting. After all, he had seen the body, and he would never describe it as the corpse of a man who had been in peak condition. Something bothered him about Knapp's manner—he felt that the man wasn't telling him everything he knew.

After letting Knapp run on, Chartrand finally directed the conversation to what he'd come to find out about. "What about the guns?"

Knapp shook his head. "Under any circumstances, I know Gig could never shoot a gun. He wasn't interested in destroying himself violently. That was not his way of living. I know he was ideally happy for the first time in his life. He wasn't capable of shooting a gun."

Chartrand decided not to challenge Knapp. He thanked him for his cooperation and said he might want to talk to him again. Halfway to the door, he said, "Harriette Douglas is on her way from California."

"You can't believe anything that crazy broad tells you,"

Knapp said testily. "What does she want to come here for? What's she saying now?"

"That she shipped four guns to Gig Young at the Osborne." Chartrand left Knapp to think that over.

Detective Chartrand tossed on Lieutenant Gallagher's desk a copy of the lab report on the tumbler cylinder in Gig Young's front door lock. Nothing in the conclusion of police expert Thomas Jackson would have raised anyone's blood pressure or expectations. Jackson had written: "Examination of the above cylinder and its inner parts fails to reveal the presence of any striations on any of its six (6) parts, thereby indicating that the lock has not been picked."

Gallagher read the report and grunted. "Guess this is an easy one—one that's just as it seems," he said. He always contended that getting a case solved by the death of the perpetrator was pure luxury. Death of the perpetrator meant no loss of man-hours in court.

Chartrand shifted his weight in the chair and agreed. He cleared his throat. He had a minor bombshell to report— something Gallagher certainly wasn't anticipating. He'd gone back to 1BB earlier that morning and located three hidden pistols.

The news made Gallagher sit up. "What took you back there?" he demanded.

"Ninety-nine percent certainty I'd find something of that kind." Chartrand filled Gallagher in on Harriette Vine Douglas's phone call.

"More to the point, why in hell weren't they found yesterday?" Gallagher inquired.

Chartrand told him how they'd been stashed away in a set of concealed custom-built drawers.

"Which were overlooked in the original search?" Gallagher was incredulous. "This department overlooked built-in drawers holding three guns in the original search?" he repeated.

"Correct," Chartrand said. "And if the chief gets bent out of shape about what we did, I'm going to tell him, 'Chief, remember where you were sitting? Well, if you had got up off your ass, we'd have moved the couch. And if we'd moved the couch, somebody would've found the drawers and the guns yesterday.'"

Gallagher chuckled. "In other words, the chief was blocking the search area?"

"Right."

"And nobody had the balls to ask him to move!"

"Correct again," said Chartrand, who proceeded to fill Gallagher in on the Lango and the two Smith & Wesson .38s he'd unearthed at the death scene.

Gallagher whistled. Four guns and all that ammunition weren't required for a simple open-and-shut case of murder-suicide. Or for a suicide pact. Was there something more here? Could someone have had an extra key? Could it have been a double murder?

"Did Young have these guns legally?"

"We'll know better when the ATF* runs down the scoop on them."

Within days, the information was in Chartrand's hands. Three of the four guns were operational. The death weapon, according to the ATF's records, was last registered to Bill's Gun Shop in Franklin Park, Illinois. The Franklin Park police department was stymied since, according to the ATF, the gun had been acquired in 1956 and the gunshop's records only went back to 1958. The Lango had been manufactured prior to 1930, before records were kept. The two Smith & Wessons, one with a two-inch and the other with a six-inch barrel, had been traced to Los Angeles. Young had

*Bureau of Alcohol, Tobacco and Firearms.

purchased them from Olympic Wholesalers: one on October 23, 1970, and the other on April 26, 1973.

"October 1970," Gallagher said. "Less than a year after the Manson murders. Those deaths must've scared him pretty good."

But why in hell would a guy supposedly incapable of shooting a gun have four pistols and three hundred fifty rounds of ammunition? Gallagher sent the manila folder marked "Young" to the CUPPI file—Circumstances Undetermined Pending Police Investigation.

Though the call was coming from Eildon, Australia, a small resort community approximately eighty miles north of Melbourne, the connection was exceptionally clear. The voice on the other end had a slight Germanic accent. Ascertaining that she had reached Lieutenant Richard Gallagher, the caller identified herself as Rosemary Schmidt, the mother of Ruth Hanalore "Kim" Schmidt Young.

Gallagher responded gently, waiting for the bereaved woman to state what was on her mind.

"Lieutenant," she said, "my daughter was murdered."

"Yes, she was murdered," he agreed.

"No, I mean they both were murdered. Ruth and her husband, Gig. I am certain Ruth was not killed by her husband."

Though by now he had concluded that all evidence pointed to a contrary conclusion, Gallagher maintained an open mind. He politely said, "I understand, Mrs. Schmidt. If you have any information that would shed light on that, we'd love to have it."

"My husband, Paul, and I believe someone else killed them. So do their close friends in America."

"I think I understand your feelings," Gallagher replied. "But right now we have nothing to support that view."

"Yes. Well, their friends are going to do everything possible to prove the deaths were not the result of murder-suicide," the woman said. "We are certain the police findings are not the truth."

Gallagher said he was sorry to hear she felt that way, and reiterated, "If you have anything you want to tell us, tell me now or call again. We are open twenty-four hours a day," he added.

Judy Washington, who had been designated by Kim's parents to represent the family in New York, was about to leave her Amsterdam apartment for the airport when her phone rang. It was the New York homicide squad. In the course of their investigation, they'd come across a packet of letters and photos. They deduced that Judy was Kim's oldest and closest friend, and they wanted to ask her a few questions.

Rushed as Judy was, she welcomed the opportunity to explain Kim to Detective Chartrand. "She could be very hard to understand. That's why she had a lot more men friends than women. Women misunderstood her. She wasn't a hard person. She was a soft person, but she found it hard to show emotion, so she seemed very self-centered. And I think women felt threatened by her."

The detective picked up on that. Could Judy think of anyone who might have had a motive for doing away with Kim? Or Gig?

Judy couldn't. She didn't know Gig. She only knew what Kim had written. And she wasn't at her sharpest today, she said. "Even now I can't accept Kim's dead. Intellectually, yes. Emotionally, no."

Chartrand said he understood. After letting her ramble on a bit about Kim's true character, he popped one more question before hanging up. Could Judy, who had known

Kim so long and so well, conceive of any circumstances under which Kim might have entered a suicide pact?

"Never, never, never!" Judy cried. "She had too much zest for life."

Did Judy have any other alternative theories or information?

"Only a vague rumor about some Vietnam veteran, a friend of Gig's, who wasn't stable. But Russ Jones in Hong Kong would know more about that. Or what about some of Gig's old girlfriends?"

Chartrand ended the conversation, arranging to meet with Judy in New York.

Judy thanked him. "What makes me very pissed off at Gig is that he took Kim with him. I'll never forgive him for that," she said.

During the month of October 1978, the *New York Times* and the *Daily News* were shut down by a strike. Except for short television and radio reports, the only news available to most Manhattan residents was in the *Post,* which had union contracts. On October 20, the tabloid's headline blared: GIG YOUNG KILLS WIFE OF THREE WEEKS THEN SLAYS SELF IN WESTSIDE APARTMENT.

Papers across the country relied mostly on the Associated Press Wire Service story, which offered little in the way of explanation. The few theories about the tragedy that did reach print drew immediate fire from friends of Gig's. Most denied that he had ever possessed a gun.

Los Angeles columnist Jim Bacon claimed he had received several calls denying that Gig was capable of violence. He reported one theory that the couple were murdered because of some incident in Kim's past, of which Gig was unaware. "It's one of those mystifying stories that will go down in Hollywood lore."

Gossip columnist Liz Smith, who had been a personal friend, wrote that no celebrity was more disturbed by his disastrous romances and shattered marriages than Gig. "So finally, Gig decided to submit to a popular analytic technique of the time practiced by many psychiatrists. . . . He entered a hospital and underwent treatment with LSD (just as Cary Grant did) in an effort to let the mind-altering drug expand his consciousness and 'release' his memory for psychoanalysis." Liz speculated that perhaps the treatments had set off a flashback, triggering a "violent depression" that ended in a tragic act.

Longtime friend Dominick Dunne says his opinion of what happened has always been essentially the same. "Out of loyalty to him, people developed blind spots. Now, Gig was a man you could have more laughs with than anyone I ever knew. But there was a sadness behind his laughter. A sadness in his face, even—and I don't think I'm saying this in hindsight. He was so sensitive, such a truly complicated man, happiness was probably always an impossible state for him to achieve. But because of their loyalty to him, people wanted to deny what had happened and insisted it couldn't be what it seemed. I think it was exactly what it seemed."

From the start, the police thought the evidence would point to "what it seemed"—murder-suicide. The coroner's report strengthened this belief. From all available information, Gig had chosen the method favored by distraught police officers and other gun aficionados when they decide to kill themselves.

"It's called sucking the gun," Gallagher told a reporter, adding that in doing the job, Gig had wisely directed the copper-jacketed lead bullet upward, backward, and slightly to the left. That way it came to rest in the left posterior section of the skull. Quite literally, Gig had blown his brains out.

Gallagher continued: "A psychiatrist explained to me

once that to these guys the barrel of that gun represents their mother's nipple. A man remembers coming into the world and being nurtured on his mother's breast, so it's almost a compulsory need to suck the metal nipple on the way out. Who knows?"

Asked whether someone could have planted the gun in Gig's hand after he was dead, Gallagher shook his head. "No way. That gun in his hand is the death print in the truest sense of the word. It comes through the ultimate spasm after the gun's fired, the total spasm followed by the final grasp. The guy involuntarily clenches the gun. Rigor mortis sets in. That implants the trigger in the fleshy part of his fingers. He gets ridges on each side of the indentation caused by the trigger. It's impossible from a medical standpoint for anybody to create those ridges in a corpse's hand. So that's the death print."

Gallagher figured that the reason so many people were denying that Gig could have killed his wife was that they thought perhaps they hadn't done enough to prevent it. When something like this happened, there was always guilt. "They feel they should have stopped it somehow," he said.

One of the most astute detectives on the New York police force had been working on the case and, after a thorough investigation, had come to the conclusion that Gig Young had murdered Kim Schmidt and then killed himself. But one fundamental, haunting question remained. Why?

"Suicides who don't leave notes are the most selfish people in the world," Gallagher told the reporter sardonically. "At that point in their lives they are thinking of nobody but themselves. They're like guests at a party who slip out without bothering to say goodbye. How rude of Gig Young not to leave a note. Not even a few words that would have made it easier on everyone—the police, his family, his friends."

What Gallagher and all the others had failed to recognize

was that Gig had left a note—his life. A clue to the tragedy could be found in any part—or all—of his almost sixty-five years. He had once observed bitterly, "You can't tell about people from the outside, because they've spent a lifetime covering their fears." He was talking about himself.

·1·

The Beginning

In the early 1920s, the residential sections of St. Cloud, Minnesota, were lined at intervals with streetlights to fight off the dark. In the golden pool directly in front of the green shingle bungalow at 10½ Avenue South, a small, forlorn figure could be seen running in circles and heard calling out plaintively, "Is enny-bodee home? Is enny-bodee home?" He would pause. Listen. There would be no response. Then he would resume running, repeating his cries in the Minnesota twilight.

That boy, born Byron Ellsworth Barr, who would come to be known as Gig Young, issued many such cries in the dark during his lifetime. In retrospect, they took on a Kafkaesque quality. Life was a maze, and he could never figure the way in or out.

Yet as an adult Gig portrayed the witty, carefree sophisticate, both on stage and off. No matter how tortured he felt, he hid it. He grew skilled at compartmentalizing his life. He kept his family and his friends separated. That way no one "knew too much," he later rationalized to his friend Harriette Vine Douglas. He became adept at this legerdemain, and well he should have been, since he'd begun practicing it in earliest childhood.

Gig's initial feelings of alienation stemmed from four major sources: his dour Scottish father; his repressed, neurasthenic mother; his strange and sadistic "Aunt" Jessie; and his domineering brother. Only from his sister, Genevieve, did he receive the unqualified love and support he craved.

There is no doubt that the whispers he often heard that he owed his very existence to a "leak in the safe," as the failure of a condom was frequently called, shook him. He felt unwanted, and his parents did little to contradict that belief. Certainly not his father, James Earl "J.E." Barr, a driven and distant man. Tall and slim, he was thirty-seven years old when Gig made his unwelcome appearance. But he felt old age creeping on, intensifying the pressures to make a success of his canning factory to the exclusion of anything else—especially his youngest child. When the boy was old enough to be around the factory, his dad's habitual manner of introducing him was "Byron's shy and a little bit of a dumbbell, but he's a good boy."

Sixty years later, the memory of that description still rankled. Gig focused on it, and in many ways, it was the first role that this sensitive little boy would seize on in an attempt to get the affection that was so rare in the Barr household. If that's what it took, Gig would be the best little boy in the world—or at least try to be. His goal would eventually be expressed in rather bizarre childhood behavior.

Visitors to the Barr home, for example, were astonished to see young Gig excuse himself and retreat to a shed in the backyard whenever faced with eating a messy food, like watermelon, or a noisy one, like celery. One guest was even more startled at Gig's timidity. Seeing him glance anxiously at the other diners, she was flabbergasted when he slid under the table to blow his nose. Curiously, neither of his parents seemed to regard this as strange, or even to take note of it.

Part of the reason Gig failed to receive the attention from his parents that he hungered for was bad timing. His birth, on November 4, 1913, came a scant two years after his father founded the J. E. Barr Pickling and Preserving Company. Struggling to expand, J.E. had little time to devote to his family. Typical of men at the time, he left the task of nurturing the brood to his wife, Emma. The one exception was the already ambitious seven-year-old, Donald, whom he constantly praised. Years later, Gig chafed over his father's inattention to him, complaining that he never read to him or showed any overt affection. The older he grew, the more such things galled him, feeding the rage that would eventually help destroy him.

That left his mother to fill the void, but truth to tell, by the time Gig made his ill-timed appearance, Emma was tired of rearing children. Don, her firstborn, fared the best, receiving her undivided attention for several years, which encouraged him to develop into a self-confident, take-charge little man even before he was old enough to attend school. Five years later, Gen came along. Gig followed in two years. With two toddlers underfoot, Emma operated chiefly on a nervous energy that sometimes got the better of her.

Half-French, half-German, with dark-brown hair, and hazel eyes set in the broad face she would bequeath to Gig,

Emma was the picture-postcard image of a Midwestern mother. But her interests centered on the larger world outside her home. An ex-schoolteacher, she assisted with PTA meetings and helped organize functions at the local Methodist church (Gig's baptism in the faith would have a shattering effect on him a little over a quarter century later). From all appearances, the Barrs were a wholesome all-American family.

When Gig was still a babe in arms, Emma stole time away from her family and household duties to resume keeping the books for her husband's business. She was a good partner for the hardworking J.E. Emma, who was nothing if not conscientious, assumed she had struck the proper balance. After all, Don and Genevieve adjusted to her going back to work without any apparent difficulty. But the younger, more sensitive Gig responded differently. He withdrew. As he matured, he held himself more and more apart from the family circle. It was as if he were sending Emma a message that if bookkeeping and, later, church affairs and school activities were much more interesting to her than he was, then he would consider her with the very same lack of regard.

Complicating Gig's relationship with his mother was Emma's emotional and physical deterioration, conditions that would later turn her into a near invalid. At first it was expressed merely as weakness and nervousness—the aftereffects of a bout with typhoid fever before her marriage. This made it difficult for her to deal with the unfettered energy of small children. When Gig was young, she took to her room with increasing frequency. She lay there with shades drawn, exhausted to the point of being physically ill. It may have been partly psychosomatic. "Ill health preyed on her mind," said her daughter many years later. Like so many other bright women, she was lonely and desperate for someone with whom to hold an intelligent conversation.

More than likely, it was this debilitating nervous condition that would cause her increasingly to withdraw from her expected role as a nurturer.

Whatever the reasons, his mother's retreat was very real—and devastating—to Gig. It's not hard to imagine him knocking at the door of her darkened room, only to receive an agonized "Go away" in reply. Where Emma was concerned, the answer to Gig's plaintive calls was frequently painful rejection. He never forgot it. Later in life, he rarely, if ever, mentioned his mother. Her absence set him searching for a substitute mother—a pattern he would follow to the very end of his life.

At a critical juncture in his emotional development, Gig found his first substitute mother: the mysterious "Aunt" Jessie. She had come into the family as the adopted daughter of Emma's stepmother. Since Jessie did not get along with her adoptive parents, the Barrs invited her into their home to look after the two younger children (Don already insisted on working at the canning plant after school). With Emma wanting to spend more time away from home, Jessie was a convenient, if not wise, solution.

Visitors to the Barr home at the time rarely saw the woman who, at her insistence, was introduced as the housekeeper rather than as a relative. When friends visited, Jessie retreated to the seclusion of her room. Though she was eventually to marry four times, she was a single woman in her late teens when she landed in St. Cloud from Lebeaux, Minnesota. That she had emotional problems, there was no doubt. But she had two assets: her availability and her talent to win any child's total devotion.

Don liked her. Gen loved her. Gig, starved for affection, adored the heavyset but not unattractive woman. Especially after he had become old enough to go to school and began having problems with his classmates. She understood him. Gig solemnly confided to Gen that next to her, he preferred "Aunt" Jessie above all others. Jessie was initially demonstrative. She always smelled wonderful. She laughed a lot with him. Jessie told him he was handsome. Jessie told him he was clever. Jessie told him whatever he wanted to hear. Gig loved and needed such flattery.

With her tacit encouragement, the impressionable child built up the fantasy that the effusive woman preferred him to her other two charges. After all, Gig and Jessie had their little secrets. Small as he was, he knew he must not share them—even with Gen. For when "Aunt" Jessie gave him his Saturday bath, she enjoyed giving his genitals particular attention. Though he was far too young to know anything about sex, he knew not to mention their "game" to anyone.

Jessie also had a cruel streak. Even though she was fully aware of her youngest charge's fantasy that she preferred him, Jessie carelessly—perhaps deliberately—made it evident by her actions and in her conversation that Don was her clear favorite. She praised Don for being a fine, upstanding young man. Gig, on the other hand, was teased about being so needy, so sensitive. In the day-to-day contests between the two Barr boys, it gradually became clear to Gig that Don was the easy victor. Gig was crushed at Jessie's treachery. First his mother's withdrawal, and now this. Gig was inconsolable, moping about the house, distancing himself even more from the family.

Gig's diffidence drew forth a tormenting side of Jessie's personality. "This isn't sexual, or maybe it is," Gig said in recounting an incident on one of the autobiographical tapes that were made at voice coach Bert Knapp's studio during the last couple of years of Gig's life. (These tapes, only a few of which I was able to locate, were an earnest but awkward attempt by Gig to analyze past and present difficulties under the guidance of Knapp.) "Now she loved me, on the one hand, and she would give me the finger, on the other." As an illustration, he vividly described an evening when the two of them were alone in the house. Hurt by something Jessie had said, the seven-year-old retreated to his room and closed the door, refusing to allow her in. Suddenly he felt his scalp prickling with fear as an envelope was shoved under the door and moved slowly from side to side.

"I cried, 'Stop! Stop! Stop it, Aunt Jessie!' But the envelope kept up its spooky journey," Gig recalled. "I knew it was Aunt Jessie, but I wasn't sure exactly what she was going to do to me." (At his voice teacher–guru's encouragement, more than fifty years after the incident, Gig concluded that had he opened the door, Jessie would probably have swept him up and cuddled him in a sexually charged embrace.)

Aunt Jessie, on the other hand, may have thought she was playing a harmless game. Indeed, any other child might not have responded with such terror. But Gig had a fertile imagination. And while imagination is a glorious possession, it can be as dangerous as any weapon when turned against the self, by either a child or an adult. In Gig's case, Jessie's sadistic teasing, plus parental rejection and difficulty adjusting to school, led to a succession of tension-induced ailments. For a brief period about this time, he suffered minor convulsions. Later on, he awoke one morning with his neck frozen in a crooked position that made it impossible for him to get up. Twice each day for the next week, the local chiropractor visited the Barr house to manipulate Gig's spine. It was an attention-getting situation, to be sure, but a painful and disturbing one.

J.E. and Emma didn't know what to make of Gig's health problems. Like most Midwesterners some seventy years ago, they knew nothing of psychosomatic ailments. And a child of Gig's age couldn't articulate that the fear he felt was brought on by various kinds of rejection. Misinterpreting what were clearly a child's desperate cries for help, Emma concluded that Gig's problems stemmed from his having too many bosses. In the void of his parents' abdication of their duties to Gen and Gig, older brother Don had stepped in. His natural assertiveness became outright aggression, demanding that the youngsters cave in to his dictates. His attitude did not change after Jessie entered the picture. Now Emma announced a hands-off policy. Jessie was to be in complete charge. Gig later said that he took this to mean his mother didn't love him enough to countermand Jessie's edicts. Gig's relationship with his parents, his brother, and now Jessie conditioned him to accept another role that, at least in his early years, he learned to play well: the victim.

In his eagerness to please, to be the "good boy," Gig inadvertently created a climate that encouraged mistreatment not only at home but also in the outside world. Upon entering Washington Elementary School, he almost immediately began to fall behind in reading and arithmetic—subjects that required a certain amount of competitiveness. As with his family, Gig simply gave up. When the forty-two pupils were divided, he was assigned to the slowest group and began to form a low opinion of his academic capabilities.

Gig managed to pass first grade, but worse was to come. It was the era of "spare the rod and spoil the child." By luck of the draw, Gig was dealt a sadist for a second-grade teacher. Spotting a "victim," she kept Gig after school and beat him with a length of old garden hose. So low had his self-esteem fallen that Gig confided in Gen but begged her not to reveal to their parents what had happened, lest he receive more punishment—from them.

The school dilemma solved itself when another student's mother visited classes. That evening she called Emma to ask whether she had any idea what was going on. "The teacher picked up a ruler to use as a pointer, and your little boy automatically held out his hands, palms up, to be cracked across them," she said. "Do you have any idea what that means?"

Emma responded immediately, withdrawing Gig from Washington and enrolling him in Riverview, a grammar school attached to the St. Cloud State University Teachers College. But the seven-year-old was now so traumatized that he was forced to repeat second grade. It was one more humiliation. Speaking as an adult of his early schooling, Gig described himself as "painfully shy" and said he'd been thrown in with the unsalvageable delinquents and malingerers. "I only had one teacher who ever liked me," he claimed. "I was so happy she did, I used to give her dimes."

Later in life, Gig recalled an experience that indicated how he began to view his unhappy childhood. The summer when he was eight, he stayed with some friends of the family whose farm was located on a lake, where he liked to fish. They were amused at his diffidence and one Sunday plied him with a glass of home brew. It was his first taste of a substance that he would later much abuse. "I began to get a little high, and it felt real good," he recalled on his autobiographical tapes years later. "It was the first time I didn't have any inhibitions, and I was out in the backyard, standing on my head. I had a ball, and they had already called my folks to tell them I'd gotten drunk before I ever got home."

Gig felt betrayed. His parents lectured him harshly, harping on his seeming inability to do anything right and pointing to Don as a shining example of the dutiful son. Criticism had become a constant, reproaches a given. He concluded on the tape that the friend had intentionally got him drunk and then called his parents. "That," he said, "was the first conspiracy against me."

Despite a growing apprehension that life was arbitrary and people uncaring, no matter how hard he tried, Gig rarely expressed resentment. In order to survive, he learned to mask his true feelings behind an open-faced, twinkling-eyed countenance. Yet he was growing more and more disengaged at home, except from the faithful Gen. Gig's plight drew the two youngsters even closer together. Although Gen has sunnier childhood memories than her brother did, she found it easy to empathize with him at the time. As their relationship grew all through grade school, the two of them made a pact never to be critical of each other. With a couple of exceptions late in life, the agreement lasted through the years, providing Gig, especially, with much-needed support.

Gig was a loner, but curiously enough, Gen was not his only friend. Acting out how he felt about himself, the boy spent hours at the city dump. His fascination with the inhabitants of the hobo jungle was more than a boy's excitement at hearing about the adventures of the knights of the open road. He also felt a desire to make life easier for them. Frequently he would bring home some hungry wanderer and cook ham and eggs for him. The Barr residence was in fact marked by a secret hobo sign, tipping off vagabonds that it was always good for a handout. The resultant string of beggars puzzled "Aunt" Jessie and Emma, but not Gen, who was aware of her younger brother's penchant for feeding the poor.

After Gen and the hoboes, Gig's most constant companion was the family dog, Shep, but Shep alone was not enough. Gig was forever trading his possessions to other boys for mutts, which he adopted. He channeled his reservoirs of affection to his four-legged friends. He had learned it was safer.

"Gig was a Mark Twain kind of boy, hanging around the

river, the city dump, and the hobo jungle with his dogs," says Gen. But of Twain's characters, Gig had much more in common with the complex Huckleberry Finn than with the sunnier Tom Sawyer.

Like Huck, Gig had his share of carefree days, mostly away from the repressive Barr household. Free from school on weekends, the boy would set off early Saturday morning for his beloved Uncle George and Aunt Addy's. Theirs was an easygoing place, with dogs, cats, chickens, and even a pet pig that ranged about freely. Emma—whose house was orderly and reeked of cleanliness, as if that alone could hold back the impinging depression she felt—looked down on her sister-in-law's laissez-faire approach to life, but Gig fully enjoyed it. He'd hang about, hoping to be invited for lunch or, better still, to stay the night. To him the food seemed tastier, the company far more congenial, than back at home.

Summers, Gig nominally worked on the huge vegetable patches outside St. Cloud that tenant farmers cultivated to supply produce for his father's canning factory. By his own account, he was lazy and so self-effacing that when asked whether he wanted a peanut butter or a jelly sandwich, he would say he didn't care—even though he preferred the former. He believed in not making waves, so he was no trouble to have as a summer guest. The farmers did their work, and the quiet, handsome boss's son with his amiable gaptoothed grin went his own way. In spite of his dislike of farmwork, he dreamed of being a farmer one day.

Summers would pass, and as fall approached, Gig would watch for his father, bouncing down the dusty road in an open-topped touring car, coming to take him home. When he spied the car, he would "take off like a deer and hide somewhere."

As Gig neared the end of his elementary school education, his father pressed him into working at the cannery, which was doing very well. At age eleven, the dutiful Don had come by after school and stood for hours at a conveyor belt, ready to dislodge potential pickle jam-ups. By the time he entered high school, he was a valued employee. Gig, who'd always resisted helping out, was another story. His employment was short-lived: a new foreman fired him for malingering, not realizing he was the owner's son. Gig's father hired him back, but as punishment cut his weekly pay from twelve dollars a week to eight.

Ordinarily that would have stung Gig, but by now he was used to being treated as the incompetent boob son. What's more, he'd grown rather resourceful in creating diversions that helped him cope with the disagreeable realities at home.

Exactly when Gig began to think about becoming an actor was his well-guarded secret, since it was not an ambition that would have earned approval from either his family or his friends. He was so intimidated by what he anticipated as Don's and his father's derisive comments that he confided in no one—not even Gen. Well into his career, he told an interviewer that he was interested in acting from the time he was in elementary school but had been too shy to do anything about it. Nonetheless he read his sister's movie magazines, which fed his love of fantasy and self-deception. Even more important, at twelve he took a job as usher at the Paramount Theater in St. Cloud. His favorite movie star, Tom Mix, may have had little to do with the sophisticated screen persona he would eventually develop, but the image of a shoot-'em-up, can-do good guy was infinitely appealing to a boy who forever seemed to be tripping over his shoe-laces. In the flickering darkness, he fastened onto characters and stories that helped fill the emptiness in his life.

When he entered Technical High School as a freshman, Gig put some of his diffidence behind him. School no longer proved to be as traumatic. Summers had matured him into a good-looking, muscular young man with a need to please. He discovered added cachet as the brother of Don, who had been a star athlete and scholar at the school. To his astonishment, his classmates apparently regarded him more favorably than he could have dreamed; he was elected class president and, shortly after, admitted to the high school's only fraternity. The fact that during Gig's freshman year the J. E. Barr company was pumping half a million dollars per year into the local economy might well have had something to do with his newfound popularity. Continuing to prosper, the business changed its name to the Barr Canning Company and burgeoned into one of the largest vegetable-preserving operations in the Midwest. Gig was flying high, with an allowance, access to the family car, and ownership of more than one good suit—not an ordinary occurrence in the 1920s in a farm community such as St. Cloud. Such flashy accessories made it a little easier for him to metamorphose from shy dimwit to dashing boy-about-town.

Moreover, Gig was no longer eclipsed by the presence of his aggressive older brother. Upon graduation from the University of Wisconsin, Don had applied for a job in Russia, advising the Soviets on canning operations during their first five-year plan. Their selection of him was surprising, because Don was still a young man, fresh out of college. Yet it was an apt choice, since Don had not only academic training but also years of practical experience in the family plant.

From the Soviet Union, Don sent letters full of brotherly advice, telling Gen not to wear short sleeves and reminding Gig to help out their mother. He also pointed his younger brother in the direction of sports, which had enhanced his own popularity. Later in life, Gig claimed to have excelled in running, pole vaulting, boxing, and basketball and, in his autobiographical tapes, said that he would have become a professional athlete had he not been injured in a football game. This claim is undoubtedly a latter-day fantasy, but an increasingly aggressive approach to sports is indicative of Gig's emotional state at this point in his life. He himself observed that it was a way of dealing with a lot of suppressed hostility. In fact, he was apprehensive about boxing, for if he got pushed into a corner, he "might become desperate and kill" his opponent. This fear of unleashed rage caused him to give up the sport.

When faced with a crisis he could not escape through sports, he at times attempted to solve it by retreating. For example, at the close of his freshman year in high school, he failed English. Feeling disgraced, he promptly sold his rifle to obtain ready cash (he had already spent his allowance) and, without telling anyone, hitchhiked to Iowa to visit relatives, thereby escaping parental wrath. His parents, who thought Gig was at home with Gen, arrived in Iowa to observe Memorial Day Weekend and were astounded to find him there. Gig returned home with them to face the music of his academic failure.

That, according to Gen, was what actually happened. But Gig, in later years, would recast the story to reflect his deepest emotional needs. In his version, he was a first grader who failed every subject and ran away to escape the humiliation of facing his family. A kindly traveling salesman, he said, sized up the situation and drove him to the Faribault, Minnesota, police station to spend the night. A policeman figured out he was from St. Cloud and notified authorities there. The St. Cloud police called his parents, who dropped everything and set out to retrieve him. The point of the story, as Gig told it, was to illustrate one of the rare occasions when his parents demonstrated their love for and concern about him. "Until they showed up, it was like I had no parents," he said from the vantage point of middle age. "But after they got me in the car, for once I felt they really cared."

Since Gig was given to outrageous fantasizing in other

areas, it is difficult to separate fact from fanciful invention in relation to his early sexual experiences. But what emerges on his analytical tapes is that he was a youth with intense sexual urges. He confessed to masturbating frequently as a preteen, as much as five or six times a day. And apparently, in spite of his social awkwardness, the handsome youth was unconsciously flirtatious enough to provoke numerous advances, beginning with the bathtub incidents with Jessie. Years later, during the Depression, a sexually aggressive college girl who roomed at the Barrs' initiated him into a tantalizing secret game called Find the Nickel. She would hide a five-cent piece somewhere on her body, and he usually found it in her bra.

Despite such claims, he said on the tapes that he dated infrequently—mostly because his mother disapproved. Remote and distant as she could be, she suddenly got very protective when she observed his interest in the opposite sex. Once when his school staged a talent show, Gig became so enchanted with a voluptuous young tap dancer's jiggle that he called her and made a date. He was proud of his boldness until the girl canceled at the last minute. His mother, seeing he was deflated, finally confessed that she had called the girl's mother, quashing the rendezvous. "She's not a very nice girl," Emma remarked.

Telling the story, Gig said, "I've never been a homosexual, but it's amazing I'm not, because my mother didn't encourage dating." Even more oddly, he said no one in the family blinked when an effeminate male teacher took to inviting him on walks and even visiting him at home. Nor was the family suspicious of the motives of an unmarried male accountant who customarily drove Gig to a roadhouse on Saturday nights, where the two of them would get gloriously drunk. Looking back, Gig concluded the accountant was often on the verge of making a pass at him but couldn't summon up the courage. He also recalled that at fourteen, he attracted the married auto mechanic who lived in the neighborhood. The fellow, in retrospect, struck Gig as a bisexual who made frequent verbal passes that could be regarded as jokes. On his tapes, Gig graphically describes these encounters, but says, "I just laughed them off. I never let any of those guys get into my pants."

At sixteen, Gig lost his virginity to a slim-waisted, full-breasted twenty-eight-year-old blond who he later concluded had been put up to approaching him by the auto mechanic. As Gig tells it, the blond spotted him leaving basketball practice and followed him home in her car. Making sure he was home alone, she called (probably getting his phone number from the mechanic) to arrange a rendezvous at the edge of town. There she gently initiated him into the rites of sex. The encounter proved so rapturous that they met several times more. But the meetings stopped abruptly when the mechanic, having heard about the trysts from the girl, mischievously warned Gig that the girl had gonorrhea. Terrified, Gig threw himself at the mercy of a higher power, praying, "Dear God, if I don't get gonorrhea, I'll never do it again. I'll never do anything again."

On a more innocent yet serious level, Gig was smitten with Mary Ellen Nichols, the daughter of his football coach. He was, he always said, "just crazy about that girl." They took rides in the Barrs' family car and sipped ice cream sodas together at the local drugstore. Then suddenly, he said, she threw him over for another boy. Years later, Mary Ellen denied ever walking out on Gig. On the contrary, she had been thrilled to be seen with him, because in her eyes he was by far the best-looking boy around St. Cloud. Inclined as he was to recast stories to suggest emotional intent, Gig may have been signaling his need to be hurt by the people he loved.

Throughout his life, Gig would seek his ideal woman, a composite of the two females who had so vividly excited his youthful ardor. She would have the uninhibited animal passion of the blond, who took what she wanted, and the virginal wholesomeness of the coach's daughter. He found a little of each, for a time, in different women he would date or marry. But something not quite right always surfaced in the picture-perfect affair, and when it did, the relationship was terminated. Twice, Gig would think he had it right. Once death would intervene. The second time, a powerful organized religion would force personal feelings to be swept aside. Still, Gig never stopped searching for versions of these two prototypes from his youth in St. Cloud. And in the background, but not out of range, was the specter of Emma, the ever unattainable woman.

As 1931 drew to a close, so did the Barr family's life in St. Cloud. The real impact of the Great Depression was beginning to be felt, and the Barr Canning Company, which had once enjoyed unalloyed prosperity, was now in trouble. Although J.E. had despaired of interesting his second son in the business, Don kept up a stream of letters from Russia, which reminded Gig of their obligations to their parents and touted the American dream just as that vision was about to be shattered in every city and hamlet across the country.

Both J.E. and Emma had thoroughly embraced the American dream and inculcated their family with its tenets. They had subscribed to the Protestant work ethic, believing that sacrifice and denial would reward them amply. Now they felt betrayed and shaken, and Gig sensed it. When the canning plant foundered, J.E. took a job as a food broker in Washington, D.C., and Gen, who had earned a teacher's certificate, accepted a position in Motley, Minnesota.

With Don still in Russia, Gig alone remained in St. Cloud to look after his ailing mother. To supplement the meager amounts of money that J.E., Don, and Gen were able to send

home, Emma threw open the house to roomers. Gig gave up
his bedroom and moved to a summer sleeping porch fitted
with storm windows for winter occupancy. Before retiring,
he would heat jars of water and place them between the
blankets to warm the bed. Gig endured the family's precipitous fall from privilege with seeming equanimity. But even
so, it was something of an endurance test.

Just as he had begun to emerge from his lonely childhood, the economic crutch upon which he had relied was
pulled out from under him. Gone was the money for gasoline
and casual socializing, gone was the confidence-building
status of being the boss's son. Like millions of Americans
during the Depression, Gig took refuge at the movies. Whenever he lacked the fifteen cents for a ticket, the manager
he'd befriended during his ushering days passed him in.
Romantic leading men like Robert Montgomery supplanted
Tom Mix in his pantheon, and he marveled at their witty
banter and charm. With his self-image as a gap-toothed and
gawky youth, he never dreamed he would realize his secret
ambition to one day be up there himself. Attracting a local
woman with hot pants was one thing; seducing an audience
was quite another.

Gig might have remained quite happy escaping the grim-
ness of home in the dark of a movie theater had Gen not
introduced him to Kay Osborne, a dark-haired, high-bred
beauty who was a student at St. Cloud Teachers College. Gig
was bowled over, and his youthful passion was reciprocated.
During the summer, he would hitchhike forty miles to
spend Saturdays with his new girlfriend. They paddled
around in a canoe on a lake near Kay's house, or took in a
movie if Gig could rustle up the thirty cents.

Kay, for her part, enjoyed visiting the Barr home. She
admired the way Gig cheerfully did whatever he could to
make life easier for his mother. Her own mother had died
young. It was assumed on both sides that Gig and Kay would

eventually wed, despite Don's ultimatum that Gig banish any thoughts of marriage until there was an improvement in the economic climate.

Then suddenly word arrived from J.E. that it was time for Emma and Gig to join him in Washington. Their sentimental treasures were locked into one small room and the rest of the house was rented out. The summons came at a bad time for Gig. He was flourishing in his junior year in high school: he was on the student council and the debating team, and he had been cast in the role of the handsome, debonair Laurie in the school production of *Little Women.* But most important, he was madly in love. The bad timing that would afflict him from time to time throughout his life was separating him from a world he had finally learned to cope with.

As usual, however, Gig showed little resentment. He and Kay planned her visit to the Barrs' apartment in the nation's capital that summer. Then on April 20, 1932, eighteen-year-old Gig jammed all the belongings he could into the rumble seat of the Barrs' gray Essex coupe. He helped his sickly and deeply depressed mother into the passenger seat and climbed behind the wheel. As he left behind the place that had tested and scarred him, Gig looked ahead with some trepidation—and hope. His parents had so imbued him with belief in the American dream that it was impossible for him to imagine that his belief in it would ever be shattered.

Youth and love obscured that possibility in the spring of 1932. For if Gig had any confidence at all, it stemmed from Kay's love. Little did he know that in Washington, he'd encounter a woman far different from Kay, who would likewise build his confidence. But she would do so in a way that would set him on a road light-years away from Kay and his life in St. Cloud.

———

Gig's immediate adjustment to city life was surprisingly smooth. His chief dissatisfaction was caused by the distance between the apartment his father had rented and McKinley High, his new school. So with his parents' approval, Gig began scouting out a more convenient location. Soon he spotted a For Rent sign in a row house near his school. Again with his parents' permission, he approached the landlady, a formidable woman, hefty, coarse-featured, middle-aged, and extroverted. She showed him the flat; he liked it—and they took to each other immediately. But she cautiously added that his parents would want to look over the rooms, and she would want to look them over, too.

The truth was that Mrs. Harry Kaines had a secret. Since a stroke had felled her husband, she had been supplementing her income by bootlegging home brew to Georgetown University students, and she didn't want any bluenoses blowing the whistle on her. Indeed, Gig's parents—the dour Scotsman and his conservative-looking wife—made her fearful, but Gig's eagerness to have the apartment carried the day.

Soon this transplanted Midwesterner and his landlady had struck up a friendship. The relationship was platonic, of course, but Mrs. Kaines became another in what was to become a long line of motherly women who would look after Gig, encourage him, build his ego—do all the things he had hungered for but failed to get as a child.

For her part, Mrs. K. thought the pictures of actors in fan magazines at the beauty shop had nothing over this strapping youth. She enjoyed listening to him talk about his track meets at McKinley; and she was thrilled but not surprised when his prowess at the 440 and the half-mile gave his school a shot at placing first in the Penn State Relays.

Gig spent his senior year attempting to redefine himself outside his father's and brother's influence. He told Mrs. K.

how he insisted on having his school records transmitted to Technical High in St. Cloud, so he could be recorded as a member of the graduating class there. A small gesture, it indicated that, at least tentatively, he was trying to take control of his life.

With his smiling demeanor, Gig was popular with the other tenants at Mrs. Kaines's, including the manager of a branch of People's Drugstores, who gave him a fountain job. His twelve-dollar weekly wages allowed him to stay in Washington after his father got a job as general manager of a canning operation in Waynesville, North Carolina. When J.E. announced his plans to move the family there, Gig balked. Small-town life held no allure for him, and he convinced his family that he should be allowed to remain where he was. Mrs. Kaines came to the rescue by offering Gig a cot to sleep on in her kitchen. The arrangement suited everyone except Mr. Kaines, who had taken one look at the handsome young roomer and decided he was competition. Whenever Mrs. Kaines left the house, her paralyzed husband would accuse Gig of lusting after her. Gig stuck it out until two young immigrants rented an apartment from Mrs. Kaines and she talked them into letting Gig share their apartment and expenses.

Eventually Gig confided in Mrs. K. his secret ambition to become an actor. She assured him that he was handsome enough to be in pictures. The gap between his front teeth might be a problem, but hell, some women thought that was sexy. She knew he could do it.

"Mrs. Kaines was Gig's earliest fan," says Gen. "I know that later, when his first movie was shown in Washington, they had her sitting in a box, taking bows. And of course, she claimed all credit for his success. Later, she did visit him in California. He said it was most embarrassing; no matter who was mentioned, she always said Gig was better, smarter, more talented, more attractive."

She certainly thought that way years earlier, while gossiping with her Washington neighbors. Long before Gig had ever taken any steps toward becoming a professional, Mrs. Kaines suggested that with his good looks he could earn a fortune teaching ballroom dancing.

During this time, walkathons were the rage in Washington. These spectacles combined variety entertainment with endurance walking and dancing. Couples would compete against one another for forty-five minutes out of the hour, twenty-four hours a day, for weeks on end, until only one couple survived. Gig and Mrs. Kaines occasionally went to Riverside Stadium, where many of the contests were held, to cheer on the contestants and enjoy the floor show. It was there that Gig saw the prototype of the master of ceremonies upon whom he would base his Oscar-winning characterization in *They Shoot Horses, Don't They?*

Mrs. K. also encouraged Gig to get experience with the Phil Hayden Players, a semiprofessional local theatrical group, which presented Broadway hits of past seasons. Although he was busy working as a soda jerk and, occasionally, as a ballroom dance instructor, Gig approached the Players' manager, who sized up the attractive young man and cast him first in small roles and then, when he showed promise, in larger parts.

Gig drank in the audience's attention and approbation. Ill equipped to meet the world on its own terms, on stage he could utilize his tendency to fantasize. The neat, well-ordered drawing room comedies in which he had roles were appealing subterfuges for a young man who, despite the developing facade, was still very much an insecure, diffident adolescent bound by his parents' opinion of him.

Even though Gig had graduated and was on his own, he was apprehensive about J.E. and Emma's response to his newly developed ambitions, and thus he delayed telling them about his work with the Hayden troupe. But when he was cast in nonunion industrial films that were being shot around the capital, the pay was so meager that in order to afford a dinner jacket for one of the roles, he had to confess he had taken up acting and appeal to his parents for funds. The money was immediately forthcoming—and so was a job interview J.E. set up through a friend.

Apparently determined to break Mrs. Kaines's influence, J.E. arranged for Gig to become an apprentice in the book-keeping department at the Hill-Tibbets Ford agency. Gig protested he had neither interest in nor aptitude for dealing with mathematical records. It soon became apparent that he was in over his head. So the office manager downgraded him to the switchboard. But Gig's concentration was focused elsewhere, on a career in show business, and even the switchboard was beyond him. "I couldn't get all those messages," he said later. "So I eventually wound up parking cars."

Although normally Gig would have been humiliated at the way he was dropping from lower to bottom echelon at the Ford agency, everything seemed unimportant compared to his burgeoning desire to get to Hollywood.

Unimportant, that is, until he developed a swelling in his testicles and jumped to the conclusion that he had contracted a venereal disease from a young woman who rented a room at Mrs. Kaines's. Rushing from one quack to another, undergoing a series of tests and torturous treatments without showing any improvement, he finally visited a reliable doctor and was informed that he was run down and was suffering from an inflammation of the epididymis, a tubular mass at the back of the testicle. The doctor's prescribed course of treatment was calcium therapy and a move to a warmer climate.

While waiting for the calcium to cure him, Gig began visiting a dentist and had braces installed to close the small gap between his two front teeth. Afterward, he flashed an expanse of teeth so white that "you could sell advertising space on it," a friend said.

The calcium therapy ultimately failed, and in 1938 Gig would undergo a vasectomy. The operation would improve his physical health but create serious emotional complications for him later in life.

When Gig finally felt ready to set out for California, he dreaded telling his parents, even though he had the excuse that it was doctor's orders. He needn't have worried. Their response was far more equable than he could have imagined. They had lost their confidence in a business career for him, since he obviously had neither the aptitude nor the self-discipline to apply himself. Besides, they knew that Gig's heart was elsewhere.

With that hurdle behind him, Gig hitchhiked to Minnesota to inform Kay that his new life plan precluded early marriage. (His dalliances in Washington had already signaled his waning interest in committing himself to a long-term relationship.) Nonetheless, the young couple had a tearful farewell. Years later, Kay was to remember him fondly.

Having concluded this painful duty, Gig buoyantly set forth, with no barriers to the new life he planned in California. If for a moment he recalled his earlier goodbye to Minnesota, as he sat beside a shattered woman clutching the sad remains of her American dream, it all must have seemed far removed from what he was confident his life was to become. Gig's demons were just beneath the surface, but they would germinate for years before coming to full term. And they would be nurtured in a hothouse of self-delusion more powerful than anything he had encountered thus far—Hollywood.

·2·

The Hollywood Scuffle

Telling his family he was sharing gasoline expenses with a friend, Gig Young hitchhiked from Washington to the West Coast. His last ride was with a truckdriver who at 4:00 A.M. deposited him in Culver City, assuring his guileless passenger that he was in Hollywood.

While Culver City may have been several miles from the geographical center of Hollywood, Gig was not far from its heart. For just a few blocks away from where he stood were the legendary gates of Metro-Goldwyn-Mayer, the Rolls-Royce of studios, on whose back lots Atlanta would burn that very year. As with every studio, inside the golden gates of MGM was a land of privilege and promise—an all-powerful dream machine that would groom, coach, cast, and publicize any actor lucky enough to have breached the formidable barrier in hopes of rocketing to stardom.

Breaking into the movies wasn't an easy thing to do. The odds of making it, according to *Reader's Digest,* were twenty thousand to one in those days. And Hollywood was burgeoning with penniless and untrained hopefuls who, like Steinbeck's Okies escaping the dust bowl, were fleeing the aridity of their own humdrum lives for the moist promise of California. Few people would have bet on the timid young man standing in the foggy chill of that California morning, wondering what to do next. There was little to indicate that he had the right stuff. William Orr, an actor who eventually became well known as vice-president in charge of television for Warner Brothers, met Gig shortly after his arrival. "He seemed like just another affable, easygoing guy," Orr said years later. "There were lots of those around. They usually didn't have the persistence to make it. I certainly didn't think of Gig as a potential star."

What Orr didn't see behind that "affable" presence were the emotional problems that had transformed more than one insecure and troubled individual into a star. Those hours of staring at the Paramount's screen and poring over fan magazines in St. Cloud had baptized Gig into a new secular religion. Like so many before him, he arrived in Hollywood under the misapprehension that the magic wave of some studio mogul's wand could solve his problems. He must have thought that his truncated education, limited job skills, economic impoverishment, and myriad other failings —real or imagined—would miraculously disappear if only a studio would sign him. If Spangler Arlington Brugh could become Robert Taylor, and Ruby Stevens could become Barbara Stanwyck, who was to say what could happen to him?

The utopian visions that danced in Gig's head converged with an ambition that was just beginning to jell when he arrived in Hollywood. It would harden through the rigors that began to test his persistence almost immediately. No sooner had he alighted from the truck than he spotted a help-wanted sign at a corner gasoline station and landed the job. If he could help it, there would be no letters home pleading for financial assistance. Soon after he'd started working at the gas station, the star-struck Gig wrote to Gen, wryly confiding: "Talked to my first movie star. Gary Cooper came into the station. Asked, 'Where's the can?' "

Pumping gas was just the first of a number of catch-as-catch-can jobs with which Gig paid his dues while working toward the mythical "big break." He mowed lawns, cleaned basements, worked as a part-time auto mechanic, and starved himself on one meal a day to save money. For three months, he worked as a waiter in a nightclub, until the manager fired him for "trying too hard." Whenever he became discouraged or deflated, he reminded himself that others had plied the same route. Taking on a job as a night clerk in the respectable Washington Hotel in Culver City, he'd pass the time searching for star signatures in old desk registers. Discovering that in the 1920s, Lucille Le Sueur, who later became glamour queen Joan Crawford, had lived at the Washington for several months was oddly reassuring. One of the good things about that particular job was that it provided lodging. At another period during these lean times, Gig shared a room in a theatrical boardinghouse with two other guys. There was only a single bed, and they had to sleep in eight-hour shifts.

These hardships transformed Gig from an easygoing, slightly scattered youth into a highly focused, no-nonsense young man. Fired from a job as a carhop because the manager's son needed work, he learned early on that nepotism was a way of life in Hollywood. He was determined to make up for his lack of connections with a charm that masked the anger he felt at being at the mercy of forces beyond his control.

Through an acquaintance, Gig secured an appointment to audition with MGM casting director Billy Grady. Grady suggested that the handsome young man get into a workshop showcase, promising that he or another MGM scout would come to see his work. There were many showcase groups in Los Angeles, but the only ones open to rank amateurs charged for the opportunity to act. Too starry-eyed to resent the exploitation, Gig landed at Ben Bard's playhouse-school, where he constructed scenery in lieu of paying the weekly tuition. His fellow students included William Orr, Alan Ladd, Jack Carson, and William Hammer.

One day, Hammer excitedly reported that every Sunday the Pasadena Playhouse held open readings for plays about to be produced. If he and Gig landed parts, they would not have to pay any fees, and they would be working with the name actors who frequently appeared there. For the next three Sundays, the two of them went to audition. Gig always hung back warily until the crowd thinned out. On his third try, he landed a small part as an old man and moved from Ben Bard's to the more prestigious playhouse in Pasadena.

The Pasadena Community Playhouse had been founded in 1917 by Gilmor Brown, an actor–pageant director–playwright–teacher–promoter. Brown, fulfilling a dream, soon began persuading silent-film stars to appear in productions with students, and he garnered a great deal of publicity. A true visionary with just the needed touch of con in him, he succeeded so well over the next twenty years that by 1937 he had persuaded the state legislature to decree his little undertaking the official state theater of California. Besides allowing fading stage and film stars to try reviving faltering careers by undertaking unexpected roles, he introduced experimental works by playwrights ranging from Eugene O'Neill to the early Tennessee Williams. He also helped launch such players as Tyrone Power, Randolph Scott, Eve Arden, Lee J. Cobb, and Eleanor Parker, endowing the operation with a cachet that was unequaled west of Broadway.

Gig immediately sensed the possibilities open to him. Immersing himself in the enterprise, he quickly became one of Brown's protégés, along with Dana Andrews, Robert Preston, and Victor Mature. Working at various odd jobs to support himself, he moved into Miss T's theatrical rooming house on El Molino Street. This former Pasadena mansion now housed married couples on the first floor, female students on the two upper floors, and males in a maze of crudely constructed rooms Miss T had added in the backyard.

"Gig didn't have a lot of time to sit out back of Miss T's in the sun, yakking," says fellow student Rita Lynn, then Rita Piazza. "When he wasn't rehearsing or studying, he was working. He was there to get a career going. So you won't find a lot of fun stories about him at the Playhouse. This was the tail end of the Depression, so people had a driven quality—and Gig had it more than most."

There was another reason Gig didn't sit around yakking. One of his first roles was as Si Tolliver in *Light from Hell*, a lab production that ran only five nights. A pleasant-looking, friendly girl named Sheila (Sheelah, for stage purposes) Stapler did a comedy role, amusing Gig by her willingness to black out her front teeth and squirt tobacco juice right and left. She threw herself into the part with a gusto that only an amateur could muster. Later, with tongue deep in cheek, Gig said, "I was overcome with her artistry."

Gig began inviting her out for coffee after rehearsals. He learned she had never had any serious intentions of becoming a professional actress. The product of a broken home, she divided her time between her mother and her father, both of whom had remarried and were living in the Philippines. Though Sheila loved them both, she liked living with neither. Her father, general manager of the Benguet gold mines, had enrolled her at Brent, a boarding school located in the mountain province of Baguio. Sheila wanted nothing more than to get away. She'd fled all the way to California.

Once Gig began dating Sheila, people speculated about what such an open-faced, twinkling-eyed dreamboat could see in her. "Listen, a match like that wasn't so unusual," says Nancy Andrews, who was at the Playhouse around that time. "A lot of ambitious pretty boys picked plain jane wives. Those guys wanted to be the beauty in the family." And given Gig's increasing recognition of his physical attractiveness, that plainness may well have been part of Sheila's appeal.

But Sheila's critics overlooked her great strength, the deeply nurturing aspect of her personality, which at that point in Gig's life fulfilled his particular need. She accepted Gig, deferred to him, bolstered his self-image if it showed signs of faltering—and it frequently did. She never criticized his ambitions and never demanded more than he was prepared to give. Sheila knew who she was and what she wanted out of life. And she wanted Gig.

Sheila's unstinting adoration was particularly reassuring to a man who had endured rejection from women throughout most of his early years. What Gig had found in Sheila was a version of Kay, the girl he left behind in St. Cloud. She was old-fashioned, self-effacing, and supportive. Taking confidence from her belief in him, Gig blossomed and mistook his gratitude for love. And perhaps in their early days together, he truly loved her. On August 2, 1940, Gig and Sheila slipped away to Las Vegas, where a simple ceremony made them man and wife. Now two people would devote themselves to promoting Gig's career.

Between February 2, 1939, and May 12, 1940, Gig acted in at least nine plays on the Playhouse's three stages. Dave Hyatt, who appeared with him in *Our Town* and *A Breed Apart,* found him puzzling. "In those days we worked closely together, and we got to be very good friends," says Hyatt. "Yet we never got to know much about each other. Except how important 'making it' was to him. I felt, as I think others did, that he was so good-looking he would carve a place out in films. But he didn't strike me as overly talented, so I was surprised by his eventual success on Broadway."

Hyatt and others may have underestimated Gig's ingenuity. For instance, when playwrights and radio writers Aurania and William Spence Rouverol, who had turned out the Broadway hit *Skidding,* the basis for the Andy Hardy series, decided to try out *Young April* at the Playhouse, Gig managed to meet them early when he volunteered to drive Gilmor Brown to a conference. The Rouverols were charmed. They saw to it that Gig was cast as Brian, who proved "brawn is better than brains—but sometimes mixing them is best of all." They assured Gig that if the show went to Broadway, he'd go with it. In the end, the play went nowhere.

But the disappointment was somewhat dispelled with his appearance in Gilmor Brown's adaptation of Charles Dickens's *Cricket on the Hearth.* His performance earned an encouraging word ("pleasing") from the critic of the Los Angeles *Times.* More important, Warner Brothers' drama coach–talent scout–test director Sophie Rosenstein marked him as someone worth watching.

Financial desperation began to creep in. In the two years since his departure, Gig had found little to brag about in his letters home. He knew that most of the family, except for the ever-loyal Gen, thought he was going through a phase. Letters from his overbearing brother invariably suggested that when he got this "foolish movie business" out of his system, there would still be a place for him wherever Don happened to be at the time. It made Gig feel defensive but determined to succeed. Sheepishly, he appealed to his father for funds with which to join the Screen Actors Guild, so that he could accept the offer he had just received — his first — to appear in a feature-length film. This should have been cause for celebration, but the film was a low-budget, minor-studio flick with the dubious title *Misbehaving Husbands.* So it's unlikely that he would have added a postscript advising the family to watch for it at the local movie house. In fact, forever after, Gig denied having been in the film.

Emma wrote to Gen, who was still teaching in Minnesota. In what appears to be a slightly wounded tone, she reported that Gig had requested "help because he had to join this Guild — so good old Daddy wired $60. . . . We haven't heard from him for several weeks. . . . He's probably too busy to write. Anyway I'm not feeling unduly elated until I know what success he's having."

What neither Emma nor Gig could possibly know was that his career was about to be launched through a bit of odd but serendipitous casting. In one of those quirks of fate, Gig was offered the starring role in a revival, at a small Los Angeles theater, of *Abie's Irish Rose,* Anne Nichols's warhorse comedy about a romance between a Jew and a Catholic. Feeling he was miscast, he wanted to turn the part down, but he needed the thirty-dollar weekly pay. Despite the heavy makeup, Gig made a rather *goyish* Abie, which dulled the play's comic appeal. Still, there was a knock at Gig's dressing room door after one of the performances. A man proffered his card, which read: "Solly Biano, Talent Scout, Warner Brothers."

"I'd like to arrange a screen test for you," Biano told Gig.

"How should I prepare for it?" asked Gig, flabbergasted.

"Just bring yourself," said Biano. "Just bring yourself."

About to breach the wall that separated the civilians from the professionals, Gig felt charged up as he arrived at

Solly Biano's office. The scout took him to Warners' famed drama coach, Sophie Rosenstein, who had seen his work at the Pasadena Playhouse. She'd been assigned to direct the screen test. Sophie sized Gig up, assessed his personality, and gave him a scene to work on. She was forthright, funny, and direct. He left her office aglow, having been told that he had two things going for him: there wouldn't be a woman in the audience who wouldn't fantasize having an affair with him; and he exuded natural elegance. She hoped to be able to capture those qualities on film.

The day of the test, his head swirled. He met the girl who would appear opposite him, then he was shoved in and out of various outfits to find the one that would be most flattering. His ruddy coloring required only a little highlighting. Then Sophie rehearsed the scene with them, made suggestions, and reviewed it with the discombobulated Gig, showing him how to hit his stage marks so that his face wouldn't be out of focus or shadowed.

On the first take, Gig concentrated so completely on hitting the marks that he forgot to act. Then he played the scene well but missed his marks. He never got it right. He knew it. The girl who was assisting him knew it. Sophie knew it. She also knew that they weren't going to get it right. But she pretended that the results were sensational.

"Now," she said, "what we'll do is what's called a personality test. Come through the door. Stand, sit, loosen your tie, do whatever makes you comfortable. Tell us about yourself. If you get stuck, I'll ask you some dumb questions. Show us the real you."

Gig hadn't spent a lifetime developing his ingratiating public persona for nothing. Using all the winning ways that had served him so well with women like Mrs. Kaines, he turned on his cocktail party charm and played directly to the camera. When the moguls saw the test, nobody cared that the prepared scene was mediocre; the boy himself had personality—the X factor that stars were made of. On March 29, 1941, Gig signed a contract with Warner Brothers. His beginning salary was the minimal seventy-five dollars per week.

To say that in return Gig gave the studio his body might seem something of an overstatement, were it not for the fact that in those days Hollywood was indeed feudalistic. Actors were, if not serfs, at least indentured servants in the setup. Ultimately, Gig would give Hollywood much more than he had originally gotten when he signed on the dotted line. Hungering for acceptance, he bought into the Hollywood fantasy in much the same way that his parents had embraced—and ultimately been betrayed by—the American dream. The intermittent rewards that were to come kept Gig's fear of that same fate at bay. But his efforts to reclaim himself would be to no avail. On that bright March day, however, the idea that he was giving not only his body but his soul to Hollywood would have struck him as nothing less than ludicrous.

Much to their chagrin, Warner Brothers found out when they signed him that their potential heartthrob had had a spouse for over a year. Out the window went a possible buildup as a bobby-soxers' idol. And when they got a look at whom he had married, the executives shrugged. The groom was definitely prettier than the bride. There would be no publicity campaign around "Who is that smashing-looking couple?" and few photo layouts of him and Sheila at home.

Ironically, in any place other than Hollywood, Sheila would have been considered pretty. She was five feet five inches tall and weighed 135 pounds, with an Irish alabaster complexion and shapely legs. Her face was square, and she had large, expressive eyes, dark brows, and auburn hair. Like many young girls of that period, she tried to look as much like Joan Crawford as possible.

From the beginning of their marriage, Sheila had been a good partner, just as Emma had been to Gig's father. She'd

found a job as a carhop to help pay the bills until Gig was
signed to a contract; she'd kept the furnished apartment
they'd rented, at 1610 North Normandie in Hollywood, im-
maculate; and she was the one who throughout their marriage would keep up the correspondence with Gig's family
back home, even though she had only met them through a
couple of crackling phone conversations. An old-fashioned,
small-town boy at heart, Gig loved coming home to his
homebody wife. The problem was that Hollywood was a far
cry from the traditional Midwestern town. After Gig signed
on with Warner Brothers, the couple were thrown into the
Hollywood social whirl. At first they responded zealously.
Gig insisted that they attend the studio's social events as part
of his career campaign. "There is more that goes into success than what you see on the screen," he argued.

Though Sheila was as naturally shy as her husband had
once been, Gig assured her that they would overcome what
he diplomatically characterized as the "common anxiety."
In his case, this seemed to be true, but Sheila invariably
reacted the same way each time—tears. She dreaded having
to attend the parties crowded with glamorous young extro-
verts from the studios, people with whom she had nothing
in common. If Gig insisted upon remaining at her side, she
feared that she was keeping him from making valuable con-
tacts and interfering with his good time. If, on the other
hand, he left her on her own, she felt he was ashamed of her.
She would retreat to an inconspicuous spot and worry that
he was succumbing to the charms of some glamour girl.
Whichever way he played it, she invariably ended up weep-
ing, and sometimes with good reason, as when actor Wayne
Morris tactlessly inquired, "Sheila, what are you going to do
when Gig divorces you?"

Eventually Gig gave up mentioning invitations to her
altogether. As he explained to friends, Sheila was a kind-
hearted person whom no one would intentionally hurt but

whom it was almost impossible not to hurt. If this hardly sounded like the rapturous response of a newlywed, it was because Gig had settled for a woman who was more a mother than a lover to him. During those early years, this is what Gig needed, and if it meant sacrificing certain social events to spare his wife and keep the peace, then so be it.

"Most of the up-and-coming young people hung out together," says Jayne Meadows. "Gangs of us kids would be driving around, and somebody would say, 'Oh, there's Gig,' and he'd be watering his lawn. He must have been very shy, because he was not with the—what I'll call the swinging performers who hung out together. We would all go out to the Press Photographers Ball or wherever you were supposed to go to get your picture taken and get publicized. And Gig was never with us, even though he did everything else to push his career."

Gig concentrated instead on entrenching himself at Warner Brothers. As head of production, Jack L. Warner was a close observer of which actors justified their salaries by working most frequently. Nonperforming contractees were placed on layoff. At option time, the unproductive ones were dropped. Also peculiar to Warners was the practice of assigning established players to minor or even bit parts. The bottom line dictated that each employee earn his salary.

Aware of this policy, Warners players scrambled to keep busy, and Gig was even more enthusiastic than most. Shortly after he started, he heard about Jack Warner's philosophy. Gig was a company man, a team player. He was the "good little boy" he'd always been: eager but not overly aggressive, dependable, likable, and cooperative—and he never haggled over money. He helped out with other people's screen tests, filled in small parts, and made himself generally useful. Being a star-struck neophyte, he welcomed his small bits in such big-budget productions as *The Man Who Came to Dinner* and *Sergeant York,* in which he was billed under his real name, Byron Barr. In *They Died with Their Boots On,* Gig gave Eleanor Parker her first screen kiss, but that kiss ended up on the cutting room floor.

Describing this period, Gig once said he specialized in "corpses, unconscious bodies, and people snoring in spectacular epics." His longest role was in *Dive Bomber,* in which he spoke only two words, "Yes, sir," while breathing with difficulty in a pressure chamber. When that film was released in Waynesville, North Carolina (where his parents resided), those two words earned Gig a write-up in the local paper, which concluded, ". . . motion picture critics are predicting a brilliant career for him." Errol Flynn, Alexis Smith, and Fred MacMurray, who starred in the film, didn't rate a mention.

Ridiculous as the "hometown" coverage might have been, Sheila and Gig preserved the copy mailed to them. "Our star's first notice," Sheila wrote to Gen. And when Gig was lent out to 20th Century–Fox for *The Mad Martindales* (eventually released as *Not for Husbands*), in which he climbed to fifth billing in the credits, Sheila wrote, ". . . in this game having Warners know someone else values you is really important."

Perhaps the most important film Gig made at the time was the air force epic *Captains of the Clouds,* starring James Cagney, Dennis Morgan, and Brenda Marshall. His role as a student pilot was minuscule, but Gig reveled in the opportunity to observe Cagney's approach to acting. The star was impressed by Gig's interest in watching and learning from each scene, whether he was in it or not. The two men became friendly during the location shooting, a friendship that was to prove beneficial to Gig later on, when his career was foundering.

On May 10, 1941, Gig wrote his draft board to tell them that he was under exclusive contract and had been assigned to *Captains of the Clouds.* "I've been instructed by Warner

Brothers to leave Los Angeles July 12th, 1941, for Ottawa, Ontario, Canada and this notice is confirming my where-abouts . . . for approximately four weeks."

The news from Europe was becoming increasingly worrisome, and war seemed imminent. Ironically, while storm clouds gathered, these were sunny days for Gig. He sensed a rising momentum in his career, and indeed, his slavish devotion to Warners would soon be rewarded handsomely. And he was happy with Sheila, despite her social shortcomings. The man the "swinging performers" saw watering his lawn had no need—yet—for the temptations Hollywood had to offer. That would come soon enough.

· 3 ·

New Acquaintances

The Japanese bombing of Pearl Harbor, on December 7, 1941, jolted Gig into an awareness of what had been going on in the world while he single-mindedly pursued his own ends in the movie industry. He at once went to the front office at Warner Brothers to declare his intentions of enlisting. Executives, foreseeing a rapid depletion of the studio's pool of leading men, urged him not to be hasty. The government might take the position that turning out entertainment to boost morale was of greater service than enlisting as a private or a seaman. Besides, his cooperation and diligence had not escaped the attention of the executives. The studio had big plans for him, especially now that the draft was scaling down the male roster.

Ingenuously, Gig bought it. He assumed that the studio had his best interests at heart. Hollywood paternalism found a willing subject in a man who had always been comfortable with people telling him what to do. The gung-ho actor threw himself into his career with renewed enthusiasm. In early 1942, he was tapped for a workhorse assignment assisting Alexis Smith, whom director Edmund Goulding was testing for *The Constant Nymph.* Determined to make his mark, Gig prepared as thoroughly as if this were *his* test. The investment of time and energy paid off. Goulding urged fellow director Irving Rapper to take a look at the young actor's work. Rapper, who was rushing to cast his next feature, *The Gay Sisters,* with Barbara Stanwyck, took Goulding's advice and was impressed with what he saw. He was looking for someone to play the dashing artist whom a vixenish Geraldine Fitzgerald tries to snatch away from her sweet, timid little sister, played by Nancy Coleman. Rapper thought he had a young Cary Grant in the newcomer and gave him the role.

Everyone in the cast took a liking to the self-effacing young actor. Aware that it was Gig's first big chance, the always-generous Barbara Stanwyck, who as the steely eldest sister had few scenes with Gig, quietly gave him tips on how to make the most of his part. The result was a characterization of roguish machismo combined with sophisticated charm. In his quest for leading-man status, Gig projected an assurance and a sex appeal that some critics feel he never again quite managed. Even though the picture now lumbers along like a turtle, it is easy to see those qualities in Gig's performance that gave the studio hope that they had another Errol Flynn on the lot—or at the very least, a Ronald Reagan.

Earning special billing in this film despite the rigid studio class system caused Gig's self-esteem to leap, and then word came down that Jack Warner was impressed with the rushes in which Gig appeared. Warner—God himself—had seen the work and declared it good! Gig immediately sensed a difference. Secretaries smiled at him, executives patted him on the back, and he was beginning to spend more and more time in the publicity office—the studio command center, which tailored the actor's personality as neatly and painstakingly as the costumers who nipped and tucked his wardrobe. If he listened closely enough, he could hear the engines of Warners' vast publicity machine warming up to send his "wholesome" story (weren't they all?) out across America.

To a modest actor who was a small-town boy at heart, the idea of a Warners publicity agent coming to his rescue was most welcome. Gig was a willing Galatea to the studio's Pygmalions. In this case, the imagemaker was Charles Einfeld, the fertile brain behind the studio's advertising and publicity machine, who had come up with a clever scheme to focus the spotlight on Gig through a name change. Thus far, he had been known professionally as Byron Barr; as Roland Reed in a couple of stage productions; and then, in his first studio name change, as Bryant Fleming. Now he was to become Gig Young, the name of the character he was playing in *The Gay Sisters.* In most of their newspaper advertisements for the film, Warners allotted space for both a photo of their new leading man and a prominent line of bold type after other players' names, reading: AND INTRODUCING GIG YOUNG AS GIG YOUNG.

On April 20, 1942, the doyenne of syndicated gossips, Louella O. Parsons (who had once lamented that Archie Leach had been "burdened with the name Cary Grant"), drew the attention of her millions of readers to the name change—and to the actor who was the cause of all the fuss. With her literary pretensions, Louella lived up to at least the last half of her self-description, "The Gay Illiterate":

Even W. Shakespeare would be surprised "what's in a name" where Bryant Fleming is concerned. Bryant has just been rechristened Gig Young—all on account of a batch of preview cards that flooded Warners after previews of "The Gay Sister" [*sic*]. I've heard about stars being renamed from numerology contests and after an old aunt. But this is the first time the amateur reviewers have turned the trick. Gig is the name of the character Bryant plays in the picture and he made such a hit everybody referred to him by that name and didn't bother to look up his real moniker on the credit sheet. For my taste, I can't think "Gig" is the most fascinating name in the world—but on him I suppose it looks good.

The reason Louella gave was, of course, a fabrication, which Einfeld had fed to the popular and powerful columnist. Hollywood was a town built on lies. Many Hollywood careers were houses of cards, swaying on a shaky foundation of hype and damage control. One false move—a marijuana bust, a sexual offense—and a star could go down in flames. On the other hand, if you played it right, favorable publicity could grease your way to the top. By now Gig was savvy enough to flatter people like Parsons, who possibly reminded him of Mrs. Kaines back in Washington. The pigeon-plump Louella may have lived in New York and Hollywood for more than a quarter century and might boast of forty million readers, but at heart, she still shared the interests and sensibilities of a Midwestern housewife gossiping over the back fence. A Cinderella story, especially a *male* Cinderella tale, quickened her romantic heart. She was always happy to encourage personable young newcomers, and Gig was more personable than most.

Shy though he was about interviews, Gig obviously had

a natural facility for projecting just the right image. Shortly after *The Gay Sisters* opened, a female staff writer for the Tampa *Tribune* tracked Gig down at Florida's Drew Field, where he was making his follow-up picture, *Air Force,* a wartime melodrama. The reporter wanted to tell her readers how Gig felt about finding himself suddenly famous. She was surprised to discover the young actor disarmingly modest and was charmed by his admission that if his "about-to-come-true dreams" went "up in smoke," he was prepared to resume making a living at one of his anything-but-impressive earlier occupations (as if he really could ever go back to being a night clerk or gas jockey!).

He did have some definite opinions about his career, he told her. He wanted to avoid being typecast. He was bored at the idea of doing only romantic leads. He hoped to be allowed to experiment with sophisticated comedy. He singled out Robert Montgomery (who, ironically, would eventually become his father-in-law), Errol Flynn, and Clark Gable as actors he would like to emulate—strange choices if he was bored by romantic leads—and inexplicably failed to mention such heavyweight character actors as Paul Muni, Spencer Tracy, or his all-time idol, James Cagney.

It seems clear that Gig was faithfully following the lead of the studio publicity machine. At the time, he was thrilled with his rapid progress, but he instinctively adopted an "aw shucks" attitude. Company man par excellence, he picked up the language of "studiospeak" fast and fashioned it as a tool with which to chip out a niche for himself in Hollywood. Just how skillfully he handled the Tampa interview and interviewer can be gleaned from the closing paragraph of the piece, which, by the way, never once mentioned Sheila.

What is he like? Well, he's got naturally curly reddish brown hair untouched by a permanent waving machine, and white, even teeth that are his very own. He's six feet one, weighs 175 pounds, and has the sort of friendly, "I'm interested in what you have to say" sort of personality that will make the girls say, "Move over, Mr. Flynn, and make room for Gig Young."

Gig earned even more fans when *Air Force,* featuring John Ridgely, Arthur Kennedy, and John Garfield, was released and became immensely popular with wartime audiences. Although Gig's part as a copilot called for little more than clamping his jaw and looking dedicated, determined, and grim, he got more than his share of attention for it. Among those who stood up and noticed were producer Henry Blanke and screenwriter Lenore Coffee, who had done *The Gay Sisters* and were now preparing *Old Acquaintance,* starring Bette Davis as a literary author and Miriam Hopkins as her pulp-writing nemesis. They wanted Gig to play Rudd, the handsome young naval lieutenant and ardent suitor of Davis, who is ten years his senior.

The filmmakers saw to it that *The Gay Sisters* was screened for Miss Davis, convinced that she would be totally taken with Gig. They were right: she was. So taken, in fact, that when Vincent Sherman took over the direction of the picture from Edmund Goulding and opposed casting Gig, Davis reportedly stormed the front office to get her way. She wanted Gig—in more ways than one, it turned out.

At the time, Bette Davis and her husband, Arthur Farnsworth, had what she described as "a classically European marriage." That allowed for dalliances, and she had one with Gig, who was flattered that such a great star should find him sexually irresistible. Since both were married, discretion was the name of the game. Farnsworth might have ignored the little affair, but Sheila certainly would not have. It is likely that Davis was the first in a long line of somewhat older women whom Gig pursued romantically over the years. She was near thirty-five; he, not yet thirty. While Errol Flynn and other matinee idols were chasing pretty young things, Gig offered homage to the seasoned actress.

Even after the romance had faded, Gig's friendship with Bette Davis flourished. During his marriages to both Elizabeth Montgomery and Elaine Whitman, Bette was a frequent visitor—she even supervised the hanging of paintings when he was married to Elaine. And in a magazine interview thirty-two years after the filming of *Old Acquaintance,* he named Bette Davis as his favorite leading lady. "I've liked many of them," he said gallantly. "But I've known Bette since my third picture. She's forthright, honest, courageous, and an interesting woman. Everyone knows where they stand with her. She's not a professional charmer. I like that kind of honesty."

Gig's clandestine affair with the film great was not the only thing sizzling on the set of the movie. *Old Acquaintance* vibrated from the clashes between the belligerent Bette and her cantankerous co-star, Miriam Hopkins. There were frequent delays. Newspapers were filled with reports of dissension. Ultimatums were issued. Scene-stealing tricks were tried, foiled, and tried again. Heel-kicking tantrums were thrown. Gig often arrived home very late, attributing his tardiness to these shenanigans. They provided convenient alibis, since sometimes they were true—and Sheila chose to believe him.

Until the end of the shoot, the battles on the soundstage of *Old Acquaintance* almost eclipsed the global inferno. But not for the draft board. They wanted Gig. So on the first anniversary of Pearl Harbor, Warners arranged for Gig to participate in a mass swearing-in ceremony, making him an apprentice seaman in the U.S. Coast Guard as soon as he finished filming his scenes.

A couple of months later, on February 17, 1943, Gig left for Alameda boot camp, riding the momentum of three hits

(The Gay Sisters, Old Acquaintance, and *Air Force)* and
feeling confident that with proper guidance he was headed
for stardom after the war. He had put his faith in Warner
Brothers, and it had paid off—handsomely. There was every
reason to expect a major buildup from the studio upon his
eventual release from the service. On the eve of leaving for
his stint in the Coast Guard, he told a reporter, "I'm trying
to think of it as a location trip."

If, as that remark indicates, real life had indeed become
one big movie set to Gig, then his years in the Coast Guard
might have been a sequence about a young man from St.
Cloud—not an up-and-coming movie star. While he was in
boot camp in Alameda, California—first as a recruit, then as
an instructor—Sheila moved to nearby Oakland and rented
an apartment at 1047 Bella Vista Avenue. There she and Gig
spent their happiest times. Away from the pressures gener-
ated by the Hollywood scene and its self-aggrandizing deni-
zens, they actually seemed well suited to each other. In view
of where life would eventually lead him, this period was a
poignant coda to the "normal" life—as normal as it could be
during wartime.

By far the most dramatic episodes during his uneventful
time in the service were the two emergency leaves he was
granted in response to his mother's illness. In May 1943, Gig
took Sheila back with him to Waynesville. His mother's
chronic health problems had been diagnosed as cancer, and
the end seemed imminent.

Gig was surprised to find that his family was acting out
a charade, pretending that while Emma's illness was serious, it was not life-threatening. But Emma may have sensed
the truth, since both she and Gig made a determined effort
to compensate for the lost years and empty spaces between
them. She cast off all her fears of appearing overly emotional and poured out her heart, finally giving him the
all-out approbation he'd always hungered for. She told him

of her pride in his success in Hollywood and her approval of the down-to-earth girl he had married. By the time Gig and Sheila had to return to Alameda, Emma had gone into remission, and the parting was relatively joyful.

A second emergency leave was granted in May 1944. This time there was no doubt as to the outcome for Emma. Once again she and Gig enjoyed the closeness that had eluded them while he was growing up. Emma showed him a couple of letters from Jack Warner, which praised her for rearing such a fine son and predicted a brilliant future for him, and she told Gig how happy those notes made her. The only thing she refused to acknowledge was the pain that was her constant companion.

With Gig's emergency leave almost over, an odd debate began among family members: should he tell Emma that he was due back at the base or simply leave? Some of the relatives were afraid that his departure might be too much for his mother to handle. The fact that disappearing without bidding her goodbye was considered a possible solution points to one way the Barr family dealt with difficult issues.

Gig finally mustered up the courage to tell his mother that he had to return to the base in California. Stoically, Emma nodded, patted his hand, and said, "That's all right. I'll be leaving soon myself." His mother's emotional resilience brought tears to Gig's eyes. At the door of her room, he turned once more to memorize her face. It was a death mask.

Three days after Gig and Sheila departed, Emma Barr was dead. Whatever unresolved feelings and conflicts Gig took with him as he left her room, he rarely, if ever, spoke of them to friends.

From Alameda in late 1944, Gig was shipped off as a pharmacist's mate aboard the U.S.S. *Admiral Capps* to serve in the Far East. The undistinguished and boring military stint—far from the hellbent escapades such as *Air Force* that Hollywood was churning out—was cut short in a matter of months when Gig was struck down by malaria. Released from the service on July 4, 1945, a month before V-J Day, Gig wanted to get back to Warners, Hollywood, and Sheila— with their new home in the San Fernando Valley—as quickly as possible.

The picture of Gig and Sheila just after the war is pure Norman Rockwell: there is the white stucco bungalow in the San Fernando Valley; Sheila's pot roasts and pies to fatten up a husband depleted by malaria; even a standard poodle named Monday to honor their new beginning. Most of America shared their optimistic vision. Returning servicemen felt confident that having vanquished totalitarianism, all of them would be rewarded by unlimited opportunities.

What was wrong with this picture? Nothing. Nothing, that is, until Gig went back to work. After just over two years in the service, he wanted nothing more than to get in front of a movie camera again. He had basked briefly in the spotlight before entering the Coast Guard, and he fully expected the limelight to become even brighter after he got out. He had every reason to believe that the studio was behind him one hundred percent. Jack Warner himself had been solicitous during Emma's illness, writing more letters to her and sending Gig a condolence telegram on her death. In Gig's polite thank you, he ended by confessing, "I spend a great deal of time dreaming of Warner Brothers. And the day I will return will be the happiest of my life."

Devoted company man that he was, Gig was ecstatic when, on October 15, 1945, Warners threw a gigantic outdoor cocktail party at the studio to welcome him home, along with Wayne Morris and Ronald Reagan. It seemed as if everyone who was anyone in the industry was there. Even Sheila was coaxed out of her shell to enjoy the ballyhooed fete.

During the party, Gig renewed his acquaintance with the vivacious Sophie Rosenstein and her taciturn husband, Arthur Gage, a successful business manager. He introduced them to Sheila, who took to the couple immediately.

At one point, Gig and Sophie got to reminiscing about how craftily she, then a relatively new employee at the studio, had guided Gig through his screen test and, once he'd signed his contract, convinced him to begin studying with her. In the course of conversation, Gig expressed concern over the fact that he'd been out of the service three months and had not yet been assigned to an A picture. Sophie impatiently told him to get off his ass and rejoin her scene study classes to broaden his horizon. Did he want to be a movie actor all his life? Try Shakespeare, and Shaw, and Chekhov. Stretch! It was the kind of bravura speech for which she was noted. Gig was inspired. Later in the evening, arrangements were made for him to sign on Arthur Gage to handle his business affairs.

Soon the two couples were close friends, getting together for cookouts and spending days at the beach. They enjoyed one another's company so much, in fact, that they jointly bought a lot ten miles north of Malibu, on which they planned to erect a weekend cottage they would share. Gig began to draw closer to Sophie, discovering in this woman, six years his senior, the same qualities he had admired in Bette Davis: forthrightness, honesty, and courage.

About a month after the welcome home party, the studio extended Gig's option and raised his salary, which was sorely out of line with the work he had been doing before he entered the service. For example, in *Old Acquaintance,* both Bette Davis and Miriam Hopkins were paid about $5,000 a week, while Gig received $250, even though he was immediately below the stars in billing and box-office importance. Warners, at the urging of Gig's business manager–friend,

Arthur Gage, appealed to the Salary Stabilization Board—a government agency established during the wartime manpower shortage to freeze salaries, keeping the economy under control—which okayed an increase for Gig. He was allowed a raise to $350 and, eventually, $500. He saw the move by the studio as a vote of confidence, and indeed it was.

His euphoria was short-lived. In his first screen appearance since his striking breakthrough in *Old Acquaintance,* he was assigned to the Errol Flynn–Ida Lupino film *Escape Me Never.* He played Caryl, a wimp who dithered and deferred to the mighty Flynn. To make matters worse, he was unflatteringly costumed in baggy trousers, wide suspenders, and an Alpine hat, which made him look like a fugitive from a Swiss tourist poster.

Years later, he told journalist Joan Schmitt that his problems began with that picture. "It started right after the war. . . . I was cast as Errol Flynn's brother in a film at Warners and if you recall at the time he was The King of the lot. If I hadn't been so naive I would have known that this would turn out to be his dull brother. But I didn't get the message until I was told to keep my hands in my lap during my big romantic scene."

An actor with any clout at all might have balked at the assignment, but Gig gamely went along despite his misgivings. And strangely, Sophie offered no advice except to urge him to keep working on scenes from Shakespeare and Shaw. So Gig continued to accept whatever roles he was offered, including 1948's *The Woman in White,* a Victorian thriller co-starring Eleanor Parker, Alexis Smith, and Sydney Greenstreet, which was out of sync with the film noir mood of movie audiences. When Warners held up releasing both this and the Flynn-Lupino picture, on the grounds that they were less than timely, Gig worried that the fans he had acquired with *The Gay Sisters* and *Old Acquaintance* would forget him. Unassertive as always, he watched helplessly as whatever career momentum he had been able to generate earlier petered out.

Had Gig examined his career more analytically, he might have concluded that he was tied to the wrong studio. The ideal spot for him in those postwar years would probably have been MGM, a company that was still making films starring handsome men in dinner jackets who sipped martinis, flicked cigarette ashes, and tossed off bons mots with abandon. At Metro, he would have had a chance at playing the type of role such light comedians as William Powell and Robert Montgomery and their successors had excelled at.

At Warners, there was a rougher tradition past and present, with leading men like James Cagney, Paul Muni, Edward G. Robinson, Humphrey Bogart, and Errol Flynn. Had he analyzed it, Gig would have seen that a script fashioned for one of them would, if the original star was unavailable, be passed on to such rough-and-ready players as John Garfield and Dane Clark. Gig simply was not the rugged type Warners favored.

At first, he was philosophical. Regarding the slump as temporary, he told a reporter from the San Fernando *Valley Times* that, sure, the war had put a "crimp" in his career, but then "everyone obviously lost in the war—many lost their lives." In later years, though, he became increasingly bewildered over what had happened to his promising future, as when he told Louella Parsons in 1952, "You know I was doing fine at Warners until I went into the army [*sic*] and my career suddenly ended. When I came back, there didn't seem to be anyplace for me. I could only get parts that meant nothing."

Why didn't Jack Warner, who had seemed so firmly in Gig's corner, lift a hand to help him? Warner, it must be remembered, was a businessman, who kept his eye fixed on the bottom line, and when Gig had turned out to be an investment that seemed likely to pay only limited returns, the executive's enthusiasm adjusted itself.

Playing the good sport in public, Gig masked the anger and depression he felt at this treatment. While projecting an upbeat image, friends say, he dealt with his anxieties in two ways.

The instant response was to find some unattached male at the studio to go girl-watching with. Writer Peter Brook, formerly of Warners' casting department, says, "I used to love going on the town with him. He was really funny and very picky. He was not just a guy who wanted to get laid, frankly. It was the chase he enjoyed. He was extremely entertaining when he did make a pitch for a gal. I'd sit there and marvel at him. I used to try to learn from him, because sometimes the dialogue was something out of a Noel Coward play. He was a charmer, not one of those whistling, off-into-the-sack kind of guys. We had some wonderful evenings, but you did often feel there was some kind of sadness underneath all the bright talk. Obviously he wasn't fulfilled at home, but he wasn't yet carrying the chasing to its logical conclusion. It was the hunt that buoyed him up."

While Gig may have brought a certain art to his girl-chasing, another kind of woman altogether brought art into his life at this critical moment in his career. Armed with few strong convictions of his own, Gig throughout his life would be particularly vulnerable to "gurus," people radioactive with belief in themselves, who could give direction to his life. Confused and floundering, Gig found a safe harbor in his friend and teacher, Sophie Rosenstein. Like almost every other significant woman in Gig's life, she encouraged him, supported him, bucked him up. But Sophie went one better. She transformed him. "It was Trilby in reverse," says a close friend from that time.

Unlike most Hollywood drama coaches and test directors, Sophie Rosenstein was a proselytizer for "Art," with her antennae out "for everything new and extraordinary in American theater," as Viveca Lindfors noted in her autobiography. Those who came under Sophie's spell contracted a kind of Sophie-mania. Among her disciples over the years were such diverse personalities as Lindfors, Jayne Meadows, Frances Farmer, Rock Hudson, Hugh O'Brian, Piper Laurie, Tony Curtis, Elisabeth Fraser, and many more.

In an industry so fixated on perfectly formed, even-featured beauties, Sophie stood out as a Minnie Mouse look-alike, with long nose, receding chin, and fine-boned arms and legs. She also had vitality, enthusiasm, and generosity of spirit. The general consensus among her friends was that she was ugly but absolutely enchanting. However plain she might have been, she was able to fascinate through sheer personality. Speaking of her to Bob William, a friend in Warners' publicity department at the time, Gig said, "She is not conventionally pretty, but every time she speaks, pearls drop from her lips."

Sophie was born in Portland, Oregon, in 1907. At twelve, she was the prize pupil of Josephine Dillon, a plain, strong-minded woman who would become the first Mrs. Clark Gable. Encouraged by Miss Dillon, Sophie eventually studied theater arts at the University of Washington, in Seattle, where she earned a master's degree and spent ten tumultuous years on the university staff. A Pied Piper in the cause of theater, she inspired a cultlike following among her students. Teaching classes in speech and acting, she also assumed responsibility for the university's theaters.

A bohemian with left-wing leanings, she was despised by some department members and adored by others. Contemptuous of middle-class values, she urged her clique to experience life in all its variations, whether embracing Marxism or free love. Sophie practiced what she preached. While still an undergraduate, she discovered that many handsome young men's interest went beyond artistic admiration. She began cutting a wide swath on campus as a preliberation liberated woman. Though she gloried in scandalizing the department, when she chose a husband in 1928, it was the sedate Arthur Gage, a wholesaler of women's hats. What did Arthur have that the others didn't? An adventurous and generous spirit, plus a little off-campus theater, where he sponsored ambitious presentations of Continental dramatists. Sophie could mount her experimental productions there.

At the university, Sophie encountered a blond journalism major named Frances Farmer, whom she encouraged to switch to drama. Farmer later wrote that Sophie "cooed, moaned and screamed about 'The Art' until I timidly confessed I knew nothing about acting. 'To hell with what you don't know, I'll teach you,' Sophie confidently promised." With that, Farmer changed majors and, under Sophie's tutelage, distinguished herself playing leads at the university theaters. She capped it all with her work in Sophie's production of Chekhov's *Uncle Vanya* at Gage's little theater. Adopting Stanislavsky's techniques as they understood them, Sophie and the mercurial Farmer earned huzzahs even from those who disapproved of them personally.

Farmer eventually managed to visit the Moscow Art Theatre in Russia and the Group Theatre in New York before traveling to Hollywood. There this high-strung, sensitive beauty made a name for herself before tragically succumbing to mental illness aggravated by alcohol, redbaiting, and her domineering mother. In 1938, Farmer had arranged for Sophie to come to Hollywood to prepare an actress for a test. To Sophie's surprise, she liked the work (even though, like most theater-oriented people at the time, she had tended to look down on filmmaking). And since disapproval of her leftist politics and liberal ideas about acceptable sexual conduct was making her life at the university untenable, she and Arthur decided to make a permanent move south. He became a business manager, while she found herself ensconced at Warner Brothers, where her path crossed Gig's.

By 1945, Sophie and Gig had had a long working relationship, which had flowered into friendship. Now, analyzing Gig's professional problems, she suggested he try working up theater scenes as a means of expanding his horizons beyond the kinds of roles he was playing at the studio between 1945 and 1947. Gig went at it with his usual enthusiasm, and Sophie saw to it that the important producers and directors were aware of his wasted potential. To further drive the point home, in the summer of 1947 Gig received permission from Warners to appear on the La Jolla Playhouse stage for one week in a revival of S. N. Behrman's hit comedy *Biography.* On the day of the opening, Gig received a shock: Warners was dropping his option.

Negotiations had been going on for some months prior to this. Gig's agents and Arthur Gage had been pressing Warners to raise his pay from the $500 per week he had been getting since early 1946 to $750. Assessing their scaled-down expectations for him, Warners wanted to freeze his salary. Neither side would budge. So in the first week of August, the Warners' business office circulated a confidential memo to those involved in casting that Gig had been dropped from the studio. It came as a devastating blow to him. The moment he was out of work, Gig, like most actors, was sure that he would never find employment again. But not everyone thought the termination was a stroke of bad luck. On opening night at the La Jolla Playhouse, as Gig sat staring disconsolately into his makeup mirror, Bette Davis came barging into his dressing room, saying she had just heard the news. Gig managed a wan smile. "Well, congratulations!" the star spat out. "You're well out of that stagnation pit! I wish I were!"

Gig's career problems and domestic difficulties were no secret, but another source of discord in his life was so disturbing that he and Sheila kept it strictly between themselves. As long as Gig could remember, his achievements had been overshadowed by those of his brother, Don. Even after Gig's splashy prewar film debut, his brother had written to remind him that when he was in the market for a solid job, Don would find a place for him in his field.

Don seemed capable of fulfilling this offer. After his stint in Russia, followed by a year in England as consultant to British Canners Ltd., he landed in New York as vice-president in charge of marketing for Birdseye Frosted Foods. There his work caught the eye of Norton Simon, then president of the Young and Rubicam advertising agency. Simon eventually lured Don to Y&R, with the assignment to try and land Hunt Foods as the agency's first national account.

Don attacked the task so doggedly over such long hours that the tuberculosis he had contracted in his travels took a turn for the worse, and he transferred to the agency's Los Angeles office—which put him in the center of Gig's territory. Relations were cordial but obviously not close, since none of Gig's friends from that period remembers meeting or even hearing Gig speak of Don and Don's wife, Jo. Although Don succeeded in landing the account, the grueling schedule exacerbated his illness, and he was forced to direct the ad campaign by telephone from his sickbed.

Distressed by his brother's poor health, Gig attempted to give Don and Jo a hand. His efforts were met with criticism and outright ridicule, and it was only with great difficulty that Gig held his tongue and continued to help the beleaguered couple. Then, much to his relief, Don was transferred to a sanitarium in Tucson, Arizona, where Gig confidently expected him to make a recovery. But Gig's relief turned to guilt and dark depression when, on September 2, 1949, the brother he had always both admired and deeply resented succumbed to tubercular meningitis.

If there was life for Gig after Warner Brothers, it came in dribs and drabs. He rejected out of hand Sophie's suggestion that he pull up stakes, go to New York, and try to land a part in a play. Hollywood lore is full of stories of stars who have been dropped, only to rise from the ashes. Joan Crawford, for example, came back with her Oscar-winning *Mildred Pierce* after Louis B. Mayer unceremoniously dumped her. Gig wanted to follow the same course. But instead of holding out for a role that would increase his artistic stature, an insecure Gig allowed his agents to persuade him to go for the money in lackluster supporting roles. Thus he played Porthos in MGM's *The Three Musketeers,* with Gene Kelly, Lana Turner, and Angela Lansbury; and John Wayne's nemesis in Republic's *Wake of the Red Witch.* Overshadowed by stellar performers in showier roles, he was ignored in the reviews.

The unsuccessful outcome of these two attempts at free-lancing caused Gig to jump at the opportunity of a long-term contract with Columbia Pictures. Studio head Harry Cohn had promised Gig a star buildup when he played opposite Rita Hayworth in *The Loves of Carmen.* The catch was that he must first play the weakling husband who loses Ida Lupino to Glenn Ford in *Lust for Gold* (shades of his role with Errol Flynn at Warners!). But when he had finished *Lust,* Cohn, the wily wheeler-dealer, double-crossed Gig, forcing him into *Tell It to the Judge,* with Rosalind Russell and Robert Cummings. The finished picture was such a debacle that Columbia never released it in New York. Meanwhile, the promised role opposite Hayworth went to Glenn Ford.

The gritty and exploitive underbelly of the paternalistic studio system he'd sunk his trust in left Gig confused and disenchanted. In retaliation, he went on suspension and eventually broke his contract with Columbia, knowing full well that he risked the insecurity of a finished career. And having ridden a slew of mediocre roles to stasis, he hardly worked during the latter part of 1949 into early 1950. Gig desperately needed a sympathetic ear. But he didn't trust his agents, and Sheila had little insight into his problems. He turned to Sophie.

Leaving Sheila at home, Gig began seeing Sophie and Arthur Gage and half a dozen other regulars at barbecues at the home of English actor Robert Douglas and his beautiful wife, Sue. The hosts were bowled over by the romantic sparks flying between Gig and Sophie. "I remember people discussing it," says Sue Douglas. "Sophie was a wonderful friend, but I must say we were a little surprised to see this attraction developing between her and Gig. She was homely, but it was definitely a romance."

While Gig was his urbane, witty self at these gatherings, his behavior at home was another matter altogether. He and Sheila were becoming bitterly estranged. She snapped at him, timed his absences, and complained. He maintained an aloof silence between squabbles. In the divorce proceedings that would follow in 1949, Sheila invoked the catchall phrase "mental cruelty." He, on the other hand, claimed that she "mocked and ridiculed" him, "feigned illness," and "threatened suicide" if he suggested they break up the marriage. In his complaint, he maintained that being around her was adversely affecting his career and leading him to drink. Although no newspaper printed the information, court records show that both were restricted from "molesting, harassing, or annoying each other in any manner."

In truth, Gig never needed his deteriorating relationship with Sheila as a reason to drink. It is hard in these relatively abstemious times to recall the days when the double martini marked a man as cultivated and charming. Ever since adolescence, Gig had used alcohol to escape his inhibitions. In Hollywood, the cocktail glass had served him well as the indispensable prop for a man-about-town. On more than one occasion, he had heard—and believed—a friend's advice: "God, Gig, take a drink—you're so much more fun when you're drinking." Indeed, he was rarely dull after a couple of belts, but he could be out of control.

In December 1948, the long-simmering tension between Gig and Sheila erupted. She had suspected his occasional unfaithfulness for some time. But now she knew she had something more to worry about. Hard as it was for her to believe, she had come to realize that Sophie and Gig were seriously involved. Finally, she confronted him. When he returned from a bout of partying one night, a bit drunk, he shouted at her abusively. She shouted back. He went on a rampage, overturning lamps and tables and smashing furniture in the living room.

Terrified at this unexpected violent outburst, Sheila raced out of the house to neighbors, begging them to come over and help calm Gig down. At the sight of them, Gig subsided, but he never forgave her for allowing casual acquaintances to become aware of their private problems. He was horrified at risking harmful publicity if Hedda, Louella, or their ilk learned of the incident. After Christmas, Gig moved in with friends, and on the first day of 1949, he asked Sheila for a divorce.

Louella Parsons broke the news of the Youngs' marital split. Then, living down her nickname "Love's Undertaker," the columnist sat Gig down and gave him one of her Dutch aunt's heart-to-hearts. A messy divorce could be harmful to a rising young actor's career, she told him. Gig listened respectfully. Despite the blows he had taken during the last couple of years, he was still so enmeshed in Hollywood's value system that he agreed to try and reconcile with Sheila, even though he could no longer stand the sight of her. It was lip service to the powerful scribe. The reconciliation lasted only a couple of hate-filled weeks, but Louella became, as Gig must have known she would, his partisan forever.

On October 6, 1949, Sheila was granted an interlocutory judgment of divorce. In the settlement, she received a 1940 Mercury convertible, U.S. Savings Bonds whose cost value was $4,200, and twenty percent of Gig's gross weekly income, not to exceed $150 a week or $6,000 a year. Gig kept $441 from a savings account, a bond whose cost value was $75, and a new Buick convertible. By order of the court, disposition of the Malibu lot, jointly owned with Sophie and Arthur Gage, was to be settled after a year had elapsed and the divorce became final.

With his marriage dissolved, Gig now pressed Sophie to file against Gage. Since she had initiated the affair, as Sophie admitted to her friend Viveca Lindfors, Gig had expected her to be overjoyed at his divorce. He was stunned to find her anguishing over the prospect of a separation from Gage. While their marriage was now based primarily on mutual respect and companionship, she knew Arthur loved her deeply. Even during this crisis he remained civil toward her and continued to function as Gig's business manager. Sophie reminded Gig that he was thirty-six and she was forty-two. Friends warned her that in a few years she'd be too old for him. Maybe they should just settle for an affair, she told him.

Gig turned her own guns against her. Wasn't she a romantic? he chided her. Wasn't she always talking about taking chances, letting the future take care of itself? He begged her to ignore dire predictions and to trust his intentions. The decision to marry was not a quick one. Sophie wouldn't allow herself to be hurried. But in the end, she decided to take the gamble. Gig was overjoyed. On January 1, 1951, at the home of some friends in New York, with actor Arthur Kennedy giving away the bride, Sophie and Gig were wed.

When word rocketed around Hollywood that Sophie was divorcing Arthur to marry Gig, people were amazed. Some never doubted Gig's love for her. Benson Fong, actor and restaurateur, said, "Gig was deep enough to love such a person as Sophie because she was such a wonderful person inside. Looks are skin deep." Others, more cynical, cited Gig's opportunism. Gossip columnists had a field day. Running into Gig at the Brown Derby restaurant, Hedda Hopper pronounced, "Congratulations! But I thought you already had a mother." Her rival Louella Parsons bumped into Sophie on the Universal lot, where she was working, and croaked, "All happiness, Sophie! I suppose you'd call this a May and December romance."

Over the years, Sophie had developed a thick hide, but not Gig, who rankled at the loose talk he overheard when they went out together. He was particularly sensitive to the speculation about his sexual preference, aroused by the match between a man of his obvious physical appeal and a woman of Sophie's plainness. In fact, according to Arthur Gage, Gig was getting downright paranoid about the aspersions on his manhood.

One evening, Gage joined Gig for dinner at Hollywood's Don the Beachcomber. The actor recoiled as the business manager slipped into a bamboo booth beside him. Gig instructed him to sit opposite him, not next to him.

"Why?" inquired Gage.

James Earl Barr, Gig's father, at 25.

Byron Ellsworth Barr (the future Gig Young) as a toddler.

Gig and his sister, Genevieve.

Summer on the farm.

(courtesy of Genevieve Barr Merry)

Gig in St. Cloud at about 18.

Gig's brother, Donald Barr.

(courtesy of Genevieve Barr Merry)

(courtesy of Genevieve Barr Merry)

Gig at Mrs. Kaines's rooming house in Washington, D.C.

In the Coast Guard during World War II.

The Barr family and friends in 1944. From left: J. E. Barr, Genevieve Barr Merry, Evelyn Craig, Mrs. Moody (rear), Emma Barr, Sheila Barr, Byron Barr.

Gig and his first wife, Sheila, at Don the Beachcombers.

Jo (Donald Barr's wife), Sheila, and Gen in Los Angeles, 1947.

Gig and Gen on a set (apparently someone mistakenly thought "Gen" was short for "Jennifer").

The dashing Gig Young.

SCREEN ROMANCES

DELL

LATEST SCREEN STORIES

SCOOP! First color portraits of FRANK SINATRA and DONALD O'CONNOR

DEC.
15¢

BETTE DAVIS
AND
GIG YOUNG

OLD ACQUAINTANCE... Starring Bette Davis and Gig Young
HOSTAGES... Starring Luise Rainer and Arturo de Cordova

Sophie Rosenstein and Viveca Lindfors.

Wedding Number Two.
From left: Anderson Lawler, Skitch Henderson, Faye Emerson
(a former pupil of Sophie's), Sophie, and Gig.

"Because they'll say we're queers," Gig replied.

"What makes you think sitting across from you will make any difference?" a stunned Gage retorted.

"I don't know, but I'm telling you that's the way it is."

An even more graphic and disturbing instance of Gig's sexual defensiveness came at a party in the San Fernando Valley that Gig and Sophie attended. He had had several drinks and was leaning on the piano, when the piano player, whom he didn't know, made some insinuating remarks about his masculinity. Gig went berserk, pummeling the hapless pianist until Sophie, with the aid of a couple of friends, managed to get him outside and into their convertible. As Sophie drove home, he pulled a knife out of the glove compartment, reached up, and began ripping the canvas to shreds.

Although this violence was drastically out of character, Sophie didn't appear to be unduly concerned about her husband's overreaction to these remarks about his sexuality. Given her liberated views, she prompted him to tell the story at gatherings afterward to defuse the latent and ominous feelings that triggered it. Perhaps the older men who had shown such an interest in the young Gig had done more to him than he would later admit to his armchair guru on the analytical tapes. But the fact remains that no one within living memory could recall any homosexual episode in Gig's life.

There is every reason to believe that Gig was physically devoted to Sophie, the woman through whom he was righting so many past wrongs done to him. In joining himself to her, he was gaining a loving, permissive parent, a good teacher, and an understanding lover, all in one small package.

·4·

Meskite

The picture of Gig and Sophie at the beginning of 1951 was more Edward Hopper than Norman Rockwell: Here was this older female "meskite"* paired up with a handsome Hollywood actor in a house with a swimming pool in the San Fernando Valley. Few people would have predicted success for such a match, but nevertheless, it worked. Gig was a doting husband, more so than most. He'd bring Sophie presents, among them gloves and shoes because he thought she had beautiful hands and feet. Shortly after the marriage, Sophie told her friend Viveca Lindfors, "Oh, Viveca, I'm so happy. They warned me I was making a mistake,

*An unattractive woman, literally, "ugly."

but everything Gig does makes me realize what I'd been missing!"

If Gig gave Sophie the romantic devotion she'd always craved, she gave him entrée into a world that was concerned with more than eight-by-ten glossies and press releases. On Sunday afternoons, the Youngs opened their doors to Sophie's former protégés. Jayne Meadows recalls how these informal gatherings defined their relationship:

"I always thought Sophie was a mother figure to him, just as Clark Gable's first wife [Josephine Dillon] was to him. Sophie was guiding Gig's career. He had all the self-confidence of an abused, frightened child. I think that's why he drank, to dull the pain and insecurity. But now there was Sophie to say, 'Little boy, you're handsome. You're sexy. You're talented.' I'm not saying he was aware of it, but in my opinion, those were the reasons he loved her."

Most of the talk at the Youngs' festive Sunday salons centered on films and the theater, especially with Sophie now working as the top drama coach on the Universal lot. With the emphasis at home on "Art," Gig rankled at the second-rate films he was forced to act in to hold up his share of the bills. From late 1950 into 1951, he free-lanced in such thankless roles as the Nazi masquerading as a captured U.S. airman in *Target Unknown.* There were the standard Westerns as well, such as *Only the Valiant* and *Slaughter Trail.*

Enter Sophie, to the rescue. She spoke to her friend Wilt Melnick, an actors' agent with the Louis Shurr Agency, about representing Gig. Melnick, agreeing that her husband's talents were being wasted, signed him. "I knew his work," says Melnick, "and Gig could be counted on to add weight to thin roles." Since the agent was aware that Gig had been typed by the studios as a second lead, he felt it his duty to find Gig a well-written feature role that would allow him once again to show people what he could do. The script that provided this opportunity was *Come Fill the Cup.*

There are several versions of how Gig got the part of the alcoholic composer. The version he gave writer Michael Buckley in *Films in Review* was that he was on the Warner Brothers lot one day and on impulse dropped in to visit his old friend Solly Biano. The talent scout said that he had just finished reading the script of the new James Cagney movie and there was a great role in it for Gig. Would he test for it? Gig tested—and got the part.

That sounds like a story told by a man who was tired of having people think that he relied on his wife's clout to get ahead. A more likely scenario is that Sophie and then Melnick enlisted a network of well-placed friends to be alert when reading scripts for any part that would offer Gig an opportunity to show what he could do.

In the film, Cagney plays a reporter, a reformed alcoholic, who is given the assignment of getting his publisher's nephew off booze and on the wagon. The nephew, Gig's role, is a self-indulgent composer who is married to the reporter's ex-girlfriend and at the same time is romantically involved with a nightclub singer, who is herself romantically entangled with a gangster.

Shortly after the film began shooting, a rumor spread that the front office, having viewed the dailies, was dissatisfied with Gig's performance and wanted him replaced. An irate Jimmy Cagney stormed into producer Henry Blanke's office and delivered an ultimatum. If Gig was fired, he'd quit. Gig was retained, but Cagney sensed that the actor's confidence was shaken. Gig was deferring to him as the star. Following several takes on an important scene, Cagney draped his arm over Gig's shoulder and walked him away from the others. He didn't know what kind of actors Gig had been working with, he said, but on this set, when it was his scene, Gig had better take it or Cagney would wipe him right off the screen. The result was a memorable portrait, especially in two scenes—Cagney cuffing the drunken composer around and the composer contemplating suicide when he can't find the liquor he has cached away.

Gig's emotional investment in *Come Fill the Cup* was so great that he and Sophie arranged to attend the preview separately so he would be free to roam the theater to study audience reaction. He knew this was his meatiest postwar role. What he was less certain of was the audience response. "What good will it do if I'm at my best but nobody sees the picture?" he nervously kept asking his agents. After a long time in abeyance, his competitive juices were flowing.

He need not have worried. Audiences loved Cagney and were impressed by Gig. Representatives from the Shurr Agency arranged to meet him at Melnick's home after the preview, for a postmortem. Sophie and a friend also dropped by. Gig was the last to arrive. "He was obviously pleased with his reception," says Helena Sterling, a Shurr employee who became a close friend of Gig's over the next few years. "And if anyone doubted that he really loved Sophie, they should have seen him that night. Most actors would have been all over their agents. He went directly to her. And there was such love in his eyes as he cupped Sophie's homely little face in his hands and kissed her as if she were a Grace Kelly china doll. He just obviously laid his performance at her feet."

After studio screenings, Hollywood insiders speculated about how much "pillow direction" Gig had received from Sophie. He tried to stanch such talk when he told a columnist, somewhat defensively, that in the interest of a happy marriage, he and his wife had agreed not to discuss each other's work at home. When the picture was released, he received exceptional notices. Gig laughed when he noted that many were predicting stardom for him. He had been around long enough to read *that* with a grain of salt. But he knew that he'd forced the industry to take another look at him. They liked what they saw. When nominations for the best performance by an actor in a supporting role were announced in early 1952, Gig was included, along with Karl Malden, Kevin McCarthy, Leo Genn, and Peter Ustinov.

Sophie and Gig were ecstatic. In February, Sophie, who had grown close to Gig's father and sister during their brief vacations in Hollywood, took time out to write Gen. She and Gig were thrilled, she wrote, that he had been singled out by the eleven thousand voters in the Academy of Motion Picture Arts and Sciences. "We don't hold out any real hope for the Oscar but that part of it is incidental," she admitted, adding, "Bunty and Sid Justin are giving a party afterward for Gig so we'll celebrate come what may."

On the night of the awards, Sophie glowed in a full-cut white mink stole, a gift from her adoring—and grateful—husband. As she and Gig had foreseen, the Oscar went to Karl Malden for his work in another Warner Brothers picture, *A Streetcar Named Desire.*

The Oscar nomination bestowed on Gig the stature of the accomplished, serious actor. But, typically, he didn't have the instinct or courage to capitalize on it. Shortly before receiving it, he'd signed a lucrative contract with MGM, who stuck him in mediocre potboilers like *Holiday for Sinners* and *You and Me.*

A more self-possessed actor might have gone on suspension, to serve notice that his talent deserved more thoughtful treatment. That Sophie did not urge him to such an action was due to her having other things on her mind—as did Gig. In fact, he had a pressing reason to accept the MGM films: there were medical bills to be paid—large ones. The woman whose face he'd so lovingly cradled in his hands the night of the preview for *Come Fill the Cup* was in trouble. Shortly after their marriage, Sophie had gone into the hospital for surgery related to a partial hysterectomy she had had years earlier. The surgeon informed Gig that the prognosis was bad: his wife of three months had cervical cancer.

Faced with this shattering news, Gig was at his best. He exacted a promise from the doctor to keep the news from Sophie and then engaged in elaborate charades designed to reassure his wife that nothing was seriously amiss. He encouraged her to return to her work at Universal and to go out with friends in the evenings. And at first Sophie kept up the pace. But Viveca Lindfors began to suspect all was not well when Gig took Sophie to an internist in Seattle and to a specialist in New York. Any attempt to talk about her friend's health, however, was met with a steely glare from Gig.

"Sophie and I would have lunch at the studio," says Lindfors. "But she only picked at her food. Today we'd immediately think of cancer. In those days I didn't. Gig believed Sophie never knew. He said she thought she had something wrong with her stomach. But she was so smart. I think each one was playing this game to fool and comfort the other."

Sophie grew weaker and finally took a leave of absence from her job. During this period, she and Gig made a trip to Portland, her hometown. Sophie was too weak to walk very far, but late each afternoon, Gig would scoop her up in his arms and carry her out to watch the sunset over the water.

As Sophie continued to lose strength, Gig began to fear that if her condition took a sudden turn for the worse, they would be trapped in Portland. Craftily, he wrote a friend in L.A., arranging for a telegram to be sent saying he was needed at MGM for a wardrobe test. "I felt guilty as hell," he later confided to Gen, "but I couldn't face having her die up there. And I knew she wouldn't do anything to stand in the way of my career. So I had the wire sent."

Throughout 1952, Sophie's health declined. By October, she was spending most of her time in bed. When Gig wasn't working, he sat holding her hand while she slept or read aloud to her when she awoke. She loved hearing him read anything but especially delighted in his reading of light comedy and Shakespearean sonnets. The idea of Gig reading Noel Coward's antically amusing *Private Lives* to a woman slowly dying of cancer might seem grotesque to some, but there was something touching and valiant in the fact that this great lover of the theater should hunger for its healing touch even in her darkest hours. She especially loved hearing it from a man whose potential for light comedy she'd immediately recognized when he first walked into her life.

Gig's richly resonant voice acted out all the parts to the plays of Coward and others, like Kaufman and Hart's *You Can't Take It with You* and Oscar Wilde's *The Importance of Being Earnest.* Visitors were astonished to enter the house and hear Sophie's weak but infectious chuckle as Gig solemnly intoned some such Wilde riposte as Aunt Augusta's "To lose one parent, Mr. Worthing, may be regarded as a misfortune; to lose both looks like carelessness."

By the night of October 24, 1952, it was impossible to ignore the fact that Sophie needed to be hospitalized. Bob and Sue Douglas came along to offer emotional support. As the four were getting into the car, Sophie turned to the place where she'd enjoyed a brief interlude of happiness and said, "Goodbye, house. I don't think I'm going to see you again."

For seventeen days, Sophie hung on. Gig remained at her side, earning the respect and admiration of the nurses on the floor, who must have wondered what strange Cupid had brought these two together. In her last days, Sophie wanted to give Gig a legacy of some sort to remember her by. She exhorted him to make good on all the hopes for his career that they had shared together. She had so wanted to help him realize his potential as a stage actor who could scale both comedic and tragedic heights. In her last moments of consciousness, she tried to buoy his all-too-shaky confidence to meet those challenges without her.

The elegiac tenderness of these desperate stolen hours

were hauntingly expressed in the sonnets Gig read to Sophie during his vigil. Shakespeare's thirtieth—a particular favorite of hers—seemed to capture the regret in that hospital room:

When to the sessions of sweet silent thought
I summon up remembrance of things past,
I sigh the lack of many a thing I sought,
And with old woes new wail my dear time's waste.

On November 10, Sophie slipped into a coma and died. Gig took her eighty-year-old father, who lived about three hours away in Lake Elsinore, California, back to the San Fernando Valley house to stay until after the funeral, which, according to Jewish custom, was scheduled for the next day. Aware that Sophie had sent her father a monthly check, Gig tactfully assured the old man that his daughter had arranged for the checks to continue. She'd done no such thing. "But," says his friend and business associate Helena Sterling, "it was a very Gig gesture."

After the funeral, Sue and Bob Douglas took Gig to Lake Mead near Las Vegas to distract him. Neither had ever seen a man so totally devastated. Taking long walks along the lake, Gig tried to recover from the shock of losing the first woman who had been able to fill the emptiness he'd felt from earliest childhood. Sophie had understood him, praised him, inspired him. If he had been sure of anything in his relationship with her, it was that she'd never leave him. This trust had led him to let down his guard, to open himself up to life's possibilities. Now, incredibly, improbably, she'd abandoned him too. With Sophie's death came the suspicion that he'd been born under an unlucky star.

Weeks after Sophie's death, friends noticed that when Gig was talking about something far removed from his tragedy, tears would suddenly well up in his eyes and course down his face. Years later, he still couldn't speak Sophie's name without stammering. Work took on the added function of distracting him from his unhappy memories. It didn't matter that the film *The Girl Who Had Everything* wasn't very good. It didn't matter that Elizabeth Taylor, as the spoiled daughter of a criminal lawyer (played by William Powell), jilted him for one of her father's crooked clients (Fernando Lamas). It didn't matter that Taylor, Powell, and Lamas were billed above him. What *did* matter was that he had something to keep him from thinking about his loss.

A couple of months later, Gig was in Chicago, having been lent out to Republic Pictures by MGM to play the lead in a documentary-style melodrama, *The City That Never Sleeps*. He liked the script despite its debt to the recently successful *Naked City*. Besides, its bluesy mood converged with his own feelings. Sophie was never far from his thoughts. He kept photos of her on the bedside table in his hotel suite. Her memory, in fact, had begun to take on an almost mystical aura.

One evening, he was waiting for the cameras to set up for the final scene of the day, in a local strip joint. Jazz was playing in the background, and getting carried away by the music, he began to free-form dance by himself. Ever since his ballroom dance teacher days in Washington, he could express in movement the feelings that he otherwise bottled up. People who knew him were always amazed when suddenly, in a club or at a gathering, he'd begin an interpretive dance, totally oblivious to his surroundings. It was a sensual side of Gig that few had ever seen.

Now, in this tawdry Chicago club, he was a striking, lonely figure gliding up and down the aisles, responding to the music from moment to moment. Then, quite spontaneously, one of the strippers fell in behind him, never impinging on his space. When the music stopped, they stood together, chatting freely. Then the music started again, and they resumed their strangely intimate pas de deux. Although the greatest intimacy he had allowed himself since Sophie's death was a shared dinner, he invited the stripper back to his hotel, telling himself, he later confided, that after all, she was attractive and he was not a monk.

They arrived at his suite. He poured drinks and excused himself to shower. When he returned, the girl was lying nude on the bed, and all of Sophie's photos were facedown on the bedside table. He became angry. Why had she touched Sophie's pictures? Was she squeamish about making love in front of his wife? He looked at her, and her arms and legs appeared strangely shaped. *It's a green frog!* he thought. He wanted her out of his suite, but how could he manage it without hurting her feelings?

Excusing himself, he rushed into the sitting room, quietly dialed the unit publicist, and asked him to call on the bedroom phone at once. Then he hurried back to the girl. Seconds later, the phone rang. Gig picked up the receiver, listened, groaned, feigned disappointment, agreed, and hung up.

He informed the stripper that there had been a reshuffling of the shooting schedule. He had to prepare a new scene for the first thing in the morning, and so, reluctantly, he would have to send her home. They got dressed; he gave her far too much cab fare and walked her to the elevator. "Then I came back to my bedroom," he later told Helena Sterling, "set Sophie's pictures up the way they belonged, and hopped into bed greatly relieved."

When he returned to Los Angeles after the shoot, Gig felt lonelier than ever, but Helena came to the rescue. She had lost her husband almost a year earlier, so they were able to commiserate with each other. Neither wanted to date, but they needed each other's company. The relationship was platonic and satisfactory for both of them.

"Gig's problem was that when the sun goes down in Los

Angeles, it goes down quickly," says Helena. "He was living at Olympic and Spaulding in an apartment, and he'd come home and check the answering service. Now, if the Douglases or some of his other friends hadn't called to invite him to dinner, I'd suddenly get a call, and in a desperate voice he'd say, 'Have dinner with me.' I knew what was happening. I said, 'Gig, do me a favor. The minute you get home—I don't care if the sun is still out—put on the lights in the apartment.' Because the loneliest hour comes when nobody's invited you out and you're there with your memories."

On those nights—and there were many—Gig would mix a shaker of martinis, pick up a book, and try to blot out his sorrow. Complicating Gig's loneliness was that aside from a few intimates, like Helena, people simply would not believe that the man with those dancing eyes and that crooked smile could be suffering. After Sophie's death he found himself plagued by insomnia. Desperate, he went to his druggist, a personal friend, and confided that he needed Miltown to help him sleep. The druggist smiled and refused. He said, "You know, Gig, with your happy face, you don't need tranquilizers."

As much as Gig hated to hear how happy he always seemed to be, his smile was by now second nature, more a mannerism than a bellwether. He later regretted the isolation imposed by the mask he had perfected so well. "You've really got to show what is inside," he later told a friend, "or nobody cares." The dissonance between his real feelings and this facade lent him an "aura of sadness" perceived by almost everyone who knew him well.

Living in cynical, self-centered Hollywood did not exactly help. Within months of Sophie's death, his male peers would slap him on the back, wink, and say, 'Getting much, Gig?' " The same libidinous undercurrents were flowing on the set of *Torch Song,* starring Joan Crawford and featuring Gig as a playboy—his final film under the MGM contract.

The legendary Crawford was delighted with him and frequently invited him to her dressing room for a drink after a day's shooting. Things went along swimmingly until they bumped into each other on a Saturday night in Palm Springs when Gig was visiting his friends Don and Zetta Castle. Crawford detached herself from her companions and invited him to dinner. The actress listened sympathetically as Gig talked on about Sophie, the strong, brilliant woman now gone from his life. At the end of the evening, Crawford fixed her powerful eyes on him and said, "Darling, why don't you come see the lovely cottage I have for the weekend?" Appalled that she would make a pass at him, Gig tried to wiggle out of the hot spot by convincing her that his hosts were expecting him back. Crawford froze.

The next Monday, on the set, Gig was no longer "darling." There were no more invitations for drinks in her dressing room. Crawford's favorite director was handling the film, and she had him completely under her thumb. "When the film was released," said Gig, "I had three minuscule scenes and one good line—'I'll go home and curl up with a good book or a bad girl.' I still had featured billing, but inexplicably, I disappeared early in the picture." Unsurprisingly, reviewers of *Torch Song* found Gig "somewhat superfluous."

But Gig didn't care about *Torch Song* or much of anything else having to do with Hollywood. Nearing forty, he was drawn more and more to the ideals and values that Sophie had instilled in him. Without anyone to turn to for guidance, he felt confused and uncertain about realizing those lofty goals. But he drew inspiration from an unlikely source: his next-to-last picture at MGM, a trendy Western called *Arena,* set in the roistering world of rodeo. It was shot in the then-novel 3-D process and meant to be viewed through special glasses.

Gig felt his role, as a roving rodeo champion, was the best thing he'd been offered since *Come Fill the Cup.* Enthusiastic about the theatrical violence inherent in a sport that pitted determined men against wild animals enraged at being tethered and burdened, he watched with fascination as snorting broncos and wild-eyed Brahman bulls jerked around his stunt double in clouds of dust and sweat. He could identify with both man and beast. He, too, had felt the whiplash of success and failure after a decade of being a Hollywood contract player and a free-lancer. As for his personal life, he simply felt he'd been kicked in the head. But while the rodeo background was authentic, the film foundered on the sudsy and shallow story of a confused and pained man torn between his wife and the Other Woman.

Now, at the end of his MGM contract, he decided it was time to leave Hollywood for a new arena: the New York stage. Perhaps there he could fulfill his promise to Sophie.

·5·

The Stripper and the Cardinal's Niece

Making a determined effort to shake off his grief and sense of defeat, Gig arrived in New York. Brimming with enthusiasm and proud of his efforts, he checked in at the East Coast branch of the Louis Shurr Agency, where he met a forceful, opinionated young agent named Archer King. They took to each other immediately, and King launched a campaign to bolster Gig's career. "He was extraordinary. Extraordinarily handsome. Great charm. A generous kind of man, but mercurial," says the agent. "I felt if he could only get the right part, he could become an enormous star."

To buy time, King booked Gig for his first television appearance, as a guest star on *Robert Montgomery Presents*. Meanwhile, he canvassed Broadway producers for a showy leading role that would allow his client to make a splashy New York stage debut. A strong believer in the axiom "The guy that gets the goil gets the money" (he even had a sign proclaiming that truism over his desk), King read every script slated for production, in search of a romantic leading role for Gig.

In the summer of 1953, King surveyed a field that, compared to today's meager offerings, was richly diverse. The Fabulous Invalid, as the New York theater was often called, was revving up for a new season with the combination of optimism and pessimism that is endemic to Broadway theater. The pessimism was due to the fact that the smallest number of straight plays ever to open was scheduled for the 1953–54 season. Still, Gig picked up the competitive scent particular to the neon jungle of Times Square, its marquees emblazoned with some of the most distinguished artists of the time. Either running or in the offing was Rex Harrison in *The Love of Four Colonels,* Rosalind Russell in *Wonderful Town,* Gwen Verdon in *Can-Can,* William Inge's *Picnic,* and Arthur Miller's *The Crucible,* with Gig and Sophie's best man, Arthur Kennedy.

Gig saw all the holdovers from the previous season, wishing that Sophie could have been there as well, to talk long into the night afterward, critiquing, analyzing, talking of Stanislavsky and Strasberg and Stella Adler. He loved observing the sheer craft of it all and yearned to be part of the artistic family, hoping that by association he might be able to eradicate the second-rate smell that still clung to him from his Hollywood debacles. He couldn't help feeling fearful at the challenge, especially without Sophie there to coax him along. But he hoped that among the productions announced for the fall, he might find a role in one that would serve as a tribute to his late wife and mentor. Among the more promising ventures were Tennessee Williams's *Camino Real,* John Patrick's *Tea-*

house of the August Moon, and Samuel Taylor's *Sabrina Fair.*

Meanwhile, producer Cheryl Crawford and her associate Anderson Lawler, at whose New York home Gig and Sophie had been married, were experiencing casting problems with Edward Chodorov's *Oh Men! Oh Women!* This farce, directed by the playwright, pilloried psychoanalysis, analysts, and analysands. Franchot Tone was set to play the analyst, who, on the eve of taking a flaky bride half his age (Betsy von Furstenberg), discovers that she has had quite a past, including an ex-lover (Larry Blyden) who shows up to wreak havoc. Then he learns from a devoted patient (Anne Jackson) that her jealous actor husband (Marc O'Daniel) is determined to seduce the doctor's fiancée to see if the doctor can take some of his own medicine. Just before rehearsals were to begin, the producers and director reshuffled the cast to improve the chemistry, and Marc O'Daniel was fired.

Andy Lawler, who was familiar with Gig's film work and aware of Sophie's confidence in her husband's comedic abilities, suggested that Gig undertake the vacated role. This character came breezing into the analyst's office, brimming with booze and malice, and querulously unleashed zingers against anyone who crossed his path. Although King had reservations about Gig's accepting a secondary role, the part was so colorful, and Gig was so enthusiastic, that the agent gave it his blessing.

By the time Gig joined the cast, most of the other actors were already familiar with their lines and had stopped carrying their scripts. Always insecure about his memory, Gig studied nonstop from breakfast to bedtime when not at rehearsals. He even tried to enlist the aid of other actors. When he appealed to Betsy von Furstenberg to run lines with him, Betsy, who was young and inexperienced, responded, "Oh, I couldn't possibly do that, because it might ruin my performance."

Gig flushed, turned, and walked away. For weeks afterward, when Betsy tried to make friendly small talk, he responded with a monosyllabic grunt and a quick escape. She kept trying and finally broke through his angry reserve. Later, after they had become friends, she asked him why he'd initially been so curt and was surprised when he brought up what had appeared so inconsequential to her. It seemed to indicate not only Gig's characteristic habit of repressing anger but also his tendency to magnify—and even fabricate—hurt and hostility.

A painfully twisted example of this came soon after the company entrained for their opening at New Haven's Shubert Theater. Gig was in a complete panic about his performance. To reassure him, King hired a young actor to cue him, and Gig took full advantage of the service.

After a rough first full-dress rehearsal, Gig's anxiety increased further when Franchot Tone abruptly left New Haven and flew to Hollywood to attend the funeral of a close friend. Nothing could convince Gig that there actually was a dead friend. He was gripped by the belief that the funeral story had been concocted. "I'm telling you nobody died. There is no funeral," he insisted. "Franchot wants to replace me. Can't you see what's up?"

In the grip of that delusion, Gig stayed up running lines for two nights in a row, terrified that he was about to be fired. But even though he was temporarily appearing with Tone's understudy, his performance consistently improved. Not without great personal cost, however. After the third New Haven performance, King and an old friend, director Robert Lewis, were dining at Casey's, across from the Shubert Theater, when Gig showed up. His clothes were rumpled, his skin tone a pale gray, and his tongue appeared black.

"Bobby Lewis looked at Gig and told him the pressure was too great, he shouldn't put himself through it," King remembers. "But Gig disagreed and persisted. I admired that. There are times when you can quit, but if you don't quit, that shows who you are."

Gig had suffered from the jitters before, blowing take after take in front of the cameras, but in the theater, the humiliation would be far more immediate. He did not want to let the rest of the cast down. Gig in some ways was simply enduring the anxiety of every actor who makes the jump from film to stage. But for Gig, who had been browbeaten to believe his best was never quite good enough, it wasn't hard to imagine Franchot Tone as a spin on his older brother, Donald, with his relentless faultfinding.

After Tone's return to the cast, the pressure Gig was creating for himself subsided. The play moved to Philadelphia to continue fine-tuning. As the tryout proceeded, Gig's work took on a high gloss. If he could only maintain what he had created, his gamble would pay off.

The curtain went up on December 17, 1953, at the Playhouse in Manhattan. And Gig came through with flying colors. The critics were unanimously enthusiastic. Robert Coleman of the *Daily Mirror* wrote that Gig's "ingratiating performance in *Oh Men! Oh Women!* is one of the season's most amusing. He had first nighters howling with his querulous analysis of Ibsen's *A Doll's House.*"

Playing the resentful husband, Gig came barging into the analyst's office, bursting with venom, affronted with what he perceived as a plot to break up his marriage. With timing, body language, and highly polished acting skills, he managed to turn a moderately amusing comic aria about *A Doll's House*—in which he suggested the doctor substitute a picture of Henrik Ibsen for one of Sigmund Freud—into the high point of the play. Raging about Nora and her husband in Ibsen's classic, he wanted to know what happened after she slammed the door and walked out on their marriage. He thought no one, especially not a psychiatrist, had the answers to the male-female question.

As the bombastic Arthur Turner, Gig said, "I can tell you why men and women never get together, Doc. Each wants something completely different. A man wants a woman, a woman wants a man. Impossible!"

The passage, which invariably evoked laughter, would later find particularly tragic resonance in Gig's life. As Gig implied on his self-analytical tapes, male-female relationships were almost insoluble. The tally of proof would eventually include countless unsuccessful romances, three disastrous marriages, and two more ending in tragedy. Gig would indeed find the male-female problem "impossible." For now, however, the actor could laugh at it.

From December 17, 1953, to mid-June 1954, when Gig returned triumphantly to the West Coast to fulfill a film assignment *(Young at Heart)*, audiences rewarded him with applause that embarrassingly was often greater in volume than that for star Franchot Tone. Six nights and twice on Wednesdays and Saturdays, a phenomenal outpouring of love came rolling over the footlights to Gig. Still, it wasn't enough. While he continued to mourn Sophie, he wanted to share the dream with someone special. Besides, he found celibacy not restful but tiresome. In the months that followed the opening, Gig engaged in two love affairs that eerily paralleled those of his youth, when the free-spirited twenty-eight-year-old, following him back from basketball practice, had initiated him into the joy of sex; and, later, when the virginal daughter of the coach had introduced him to the sadness and frustration of love.

One night, a raven-haired glamour girl with beautiful skin and one of the most admired figures in New York came breezing backstage at the Playhouse to visit Franchot Tone. Her name was Sherry Britton. She was a big-time stripper, a beauty with a flat stomach, long legs, and a 38-18-33 figure that made her look like a Varga Girl pinup. Before the visit was over, she had met and, as a lark, made dates with the two other unattached males in the cast—Larry Blyden and Gig. Everyone joined in the spirit of things as Sherry rotated the three suitors. Life was a smorgasbord. "Is it my night tonight?" the fellows would chorus as she appeared backstage to meet the man of the evening, and Sherry would sweep off with her choice. Juvenile as these antics may sound, they suited everyone's purpose. Sherry liked all three actors.

Tone soon removed himself from the running by telling Sherry he was impotent. Blyden finally admitted he was seriously involved with a longtime girlfriend. So that left Gig—which thrilled Sherry.

Given her sultry exoticism and Gig's suave demeanor, they appeared to be the perfect couple, and in the fifties, scintillating Manhattan was the perfect backdrop for a lighthearted tango. Whether they were at the Onyx, at Tony's on Fifty-second Street, or at an Irish bar somewhere, they were affectionate, high-spirited, and bantering. Neither gave the impression of having a care in the world, and that extended, at least at first, to their affair. Neither was prepared to handle more than the most superficial sort of relationship. Gig was still doing his slow, dreamy impressionistic dancing alone; he'd just found another dancer to fall in with him.

Whatever its real origin, Gig chose to attribute his fear of intimacy to the trauma caused by losing Sophie. And Sherry, for all her breathtaking beauty and ebullience, suffered the same fear of emotional sharing. In retrospect, after the passage of thirty-three years and countless hours of analysis, she said, "I kept my private feelings pretty much secret—even from myself."

Sherry was a survivor of two orphanages and five foster homes in New York City. At fifteen, she was sweet-talked into a "marriage" that she later learned had never been registered. By sixteen, she had made her debut at the People's Theater on the Bowery, where she learned the art of striptease. She graduated to Minsky's Gaiety at Forty-sixth and Broadway. Her long run at the Gaiety was punctuated with appearances on the Subway Circuit theaters in revivals of *Stage Door* (with Nancy Carroll and John Forsythe) and *Getting Gertie's Garter.*

After leaving Minsky's and the Gaiety, Sherry moved to "Swing Street," New York's famous Fifty-second Street, where for seven and a half years she was the featured stripper at Leon and Eddie's splashy cabaret. She was a class act, timing her clothes-shedding to the beat of classical numbers like the "Warsaw Concerto" and the "Fire Dance." She was known as the "Little Princess," because she wore a tiara on her head. Whatever else she dropped, that always stayed on. Needless to say, when Sherry was on stage, few of the men in the audience paid attention to their thick sirloin dinners. What they couldn't know was that this voluptuous knockout in front of them was no bimbo. She could quote from *Peer Gynt* and would eventually graduate magna cum laude from Fordham University's prelaw program.

In the fast-moving world of Broadway nightlife, Sherry found Gig refreshing. He wasn't pushy. In fact, they dated for weeks on a platonic basis. Some nights he talked and laughed and enjoyed dancing; others, he was vague and preoccupied. But whatever his mood, he was, in Sherry's view, sweet and giving. Their respective fear of intimacy kept them comfortably at arms' length. Then, a few weeks after they started dating, Gig stunned Sherry. She remembers it very clearly as the night they fell in love. They were at Reuben's, having a late supper after the theater, when Gig suddenly declared his love for her and asked for a kiss. She consented.

"There was great warmth. I felt very loved, very protected," Sherry remembers. "I felt as if I were in a warm, loving cocoon, which evidently was enough for me at the time. I guess I was so needy in those days that if anyone said, 'I love you,' those were the magic words. I had had a great deal of adulation, but I don't know how much genuine affection I'd had, because having Gig say, 'I love you, and I want to kiss you,' evoked such a response in me. Evidently I felt 'I love you too,' but I don't remember actually saying the words 'I love you' to Gig or anyone else until many years later."

Gig and Sherry spent most of their intimate moments at her apartment. She found his hotel room dark and depressing, strange for such a seemingly cheerful guy. "But wherever we were, he was a sweet, tender lover," she says. "I don't remember any negative notes in what he said or did. I think he realized the importance of showing his affection."

Gradually, Sherry dated only Gig. She did it voluntarily. He didn't request that she do so. "Gig was a special person. The only note that struck me as odd was that he could make love as frequently as he did to me over a period of months and never have an orgasm," she says. "I'm Freudian, and so, of course, I look for all kinds of reasons. But I have wondered whether his lack of orgasm had something to do with the fact that Sophie had had cancer of the cervix. Or whether it was another way of withholding intimacy. Oddly, he didn't seem to mind. Even odder is the fact that I never once asked him about it. It shows you how strange our relationship was. The only explanation I can give is that partly, I think, I preserved his privacy because I did not want anybody to step over a certain threshold myself. I did not open doors to anyone, and I didn't want anyone to open doors to me."

One day, Gig stunned her. "Marry me," he said. She was unprepared for the proposal. Frightened by commitment, she responded in the only way she knew how—with hostility. Immediately the relationship began deteriorating. Gig, bewildered, inquired what had happened. "I'm great to be engaged to, but married to—no!" she told him.

Gig pressed his suit, but Sherry warned him to give up. Still, he persisted. Feeling the need to cut off the relationship, she did the unforgivable. "I picked out another actor and went home with him," she recalls. "Then late at night this other fellow and I called Gig. We both got on the phone and joked with him. Naturally, he was terribly hurt."

Looking back thirty years later, Sherry says, "It was dreadful behavior on my part. But it wasn't the only time I did it, so I can't say Gig was the only one I hurt. But that was part of my sickness at the time. I feel badly when I think about it, but you have to understand our whole relationship was based on the needs of two deeply neurotic people. So even though the way it ended was wrong, ending it was right."

While the other men on the receiving end of Sherry's cruelty might have responded with rage and furious insult, Gig did not. In fact, he even saw Sherry a few more times. Emotionally fragile as he was, he remained, at least on the surface, as nonjudgmental as ever. In his habitual fashion, he displaced whatever anger he felt, as though that emotion were too unseemly for the urbane gentleman he now thought himself to be. If life indeed were one big movie set against which he played out his peculiar dramas, then Sherry was just a naughty romp through Swing Street. As for the ending, well, if he had responded as he truly felt, that would have meant acknowledging how cruel she'd been to him. By not reacting, he could effectively let the scene hit the cutting room floor. Gig was learning to edit expertly.

If Sherry was the archetypal sexually liberated lady Gig first encountered after basketball practice in St. Cloud, his next love was a grown-up version of the coach's daughter, reincarnated in New York as the cardinal's niece.

With Sherry out of his life, Gig gravitated toward the bar at Sardi's to wind down after evening performances of *Oh Men! Oh Women!* Broadway success had supplanted the self-conscious, self-doubting Hollywood Gig with an impeccably dressed bon vivant whose offbeat wit helped make late evenings livelier. Sophie's memory still haunted him, but he no longer retreated to his hotel room each evening with a book and a pitcher of martinis to lull him into oblivion. Now he lulled himself publicly, at the sort of New York parties that Truman Capote would spin into myth in *Breakfast at Tiffany's.*

One night, Gig was holding forth at Sardi's when Edward Chodorov, the author of *Oh Men! Oh Women!,* mentioned that he and half of the theatrical community had been invited to a party at Elaine Stritch's. Chodorov, who was smitten with Elaine, suggested that Gig come along. "She'll be enchanted with you," he promised. Gig demurred. But a telephone call to Stritch brought word that "of course one of the best-looking men in the whole world" was always more than welcome at her parties.

Stritch was the Holliest of the Golightlys on the scene. She was also the holiest. The tall, champagne-blond singing actress was a Catholic playgirl who was determined to guard her virginity at all costs. Born in Birmingham, Michigan, she was convent educated and, from an early age, hell-bent for a career on the stage. Rooming at a convent on Ninety-sixth Street upon her arrival in New York, she soon found her way to the New School's Dramatic Workshop in Greenwich Village. There she enrolled in an acting class that included, among others, Marlon Brando. Encapsulating her early New York life, she once said, "I had Marlon in the morning and Mother Superior at night."

Before long, she had captivated a goodly share of the

eligible young men in theatrical circles and made an indelible impression on theatergoers with her appearance in the Paul and Grace Hartman revue *Angel in the Wings.* The way Stritch belted out her songs—especially the humorous "Civilization"—convinced theatergoers and fellow performers that the "new Merman" had arrived. She was a show-stopper.

She followed *Angel* with a tour-de-force performance as a newspaper reporter satirizing an intellectual stripper in the Vivienne Segal–Harold Lang revival of *Pal Joey.* Her entire role, including the song "Zip," took twelve minutes of playing time and, on opening night, earned her a six-minute ovation and ten curtain calls. Her triumph reinforced the old saying that there are no small parts, only small actors.

At the same time she was appearing in *Pal Joey,* she was allowed through special arrangement to hire out as a standby for the undisputed queen of musical comedy, Ethel Merman, who was playing "the hostess with the mostest on the ball" in *Call Me Madam.* Merman was blessed with such good health, dedication, and determination that Stritch never got a chance to show her version of the party-throwing ambassador in Merman territory. But clearly Stritch was a woman with such personality that almost everyone in the theater wanted to meet her.

And Stritch wanted to meet almost everyone in show business, which was the reason for the party she was giving. As she tells it, "I was in my second grownup's apartment, on Fifty-second Street and the East River, next door to Garbo. So I decided to give a party like grownups." With that in mind, she invited every entertainer she had met or simply dreamed of knowing: Greta Garbo, Judy Garland, Frank Sinatra, Leonard Bernstein, Ethel Merman, and almost everyone else who had ever popped into her dressing room to congratulate her on her performance.

"Nothing but the best," Stritch says. "So I had it catered

and got Dom Perignon. It was a tiny apartment, of course, but those were the best parties—when you couldn't afford what you were doing but did it anyway. You see, it was sort of straight-out Fitzgerald time.

"Everyone was dancing and drinking and playing games, except Leonard Bernstein, who was in my bathtub, having a bath with some bubble bath he rather liked. Ethel Merman and Judy Garland arrived together. This was at a time when they were sort of palsy-walsy and were running around and around and around.

"I should say right here that at the time I was madly, madly smitten with Billy Harbach" (the son of famed librettist Otto Harbach and later a television producer). "I was from the Midwest and didn't put out; and Billy was very Sands Point, and when he didn't get what he wanted he looked elsewhere. You might say I was having a delayed childhood in my twenties.

"Anyway, finally the door opened and in came Eddie and Gig. Eddie said, 'Gig, this is Elaine,' and I said, 'How do you do. What would you like to drink?' and everybody was off and running.

"The party went on until four o'clock in the morning, naturally. Finally, everybody was saying goodbye and thank you, Elaine, vum-vum-vum-vum." Stritch mimics air kisses. "I shooed the barman out. And because I'm from the Midwest and can't stand waking up to a lot of dirty dishes, I was rinsing glasses. When I looked up from the sink, Gig Young was still there. So he helped with the dishes and spent the night in my apartment. I had twin beds in the bedroom, and Gig went to bed in his bed— In *his* bed, don't you love it? The first time I ever met him, and it's *his* bed! Now, I could tell you this racy story, but it wasn't. It was 'Good night. Did you have a good time? I'm glad you came,' and then we both went to sleep."

The next morning, Stritch made breakfast for the two of

them. She now says she wasn't "flipping in her mind." She was simply thinking, "Isn't it wonderful he stayed over?" because she didn't like being alone. Gig, for his part, *was* indeed flipping in his mind. He was bowled over with this enchanting creature. On his way to the theater for a matinee, Gig dropped Stritch off at "21," where she had a luncheon date with hotel magnate Conrad Hilton. Later, he told her that when she got out of the cab and went into "21," he said to the cabdriver, "I'm going to marry that girl."

"That was Gig's line. That was his romanticism. Gig was a deeply romantic man, but there is a price to be paid for romanticism," says Stritch. "Most people who are wonderfully romantic, and have wonderful dialogue, and everything about them is exciting—underneath there's something that's driving them crazy. But I really didn't understand about that then."

Stritch, with a "sneaker" for Bill Harbach, wasn't eager to date Gig. At the beginning, she saw him out of default, since Harbach had little patience with a girl who wouldn't come across. Gig, on the contrary, was patient and persistent. He was also very Midwestern, which was to say that he had an elevated opinion of women. After all, this was the man who had waited weeks to ask a stripper for permission to kiss her. He struck Stritch as romantic in a low-key way.

"I mean flowers," she says. "He used to kid me later: 'Gosh, I sent you a dozen roses, and you just accepted them as if they were due you. You never said, "Thank you for the beautiful roses, kiss, kiss, kiss." You just said, "Hi," and the roses were in a vase, beautifully tended, but you never said, "Thank you, darling." ' " Stritch shrugs. "I guess I just accepted them as my due."

Stritch describes the two of them as being like a couple of pep pills when they were together. "Sure there was a lot of drinking," she admits, and adds, "But it wasn't *Days of Wine and Roses* time. It was Sardi's, Billy Reed's Little Club,

'21,' P. J. Clarke's, El Morocco. And it was still innocent. I'm sure everybody else we had drinks with was sleeping with somebody, but not Gig and me. I was young enough at that point not to be able to come across outside marriage. That made us unhappy. So we drank."

Then all of a sudden, because of Gig's persistence in pushing his suit, Stritch began to fall in love with him. "We've all seen that happen in Jimmy Stewart movies," she muses. "The girl's in love with some smartass and overlooks the good guy, the sincere guy. But the smartass doesn't win. The Jimmy Stewart guy keeps persisting until the girl finally sees the light. And he wins."

This went on until summer, when Stritch was asked to do *Call Me Madam* with Russell Nype and Kent Smith at the St. Louis Municipal Opera. Her mother and father made the trip down from Birmingham, Michigan, and Gig called to say he was coming to see her in *Madam* because he wanted to marry her. "I said, 'You want to see me in *Call Me Madam* just to make sure?'" She laughs. "And he said, 'Oh, be quiet! You're going to marry me, and I want to meet your mother and father and have them know about me. I want everything out in the open.'"

Stritch had told Gig early on that she would never marry outside the Church. Her parents, particularly her father, were adamant that marriage was difficult enough without having the added burden of religious conflict. Marriage between a divorced Protestant and a devout Catholic, especially in the mid-fifties, was rife with obstacles. Gig's second marriage, to Sophie, was no problem (they had been wed in a civil ceremony), but his first, to Sheila, which had ended in divorce, could prove insurmountable. Their one hope was that the Catholic Church would invalidate the marriage by proving that either Gig or Sheila had not been baptized. In that event, Gig's first union, in the eyes of the Church, would be considered "nonsacramental," and Stritch could apply for "a special privilege solution" whereby the Church would effectively consider Gig's first marriage dissolved.

In St. Louis, Gig took the Stritches to dinner. After heaping praise on Elaine for her performance, Gig told her parents that he was going to find a way in which he and their daughter could be married in the Church. His plan was to continue on to St. Cloud to introduce his fiancée to his sister and her husband, then proceed to California, where Gig had a job lined up and Elaine would look for work. "I'm going to convert to the Catholic faith," he told them.

"It was like a scene from an old movie," Stritch says. "It was so old-fashioned that I began to fall even more in love with him because he reminded me of my father, which is why every girl gets married anyway. I got very emotional when I said goodbye to my parents, because it was the first time I'd thought seriously about marriage. Daddy was saying, 'Think carefully. This is for life.' Mother's saying, 'God, he's the most attractive man. Marry him in a cornfield if they won't allow it in the church.'"

In Minnesota, Stritch met Gig's sister, Gen, and her husband, O. M. Merry, both schoolteachers. Gig went to the Methodist minister in St. Cloud to see whether there was any record that he had ever been baptized. He knew that if he had not been, there was a very good possibility that the Catholic Church would look with favor on his marriage to Stritch. A lot was riding on what he'd find out—in fact, nothing less than his and Stritch's future together.

Since Sophie's death, Gig had not been as happy as he was now with this vibrant, funny, and talented woman. She had been able, if not to erase, at least to ease his haunting memories of Sophie. Coming after the emotionally devastating affair with Sherry, she'd rebuilt his masculine confidence and appeal. And unlike Bill Harbach, Gig admired her old-fashioned principles. He just wasn't the kind of guy for whom sexual abstinence was some holding pattern until the woman had been softened up.

The minister told Gig that there was no record of his baptism. Though the story was whispered that Gig had charmed the minister into this crucial conclusion, the exultant couple left St. Cloud for California, confident that they had cleared the biggest hurdle.

Flying to Los Angeles, Gig and Elaine checked into separate rooms at the Beverly Hills Hotel. Gig began preparing for his part in the film *Young at Heart,* with Doris Day and Frank Sinatra, while Elaine and her agents were on the lookout for a suitable role for her.

Recalls Stritch: "When we got settled, Monsignor of 'Our Lady of the Cadillacs' in Beverly Hills told Gig, 'Since you've never been baptized, I guess we can take you on to study the Catholic religion.' And Gig started taking instruction from Father Ford, the best-looking priest I've ever seen in my life. One day, when I picked Gig up after instruction, he got in the car while Father Ford, who looked like a male version of Ingrid Bergman, stood in the entrance waving goodbye. Gig looked at him, then at me, and grinned: 'That guy's so attractive, I may overshoot the runway.' "

While Gig took instruction, Elaine waited for work and lounged around the hotel. "As far as I'm concerned, everything is terrific. I'm living like a hooker, and I've never been to bed with a man." Stritch smiles. "It was wonderful. Gig and I used to laugh about it. I'd charge a bathing suit at the hotel, and Gig'd say, 'You know, Elaine, women do this when they're giving out every five minutes. I can't believe you're getting away with it. Now, I'm not saying I'm tired of kissing you, but . . .' "

To cut down on expenses, Gig rented an apartment. While Stritch kept her room at the hotel for appearance sake, she began spending most of her time at the flat, even sleeping there. Still, she refused to "go all the way."

People, at least those who were in the know, were somewhat puzzled by Gig and Elaine's relationship. "Friends would ask incredulously, 'You live with Gig Young, the cocksman of the world, innocently?' Well, we loved each other," she explains even now. "So we were preparing for a marriage of perfection. One of the wonderful things then, unlike now, was that people were patient."

Not that strains didn't develop. One weekend they drove to a resort south of Los Angeles, where Stritch had made a reservation for them to share a suite. "That's when I really found out how frightened Gig was of public opinion," she says. "He panicked. 'Are you crazy?' he asked me. 'If Hedda Hopper or Louella or doo-be-doo finds out, it could kill my next movie.' So I could see how the lovely, compassionate St. Cloud fellow was buying Hedda and Louella's and the industry's values."

Though there were few such disagreements, even the most patient suitor has his threshold. After a year of celibate courtship, Gig and Elaine were driving back from a day trip to La Jolla and he put his hand on the nape of her neck. "It was wonderful, a kind of secure feeling, a sweet feeling," she says. "He said, 'What if we don't go home tonight?' I said, 'Whatever you think is fair, Gig.'"

They stopped, had a romantic dinner by the sea, and, primed with a couple of martinis, drove to a rather chic motel. "And . . . that was my first affair, so please be kind," recalls Stritch warmly. "It wasn't the south of France. It wasn't Wiesbaden. It was a motel in Malibu, scooby-doo.

"Every single moment I had thought about romantically came alive because of the human being I was with. And when you get it right, it *is* the south of France, even though it's Malibu. And God really must have looked down and laughed because with all our holding out we ended up in Malibu." She chortles.

The next morning, back in Beverly Hills, a barrier had been broken. Stritch felt a little guilty but happy; Gig just felt happy. This man who had always imagined that life was one big movie set was now in a Neil Simon comedy, going to parties, drinking martinis, running barefoot through the park, living life to the hilt. For once, the suave, debonair charmer who was Gig's film persona dovetailed with the person at home. As long as he was with Stritch, his darker side was held in abeyance, even when the self-described "spoiled" woman tried his patience. "I had one of the best-looking guys in the whole world. And he liked me. And I *adored* him," she says.

Suddenly the idyll exploded. The wicked witch came in the form of a secretary from the Barrs' family church in St. Cloud, who contacted Monsignor Ford in Beverly Hills and told him Gig had been baptized and she could prove it. Whether she was motivated by true religious conviction, personal frustration, or spite, nobody knows. No one remembers whether she had ever even met Gig. But when she sent Father Ford the certificate, he concluded that the actor had been lying to him and discontinued the canonical marital process. The couple were devastated.

Says Stritch, "That St. Cloud spinster ruined everything. Gig said, 'Screw it!' and I said, 'Screw it!' and we drank ourselves into the middle of next week. Life went on with martinis and Gibsons and no hope. The arguments between us started, and finally our love affair dwindled into burned-out ashes."

Stritch reluctantly decided to go back to New York. Gig drove her to the airport, and they said goodbye. " 'All of a sudden this dies so quickly,' as Tennessee Williams said," Stritch sighs.

Yet Gig and Elaine remained friends. "It was a long time between laughs," she recalled many years later. "But after I married and was living in London, Gig came over. He called and he met my husband. It was like a Woody Allen movie. When he met John, he hugged him and said, 'How wonderful you've found Elaine.' "

Stritch remained married to John Bay until his death in 1982. She had indeed taken her father's admonition, "It's for life," to heart. In view of Gig's wrenching marital struggles after Stritch, it's tempting to speculate how she might have saved him. But once more, fate had intervened, as it had with Sophie's untimely death, to drive Gig inexorably toward his destiny. This time it had come in the form of the Catholic Church. Long after they had split, Gig told Stritch that he wasn't sorry they'd thumbed their noses at the Church's ban on premarital sex, because, he said, "unless you consummate a good feeling, you will go to bad feelings."

Frustrated in his desire to marry Stritch, Gig indeed would "go to bad feelings." But before that, for a brief moment, he had revealed his best, perhaps his truest, self. Confident in Stritch's love, he had considered her feelings with tenderness, admiration, and remarkable restraint. "I didn't know anybody else in the world who loved a woman so much he'd live with her for a year before having an affair," says Stritch. "I'll never forget that compliment. Gig loved in a special way. And I don't think that happens too many times in the world anymore, anymore, anymore."

·6·

Gig Bewitched

His romance with Elaine Stritch at an end, Gig divided his time between Hollywood and New York, pursuing a career that was proving to be no more successful than his thwarted personal life. Had Sophie lived, she undoubtedly would have reminded Gig of his artistic aspirations, encouraged him to stand fast until he got the roles he wanted. After all, he had put himself through hell to succeed on the Broadway stage, partly to justify her belief in him as well as to get better roles.

"You're a handsome fellow," Gig's New York agent told him over and over. "Not like most second leads, who look like the guy who loses the girl. If you got a well-written lead, audiences would not only believe the girl'd choose you, they'd root for her to. And remember, the way this industry is set up, you won't become a major star unless you get the girl."

Gig agreed. But now, in his forties, he wasn't sure how long all this would last. Poised to capitalize on his Broadway success, he suffered a loss of nerve. In the end, he panicked. With television now beckoning with tempting money offers, he came up with the rationalization that he could take a mediocre part and through sheer effort elevate it to art. "Hell, anybody can play a great part," he said. "The secret is to take a lousy part and bring out as much as you can."

The argument was simply an excuse. Even after his Broadway success, Gig couldn't resist the siren call of Hollywood, the gilded mistress who tempted him with the good life—a house with a pool and tennis court, a Cadillac convertible, fat paychecks, recognition, and enough distractions to keep his loneliness at bay. But beneath the surface, there were distinct echoes of another time and place, when a teenage dandy with two suits, access to the family's big touring car, and pockets full of spending money had had all those things—including the family home—snatched from him by the whirlwind of the Great Depression. The trauma had eventually abated, but the insecurity had never completely vanished from Gig's consciousness. He'd never be able to withstand the lure of big money for performing an unrewarding role. So for all his good resolutions, Gig drew his self-worth less from good work than from the accumulation of material things.

In 1955, after having scored on Broadway in *Oh Men! Oh Women!* and having accepted a thankless part in *Young at Heart,* a musical version of the 1930s hit *Four Daughters,* he reluctantly allowed himself to be talked into hosting *Warner Brothers Presents,* a television series featuring hour-long segments based upon the feature films *Kings Row, Cheyenne,* and *Casablanca.* At the end of each episode, Gig would interview the biggest star working on the lot any given week. It would be undistinguished work, notable only for his high salary ($2,000 a week—three to four times what the series stars would earn) and for an interview with James Dean, during which the screen legend admonished viewers to drive carefully, because the life they saved might be his. Shortly after, he died in a head-on collision.

To celebrate signing contracts for the show, the studio staged a dinner at the Beverly Hilton Hotel. Gary Stevens, then a Warner executive, requested that Gig attend. Gig agreed, then asked: "It will be for two, won't it? I don't know who to bring." Stevens suggested Elizabeth Montgomery, who was making *The Court Martial of Billy Mitchell* on the Warners lot. The fortyish actor had reservations, wondering whether he would appear to be robbing the cradle. Assured that he wouldn't be taken for a lecherous old man, he decided to escort her.

She was thrilled at the idea of dating Gig. Since the first time she had seen him in a film, the impetuous Liz had told anyone who would listen, "I think he's the most attractive man on the screen, and I intend to marry him." Most laughed off the remark, attributing it to the fact that his appearance and mannerisms were strangely similar to those of her father, Robert Montgomery, who had met Gig when he guest-starred on Montgomery's television show shortly before appearing on Broadway.

Fate seemed to play against Liz's hopes for a romance, let alone a marriage. At the time of their first date, she was scheduled to return to New York shortly to begin rehearsing a play. More important, she was not legally free from her first husband. But for anyone who knew her, these seemed minor obstacles.

Bicoastal from birth, she was equally at home among Hollywood stars and Eastern society people. After attending the Spence School, she spent two years studying at the

American Academy of Dramatic Arts, preparing to be an actress (as her mother, Elizabeth Allen, of Lexington, Kentucky, had been before her marriage). Liz's performances in student productions always drew the most stringent criticism from her father. Yet even before she attended drama school, at sixteen, he cast her to play his daughter in a segment of *Robert Montgomery Presents.* Her performance elicited excited responses from various producers. Eventually she made her Broadway debut as the ingenue in *Late Love,* starring Arlene Francis.

At twenty, she married Frederic Gallatin Cammann, a Harvard-educated casting director. The marriage was a rocky one, according to friends. Cammann had strong family ties; Liz had weak ones. When they had their first tiff and he packed his bags and went home to mama, Liz was reportedly astounded. He returned, and all was well until they had their next quarrel. This became something of a ritual. After a year, he again began packing. This time Liz reportedly sat on his suitcase to make sure he got it fastened and left. Then she filed for divorce. At least this is what Gig later told his sister. (Elizabeth Montgomery ignored all letters requesting an interview for this book.)

While awaiting her divorce, Liz went briefly to Hollywood, where she met Gig on the blind date arranged by Stevens. Gig was immediately captivated with her social ease and flattered by the attention she showered on him. When she returned to Broadway to replace the ingenue in *The Loud Red Patrick,* she and Gig were constantly on the phone. After finishing his stint on *Warner Brothers Presents,* Gig received an offer to go into Jean Dalrymple's revival of *The Teahouse of the August Moon* at the New York City Center. He leaped at the opportunity to be near Liz. The revival didn't fare well, but the romance heated up.

Liz was a honey-haired little beauty with a to-the-manor-born assertiveness, which often gave way to a beguiling enthusiasm that lit up any room she entered. She was the kind of girl that Gig found fascinating, faintly intimidating, and ultimately lovable. The kooky young enchantress dispelled Gig's loneliness and loosened him up socially. At times they resembled nothing more than two children tearing up the nursery together—although according to Bob Douglas, a bystander sometimes needed to keep his sense of humor.

One weekend, for instance, Liz took Gig and Douglas to her family's attractive country house near Patterson, New York. When they got there, they had several drinks. Finally, Gig asked, "What about dinner?" Liz went into the kitchen, came back, and reported, "Well, we really don't have much of anything." They discussed going to a restaurant, but she urged the men to have another drink while she fixed something.

"After a time, she appeared with three plates, on which were three hamburgers," Douglas recalls. "We tasted them, and Gig said, 'Mmmmmm, don't think muchathese.' Liz said, 'What?' and Gig repeated, 'I don't think much of these.' Well, they were absolutely filthy. She'd made them out of dog food."

Out of such startling capers as this their romance grew and became serious. Liz pressed for marriage, according to the Douglases, but Gig was apprehensive. Sharing the secret of his 1938 vasectomy with her was not easy. Sheila had accepted the information calmly and seldom referred to it. With Sophie, the problem was nonexistent, since she had undergone a hysterectomy prior to their marriage. Elaine Stritch had assured him she was marrying him, and if it was impossible for him to father children, then she would simply have more love to lavish on him. But with Liz, he hesitated. As he grew older, he became increasingly concerned about his masculine identity, which, in his mind, was diminished by the vasectomy.

After much vacillation, he screwed up his courage and

confided his secret. Liz, too, brushed aside his concerns. They would breed dogs, she said. "She went into the marriage with her eyes wide open. She was so nuts about him, I don't think anything would have made any difference," Sue Douglas says. "I think he was a little scared of the marriage, but not Liz. She adored animals and in some way believed they would take the place of children, which, of course, is ridiculous thinking."

When the news spread that Liz and Gig were marrying, Robert Montgomery was beside himself. His relationship with his daughter was an off-again, on-again thing, but he was determined she was not going to throw her life away on "someone almost as old and not one quarter as successful as I am." But after Gig completed the two-week run of *Teahouse of the August Moon,* he and Liz were married. The simple ceremony took place on December 28, 1956, at First Presbyterian Church in Las Vegas, with Don and Zetta Castle as attendants. Robert Montgomery did not attend. Liz was twenty-four; Gig gave his age as thirty-eight.

The bride and groom and their attendants returned to Palm Springs, where the Castles had arranged a reception. After spending the weekend in the desert, the newlyweds returned to Hollywood so that Gig could begin work on *The Desk Set.* He accepted the secondary role only because he couldn't resist the opportunity to work with Spencer Tracy and Katharine Hepburn.

Gig and Liz regarded New York as home, Hollywood as a place to work. They preferred the tempo and the style of the East, and both were reading play scripts, hoping to find a quality project they could appear in together. Also, if they were going to do television, they insisted it be live—and most live telecasts originated in New York. Liz, ironically, denigrated the medium in which she would later gain national prominence as the popular star of *Bewitched.*

"The marriage seemed to be a good one, especially at

first," says Archer King, who represented both. Producer Howard Erskine, a close friend of the couple, agrees. "It was initially a good relationship," he says. "She had been disappointed by the outcome of her first marriage, and Gig had been saddened by his torpedoed romance with Stritch. Now they both seemed to bloom."

Spontaneously, a group of loosely connected couples from the entertainment field converged around Gig and Liz in New York. "'The group' just naturally came together," says Dominick "Nick" Dunne. The people who constituted it were all of the same era. Most were successful or well-to-do. And at least one partner in each couple had some connection with show business. A lot of them had known one another for some time, but after Gig and Liz's marriage their ties became closer. The regular members included Nick and Lenny Dunne, Howard and Lu Erskine, Betsy von Furstenberg and Guy Vincent, and Bill and Fay Harbach. Initially, besides their shared affluence, they seemed to have been drawn together by a love of jazz music, dancing, and having a good time. Also, in an inexplicable way that Gig demonstrated later in life as well, he managed to insinuate to each couple that they were his closest friends.

Guy Vincent, then the husband of Betsy von Furstenberg, was one of those friends in whom Gig confided. "We talked about everything in our lives," Guy says. "At the time, Gig was very much affected, I think, that he couldn't father children. Because Liz wanted babies badly." So badly that, in an especially confidential moment, Gig told Guy that he had undergone corrective surgery to reverse his vasectomy. He was optimistic about the prognosis and hoped he could give Liz the children he thought she needed to be completely fulfilled. Whether or not he actually attempted the reversal or simply fantasized it has never been verified.

In early March 1958, Gig and Liz appeared together in the teleplay *Dead Ringer.* It was an ill-conceived, scathingly reviewed production, which was happily overlooked ten days later, when cheers greeted Gig's performance in *Teacher's Pet,* starring Clark Gable and Doris Day. The film gave him a genuine comedic role that he exploited to the hilt. Critics praised Gig's turn as Day's psychology-instructor boyfriend, who loses her to Gable's hard-bitten city editor. Director George Seaton told Gig that his work was polished enough to win him an Oscar nomination, but Gig disagreed. "Light comedy may be harder to play than drama," he said, "but how many Oscars does Cary Grant have at home? The Academy voters aren't impressed, because part of the goal is to make it look easy."

Seaton was right. Gig indeed received his second Oscar nomination, but this time he lost the prize to Burl Ives *(The Big Country),* who was riding the momentum of his role as Big Daddy in *Cat on a Hot Tin Roof.* At the ceremony, Liz was on hand to give her husband a consolation kiss when the winner was announced. She was especially thrilled with the recognition that Gig received, grateful that it stilled—at least for a while—her father's vituperative comments about his new son-in-law.

Even with the passing of time, Robert Montgomery's dislike for Gig did not cease. Gig and Liz were well aware of this fact and often devised little schemes to irritate him. Lenny Dunne remembers an evening when Montgomery was visiting the West Coast and took Liz, Gig, Nick, and herself to dinner. It was not the easiest of evenings, because neither Montgomery nor Gig was able to muster any camaraderie—real or otherwise. "But after we finished dining, Nick and I invited everyone back to our house for a drink," Lenny Dunne says. "They came. Some more eagerly than others."

After a respectable length of time had elapsed at the Dunnes', Elizabeth announced that she had to be going because she had an early call the next morning. She and Gig stood up. Liz went over and kissed her father, saying, "Good night, Daddy Bob." Then Gig parroted, "Good night, Daddy Bob," as he suddenly leaned down and planted a smack on Montgomery's lips. "Well," says Lenny Dunne, "I thought Robert Montgomery was going to have a stroke."

The Oscar nomination for his work in Paramount's *Teacher's Pet* earned Gig a considerable amount of work: at MGM in *Tunnel of Love* and at 20th Century–Fox in *The Story on Page One,* culminating in the long-sought above-the-title billing at MGM in *Ask Any Girl*—a comic caper co-starring David Niven and Shirley MacLaine. All these assignments made the West Coast look like a much friendlier place, and in late 1958, the Youngs decided to make it their primary residence. Liz located an attractive small house on the San Fernando side of Laurel Canyon, and Gig's confidence in his renewed career materialized into a snazzy Jaguar Mark IX, in which he buzzed around town. Most of the New York "group" had moved west as well, augmented by Bob and Sue Douglas and such new inductees as Mitzi Gaynor and Jack Bean, Jayne Meadows and Steve Allen, Ginger and Johnny Mercer—to name a few.

Through Bill Harbach, Gig also fell in with the "croquet crowd," a group of enthusiasts who played the genteel sport on Samuel Goldwyn's court. The entourage of killer players included Louis Jourdan, Tyrone Power, Jean Negulesco, Howard Hawks, and George Sanders. "Gig was a hell of a good shot," says Harbach, who introduced him to the game. "He'd kill you at eighty feet." Gig became so merciless that he was initiated into the U.S. Croquet Hall of Fame, receiving a plaque and a red jacket, which he wore with pride. Says Harbach, "He was a golden personality."

If the Young-Stritch affair played itself out as bittersweet Neil Simon, then Gig and Liz's mad marriage radiated Noel

Coward savoir faire: communal dashes to the martini fountain after screenings, croquet matches and other games. To those who knew them both, it seemed that Liz was intent on matching Gig's capacity for drink as though it were some kind of contest. Meanwhile, Gig's tolerance seemed to grow, adding conviction to the drunkard roles he played: a brilliant lawyer whose alcoholism turns him into a Bowery bum in a CBS television movie, *Jacob and the Angel,* and in the Doris Day film *Tunnel of Love.* His engaging philandering tippler nearly stole that film and reinforced his reputation as "a topflight comedian of the light-sophisticated kind," according to Richard Coe in the *Washington Post.*

"As a couple, Gig and Liz were a delight," recalls Martin Baum, who would later represent the Youngs. "There was a childlike innocence about him that was totally refreshing. There was little guile, no jealousy or resentment of others who were doing well. A dear person. Of course, that was the surface Gig. I noticed when we were out on an evening socially, he drank excessively by my standards, and Liz was drinking right along with him. But they seemed happy."

The couple appeared especially happy with the house they acquired on Rising Glen Road, which they furnished in Early American. And they bought pets, attempting to fill the vacuum caused by Gig's inability to father children. They pampered two Italian whippets, spoiling them outrageously like treasured children.

One Easter morning, Gig rode off on his bicycle, to return a half hour later with a tiny beribboned lamb in the handlebar basket. He ceremoniously presented the lamb to Liz, who christened it Mary Chess. Everyone was beguiled by the gentle, fuzzy creature. Gig and Liz were especially crazy about it. "And then," says their friend Robert Horton, "the tiny lamb developed horns, and it grew and grew until when it leaped playfully, it would land on the table and skid across it. Cigarettes were its favorite delicacy, and after it ate all the cigarettes it cleaned up the butts."

The lamb turned into a buck and began wreaking havoc on the house. Gig and Liz couldn't figure out what to do. Having Mary Chess butchered was unthinkable. They agonized over the decision until someone came up with the suggestion that they give the animal to the children's zoo. They did this and for a time visited their former pet frequently.

Gig discovered, much to his chagrin, that his hopes that *Ask Any Girl* would help him make the career jump to leads had been misplaced. While Gig endowed his hedonistic playboy with considerable charm, he did not end up with the girl—and confirmed Archer King's dictum. Worse, he failed to receive the billing he'd been promised, though he got a nice buildup in the movie itself when, shortly after meeting him, the Shirley MacLaine character says, "I don't know why I kept staring at him. He was no better-looking than the average Greek god and no more charming than Cary Grant."

The reason Gig, despite his charm and good looks, never managed to attain the airy heights of a matinee idol came into bold relief three years later when he jumped at the chance to be featured in *That Touch of Mink,* with Cary Grant and Doris Day. As with Hepburn and Tracy on *Desk Set,* he treated his idol Grant with deference. Grant, for his part, was generous and casual with Young, urging him to make the most of the role of Grant's quasi-psychotic financial adviser. Encouraged, Gig turned it into a hilarious portrait. Yet, while he was nearly as handsome and as deft a comedian and was most certainly a better dramatic actor, he lacked the superstar's charisma.

In spite of the financial rewards of film, when Gig was offered a play, he and Elizabeth pulled up stakes and returned to New York. The role of Hogan in the Broadway comedy *Under the Yum Yum Tree* demanded lechery more than sex appeal. Ambivalent about accepting the part, Gig worried that the landlord, who engages in an all-out campaign to seduce his virginal tenant (Sandra Church), was written as a stereotypical cocksman. Though not a Method actor, Gig always spent a great deal of time constructing a detailed life history for any character he played. Digging into Hogan's deeper emotions, Gig concluded that the source of the man's lechery was his loneliness. Gig's ingenious approach was to shape the character so that with each successful seduction, the seducer lost a bit of himself, becoming even more manic in his attempts to banish his feelings of alienation.

Lawrence Roman, the playwright, appreciated what Gig was attempting but became increasingly alarmed over his failure to master lines—as did everyone else involved. The producer, Freddy Brisson, and director Joseph Anthony made it clear that they found it difficult to discern the characterization he was working toward. They had hired him because of the offbeat twist with which he customarily endowed his roles, but were impatient for him to arrive at an outline of the performance he would eventually give. Instead, he fumbled along, slowly adding and discarding things without making visible progress. Liz added what encouragement she could, but seemingly no one could help him in his search. The problem in a nutshell, says stage manager Charles Forsythe, was that "they wanted instant coffee, and he just refused to give it to them."

On the day the company set out for New Haven, expectations concerning the play's fate were bleak. Gig and Liz were in despair at the prospect of his being fired. Anthony, Brisson, and Forsythe drove up together. "I sat in the back seat and kept quiet, while Joe and Freddy discussed what had to be done," Forsythe recalls. "They had decided he had to be replaced. However, since there was a commitment at the

Shubert Theater that had to be fulfilled, they decided to let him open the play until they could get a replacement."

The dress rehearsal was a shambles. Cast morale was generally low for the premiere, but no one's was lower than Gig's as he sat in his dressing room with his hands trembling so uncontrollably he was unable to button his shirt. He dreaded facing a sold-out house—especially a house full of Yale students.

The minute Gig got his first big guffaw from this tough audience, however, he found his footing. To the astonishment of the producer and director, and a delighted Liz, no one else in the cast delivered quite the way Gig did. Even though he missed a line now and then, the audience was with him all the way. He evoked laughs no one had suspected were there. "He was like an arrow headed for the moon," Forsythe says. "He was the show. The audience couldn't wait for Hogan to appear again."

Patrons, attuned to the lying, lecherous, predatory Hogan, found him both hilarious and touching. They roared at his flamenco-like manipulation of two hand mirrors to enable him to spy into the across-the-hall apartment of his nubile neighbor. They screamed when he eavesdropped on her private conversations by putting his ear to an inverted glass placed against a shared wall; when he gained entrance to her premises with one of an endless supply of passkeys, on the pretext of watering her plastic flowers with an empty sprinkling can; and at his confession to her, when confronted, that he was a liar and a lecher. "His movements might have been choreographed by Martha Graham," Forsythe says. "It was like watching a dancer out there. Everything was so precise and perfectly timed. He would rise at just the right moment, on the right inflection of the right line. It was inspired."

Gig's doubts about his performance and his fear of being fired were forgotten. He slipped back into his public image

of the laid-back, carefree fellow who accomplished everything easily. During an interview with his old friend, the
critic Richard Coe, Gig went so far as to claim, "The first two
weeks in a part are the real work and fun of acting. In this
period you build, think and create. You try something and if
it doesn't work, you drop it and try something else."

It would be easy to attribute such statements to canny
public relations. But the truth of the matter is that Gig believed them. He was so out of touch with his own anxieties—either exaggerating or denying them—that as time
went on they would express themselves in increasingly bizarre ways.

The play opened on Broadway on November 16, 1960, at
the Henry Miller Theater. Gig was momentarily terrified,
but he came through, to unanimously enthusiastic reviews,
even though reactions to the play itself were divided. Although he'd hoped for a longer run, the show closed after
five months and 174 performances; a dejected Gig fled New
York for Hollywood, wondering once more if he would ever
work again. Liz had stood by him through it all—frequently
coming backstage to invite Forsythe and members of the
cast to have supper with her and Gig. Few would have
guessed their relationship was less than ideal.

Truthfully, it was never the "perfect" marriage portrayed in the press. The first hint that trouble was brewing
came early on, back in the "golden days" in New York.
Helena Sterling, Gig's old friend from the Louis Shurr West
Coast office, had moved to Manhattan at the Youngs' urging
and found herself spending a lot of time with Liz, whom she
at first considered scatterbrained. "Then I realized she was
lonely," she says.

One day, Liz was in the midst of complaining to Helena
about Gig, when she pulled out the drawer of one of the
Early American tables placed at the ends of the sofa. "Look!"
she told her guest. It was chock-full of pictures of Sophie.

Elizabeth asked what she should do about them, and Helena advised her to tell Gig that she didn't want him to forget Sophie, but he was married to her now; he would have to store these pictures in a box somewhere. Liz greeted this suggestion as if Helena had come up with some startling solution.

Part of the problem, of course, was the age difference. Liz lacked the maturity to understand the emotional vicissitudes of a man who traveled with photos of his dead wife. She also couldn't compete with the woman who came into Gig's life just after his triumph in *Teacher's Pet,* when he signed to do a summer stock tour in Daphne Du Maurier's *September Tide.* Her name was Doris Rich, and she was a short, dumpy, vivacious character actress in her mid-sixties, who wore her hair in flapper bangs and managed to be at once motherly and flamboyant. With her unflagging vitality and her admiration of Gig's talent, she was in the loyal mold of Mrs. Harry Kaines and Sophie Rosenstein. What's more, she sensed in the actor a quest for metaphysical meaning and encouraged it. What she'd actually tapped into was Gig's desire for a guru who could help him understand a life that was becoming more and more mystifying. She played to that side of him in a correspondence that continued until his death. In fact, two years before the tragedy at the Osborne, she wrote to him about a reproduction of Titian's *St. Christopher,* which she fancifully insisted was a portrait of him: "It is my favorite picture of you. I have seen that expression of trust and faith—that searching, looking-up-to-God inner vision—mirrored on your face many times over the years. That is the portrait of you—the Gig not everyone sees."

Doris Rich was a true believer worshiping at Liz's husband's shrine in a way that his increasingly disgruntled wife could hardly be expected to understand. Platonic though the relationship was, Liz felt emotionally short-changed. There was a distinct coolness at the Young household whenever Gig brought up the name of the woman who fed his artistic and spiritual needs.

Nor could Gig cope with what he considered his wife's father fixation. Helena Sterling found herself consoling him as well. He appeared late one night on her doorstep, and she invited him in to chat. "He had been drinking," she says. "He wasn't really drunk. It was a kind of I-wouldn't-be-telling-you-this-if-I-weren't-high kind of thing," Helena recalls. "He lay down on the couch and began talking philosophically about life, women in general, and specifically Sophie and Elizabeth. He went on and on, and I finally said, 'You and Elizabeth had a fight?' He said, 'Well, yeah.' I asked, 'Are you breaking up?' He said he didn't know. Probably not. Then he said, 'The trouble with her is she's jealous of Sophie, and she thinks she married her father.' He didn't mean father figure; he meant Robert Montgomery. Because Gig was getting more and more into the same kind of roles." What it boiled down to was that he wasn't going to allow her to regard him as a kind of Robert Montgomery clone. Gig might defer to Cary Grant or Gable or Cagney, but not to a father-in-law he despised.

Around this time, a friend and business associate who prefers not to be identified saw other signs of marital discord. He thinks Liz may have begun drinking with Gig because that was the only way she could be with him. "But," he says, "it was so wrong. Because in the middle of the night they'd get to fighting, and he would throw her out. She would come to my apartment and stay overnight until he recovered."

These episodes were kept secret, however, and did nothing to contradict the public picture the couple worked hard to present until after the closing of *Under the Yum Yum Tree*. Back in California, the marriage quickly began to degenerate into a taunting game of mild flirtations that gradually became more and more serious.

One of Gig's more conspicuous romances took place in Paris in 1962, during the filming of Anatole Litvak's *Five Miles to Midnight,* starring Sophia Loren and Anthony Perkins. Gig was immediately smitten with Sophia, who seemed to return the feelings. They toured Paris together and had a bittersweet parting. By the time he arrived back in New York on his way to Hollywood, he was ready to scuttle his marriage for Sophia. He *had* to speak to her. Enlisting a close associate to place the call, so he wouldn't risk getting Sophia's husband on the phone, Gig was in for a shock. The actress heard who was calling and hung up. Gig insisted they had been cut off. His intermediary placed a second call. Again Sophia hung up. Her message was loud and clear: the picture was finished, and so was the romantic interlude. He never saw or spoke to her again.

Liz, in turn, discovered a way to retaliate when Marty Baum set her for a movie directed by William Asher. Soon after filming started, gossip began flying that Liz and Asher were romantically involved and that Liz and Gig were separated. Both denied the rumors vehemently. But the rumors were further fueled when Gig was seen frequently in the company of a well-endowed blond.

Gig's paranoia about Liz's possible cheating escalated to intolerable proportions. Ignoring his own behavior, he self-righteously devised a scheme to entrap her. He concocted a story about having to go to San Diego for the weekend, left home, then burst into the house that night, expecting to find Liz in a compromising situation. He failed.

They separated, only to reunite shortly after. Apparently they still cared for each other but were inexorably pulled apart. "At first I couldn't express what I felt about their battling," says Sue Douglas. "The marriage had started out so well, but gradually it degenerated into playing games. They were like two children getting back at one another." Howard Erskine, who had been close to them before their marriage, says, "Who knows what goes on between a man and a woman, but each just seemed to be trying to show the other."

Whatever the immediate causes, the crosscurrents of resentment regularly escalated into quarrels that punctuated their days. Once, the door of the house was accidentally left ajar and one of the beloved whippets ran onto the road and was killed by a passing car. Gig, beside himself with grief, lost his temper and blamed Liz. During the angry exchange, he accused her of having an affair with Asher. Her response was that if that was what he believed, then she would oblige. In retaliation, rumor has it, he arranged for her to come home shortly afterward and find that someone had used her douche bag. The blithe Noel Coward comedy had deteriorated into an Edward Albee emotional slugfest.

After a climactic quarrel, Liz stamped out of the house, and so did Gig. When, twenty-four hours later, neither had returned, a friend began worrying whether the surviving whippet, Mr. Boo, was being cared for. She hopped into her car and sped to the Youngs' house. There a chaotic scene greeted her. A table lamp was tipped over and smashed, upholstery was shredded, and stuffing was strewn about the house. The pampered Mr. Boo, spiteful and half crazed by fear and loneliness, cowered in a corner, forgotten by the people who loved him.

"What an awful end to a marriage," Nick Dunne said years later. "Doing that to a dog they worshiped—and both forgot."

The pretense that they were still together ended on March 25, 1963, when Los Angeles *Herald-Examiner* columnist Harrison Carroll printed this item: "After repeatedly denying that they were even separated Elizabeth Montgomery today finally admitted she got a Juarez quickie divorce last January from film star Gig Young."

The collapse of his third marriage was humiliating to

Gig. From his point of view, he had lost Liz to another man, William Asher, who could—and would—give her the children that Gig could not. Dogs were no substitute for children. Liz might have argued that Gig had not so much "lost" her as driven her away. Whatever the case, the sour ending between them left him feeling emasculated and impotent, reviving the childhood fear that some part of himself was unlovable, incapable of keeping people from leaving him. The emotional scars his mother had inflicted on him were repeatedly coming back to haunt him in his relationships with women: the mismatch with Sheila, the burden of coping with Sophie's fatal illness, the psychological battering from Sherry, and the loss of Elaine Stritch because of her religious scruples. The ten-year-old Gig was forever dogging the adult Gig, a theme that the actor would play out in one of his best, and least-known, acting assignments.

Back in 1959, Gig accepted what he then considered to be just another job. In fact, it turned out to be, next to *They Shoot Horses, Don't They?,* his most enduring achievement. It was a half-hour fantasy segment on Rod Serling's *Twilight Zone.* In "Walking Distance," he played an advertising executive who steps "through the looking glass" in an attempt to prove that he can go home again to enjoy band concerts, merry-go-rounds, and a gentler life. Once transported back, he encounters his family and his childhood self. In his eagerness to make contact with that youthful self, he injures the child. His father orders him to return to the present, since there is no place for him in the past. "Maybe there's only one summer to every customer," his father says. Reluctantly, the executive returns to his hectic world, bringing back with him only the limp he inflicted on the boy he once was.

Now, as Gig was nearing his fifties, he would try to recapture the "summer of his youth" again and again through dalliances with beautiful young girls and flirtations with the psychedelic drugs that would set trends in the 1960s. Byron Barr had come a long way from his simple Minnesota beginnings. But the boy of ten, in a reverse of the *Twilight Zone* episode, would haunt the man of fifty, eventually injuring him beyond recovery.

·Part Two·

*"You don't know what hell
there is in life, do you?"*

· 7 ·

LSD Trips and Orgone Boxes

"You don't know what hell there is in life, do you?"

Bill Harbach was startled at Gig's question, which seemed to come out of nowhere.

"You're so lucky. You don't have any idea what hell life can be," Gig said and walked out, leaving his longtime friend standing there.

They'd spent the afternoon playing croquet in the warm California sunshine and then stopped off at a bar. Gig had been his usual charming, suave, and delightful self. He'd been a "killer" on the court but in a jovial mood afterward. At first Harbach thought Gig was joking, but his features were clouded with an anguish Bill Harbach had never before seen in his friend. Showing the face of his despair was an aberration for the cool charmer of fifty. But since Gig had recently emerged from the debacle of his third marriage, Harbach simply concluded that the wounds from Gig's wrenching disappointment over Elaine Stritch and his bruising fights with Elizabeth Montgomery had never healed.

Picking up on the nascent tempo of a decade cartwheeling to the liberal maxim "Do your own thing," Gig set out to drown his troubles by doubling his doses of alcohol and women. The pleasures of drinking he'd discovered in his boyhood accelerated to proportions that would have been alarming in more abstemious times, though the good times in Hollywood were always well lubricated. "When I discovered liquor," Gig often observed regarding his "serious" drinking, "I thought I'd found the magic potion."

Women were more troublesome. In his autobiographical tapes, Gig insists that with many women he was only looking for friendship but was maneuvered into affairs. Yet tales of his many sexual adventures circulated freely around New York and Hollywood. And for a man who was overly concerned with his virility, he had done little to discourage the stories of his indefatigable prowess.

Shortly after his divorce from Liz, Gig enlisted a friend to drive him to a funny little house on an unpretentious residential street in Pasadena (his own car was in the shop at the time). Gig instructed his companion to drop him off, go to the end of the block, turn right, turn right again, park on the street in back of the house, and wait for him. Before the man behind the wheel pulled away, the door of the cottage swung open and a beauty in a robe greeted Gig. Forty-five minutes later, the back door of the house slammed and Gig sprinted toward the car. He leaped into the front seat as a shot sounded. A man came roaring down the lawn, brandishing a gun. "Old Gig," says his friend, "was quite shaken up." No explanation was offered—nor was one needed.

The same friend, who chooses to remain anonymous, also recalls an afternoon when he and Gig were playing croquet at the end of Coldwater Canyon Drive. A beige-and-pink Cadillac convertible approached very slowly, its driver observing the game. Her blond hair blew loosely in the wind, and her cleavage was spectacular. "Look at that over there. That's something to see," said Gig with a laugh, and he hit his croquet ball near the car. "And as far as I know, that was the first time he ever laid eyes on Elaine Whitman," says the friend.

This is only one of several stories about how Gig and Elaine met. A popular version is that she sold him a house. Elaine says she showed him several houses, but ultimately he bought one from someone else. At the time they met, Gig was still married to Elizabeth, and Elaine was the wife of a young Los Angeles real estate salesman, Danny Whitman. Elaine was a handy weapon in the wars of escalating jealousy between Gig and Liz. Reports of Gig and Elaine having coffee or lunch would reach Liz and send her into a fury.

Gig may well have decided that after Liz, he'd put marriage at arms' length for a while. But his resolve would prove to be no match for a woman as effusive and vibrant as Elaine. Born Elaine Garber, the daughter of a minor movie executive, the petite blond with the Jayne Mansfield figure was determined to make a big success in Beverly Hills. After a short stint at UCLA, she withdrew into the arms of the first of five husbands and earned a license to peddle real estate on the Sunset Strip in Los Angeles County. Although still a journeyman, she was consumed with ambition, arriving at the office by seven o'clock six mornings a week, no matter how late she was out the night before. She had the reputation of being a promising real estate agent: aggressive without being pushy and flattering without being obsequious. She also knew how to dress to attract attention, whether at a party or just sitting at her desk behind the window of

Archer Realty on Sunset Boulevard. One of the many rumors had it that Gig first noticed her at that desk on his way to work and slowed down the car to drink her in.

As Elaine tells it, she'd been married to Danny Whitman for three years when she met Gig, who was in the market for a house. Of course, she knew who he was and had always admired his soigné screen persona, but twenty-five years later, she insists that at first she and Gig were "platonic friends." A few months after they met, her marriage had "fallen apart" and she filed for divorce. She says the actor had nothing to do with it. Soon after, word came over television that Liz had secretly divorced Gig in Mexico. Elaine immediately informed friends that she "just knew Gig would be phoning." She was right. The next day, he called to invite her to a party at his modest beach house on the 1900 block of Pacific Coast Highway.

She accepted but balked when he told her what time to be there. "I'm old-fashioned in some ways," she informed him, insisting that he pick her up. It turned out to be a mistake. There was a good deal of drinking at the party, and she had to find someone else to give her a lift home. She was very angry.

Gig repeatedly called to apologize, but she waited until the fourth or fifth call to forgive him. Explaining her decision, Elaine enthuses: "I did because Gig and I had been such good friends, and I liked him so much. I mean, he was so charming and wonderful. I thought I'd just give it a chance."

One of the things they had in common besides the movie industry was a love for the sea. "We took [Gig's boat—a thirty-four-foot Vega] to Catalina almost every weekend," she recalls. "I loved to swim. And Gig said most girls he knew didn't want to get their hair wet. But I didn't care. That boat was an important part of our life together. I think it was my most fun time."

Gig's spirits noticeably lifted once he began dating Elaine. Bob Stephens, a yacht captain, actor, and stunt man who was a good friend of Gig's, thinks Gig probably found Elaine's "Southern California–girl enthusiasm" an exciting contrast to Liz's "Eastern finishing school sophistication."

"Elaine was pretty cute," Stephens says. "And unlike Elizabeth, Elaine went along with our driving the little race cars I built for us and going boating. She wasn't afraid of a little grease. So many of the other girls were prima donnas, not wanting to get their nails dirty. To find somebody who was kind of earthy—I think Gig thought he was in love."

In many ways, Gig's outlook on relations between the sexes still reflected St. Cloud's mores rather than Hollywood's. Nowhere was this better illustrated than when, after steadily dating Gig for several months, Elaine discovered she was pregnant. In St. Cloud, if a man impregnated a woman he either married her or ran off and joined the navy. In Hollywood, "nice guys" drove their girls to and from abortionists and then paid the bills; "cads" often gave them the name of "a doctor" and a packet of cash and left them on their own.

When Elaine informed Gig of her condition, he was overjoyed. He concluded that the attempted surgical reversal of his vasectomy, which he had undergone in a desperate attempt to save his marriage to Liz, had resulted in a medical miracle, allowing him to father a child with Elaine. At last, he exulted to columnist Marilyn Beck, he had found the right woman for him, a woman who was gentle and loving. He decided to marry her.

Many people felt the relationship was one of oil and water. As Gig's press agent Jay Bernstein (who knew and liked Elaine long before he was hired by Gig) puts it, they were "just wrong for each other." Friends were uneasy that Gig was jumping into the marriage-go-round again so soon. Even while acknowledging that he was the "marrying kind," they wondered if the nuptials weren't a spur-of-the-moment decision fueled by too much alcohol. They also worried about the twenty-year age gap. Elaine was twenty-eight; Gig, claiming to be forty-five, would soon be fifty.

Had the friends known about the visit Gig paid to his lawyer, their doubts might have been put partially to rest. Perhaps remembering the acrimonious squabbling over his first divorce settlement and having recently and reluctantly surrendered to Liz a clear title to their house, Gig somewhat shamefacedly arranged for a prenuptial property agreement to be drawn up and signed by Elaine and himself.

After returning to Los Angeles from the nuptials in Juarez, Mexico, on September 18, 1963, Gig telephoned several relatives and close friends to introduce his bride, claiming that this marriage really would be forever. When a friend who had visited Los Angeles recently and was aware of Gig's early vasectomy bluntly inquired, "But isn't she pregnant?" Gig couldn't resist wisecracking, "Yeah, I think I saw a star in the east."

Even Gig must have marveled at being able to father a child after all the years he and Liz had tried. The scenario, however, fit neatly into what he wanted—or thought he wanted—as he segued into middle age: a wife-baby-home-with-a-picket-fence fantasy, proof of his virility, and a role as father-provider that would distract him from the specter of failure and perhaps even help spur him on to success.

"I think Gig always expected or hoped he could father a child," says Irving Apple, his lawyer. "I think, with him, it was psychological. He wanted to believe that he could."

Gig's dream became true on April 22, 1964, when, at St. John's Hospital in Santa Monica, Elaine gave birth to a five-pound-eleven-ounce girl, whom they christened Jennifer. Three weeks later, a smiling Gig and a radiant Elaine introduced the baby to the press. Wire services carried the photo worldwide, leaving the impression that Gig's most satisfying role to date was that of a real-life parent.

Over the next few months, Gig gave frequent interviews portraying himself as a successful star who had at last found contentment as a father and a pillar of the film community. He told Marilyn Beck: "Can you imagine after all these years, my being a father for the first time? . . . I thought about the kind of home we'd be bringing Jennifer to. And I thought about how horrible it would be to raise a child in an atmosphere of bitterness and frustration. . . . Happily I don't have to worry about such things. Elaine and I have a wonderful relationship. She's a marvelous girl. . . . I'm lucky to have found a woman who can give me everything I need. And Jennifer is lucky, too, for she's going to be raised in a home where love rules and where she won't have to be exposed to tempers and violent arguments. I'm not sorry about my past mistakes. I learned from them and profited."

Mindful that he should back up his beliefs with action, Gig perceived the prenuptial agreement as casting a shadow over his marriage. "How can we develop a mutually trusting relationship with that paper hanging over our heads?" he demanded. Ignoring legal advice, he dramatically destroyed the agreement, determined to play this marriage for keeps.

Gig and Elaine set up housekeeping in a small house on Heather Drive, just outside of Beverly Hills. Gig soon began to dictate some changes in Elaine's lifestyle. Convinced that their best chance for a happy marriage lay in her limiting herself to being a housewife and mother, he insisted she give up her realtor's job. He urged her to concentrate on domesticity; cooking classes would turn her, in her words, from "a sandwich girl into a gourmet cook." At first Elaine accommodated him. If she was turning in the beige-and-pink Cadillac for a station wagon, at least there were compensations. She delighted in hobnobbing with the

Hollywood crowd, now as an insider, playing hostess to the likes of Bette Davis, who was a frequent visitor.

Just as Gig made changes in Elaine's life, she was soon attempting to modify certain habits of his. "I knew he drank too much from our first date, but like every other woman in the world, I thought love could conquer all," she says. "I didn't know alcohol was a disease. I soon found out. I knew nothing about AA, nothing about that stuff except I was going to leave him if he continued drinking."

In a matter of months, trouble began to develop. Elaine remembers that while they were still living in the Heather Drive home, they came home from a party slightly drunk. Gig took his motorcycle out for a spin and, an hour later, returned bloodied from a spill. Realizing he had an interview for a TV series coming up, Elaine exploded. A marital battle ensued, in which she claims she told him for the first time that she wanted a divorce.

"The next morning, as with all drinkers," Elaine says, "it was, 'I'm sorry. What can I do? I love you,' and I said, 'You've got to get help.'" A friend recommended AA. Elaine urged Gig to go. Three weeks later, he went. "In those days it was difficult because people didn't understand. Studio executives would come up at parties and say, 'God, Gig, have a drink. You're really boring tonight. You were much more fun when you drank,'" Elaine recalls. "In our world, AA wasn't a big thing like it later became."

Despite Gig's initial optimism, the relationship was, almost from the beginning, obviously in trouble. It was aggravated by career problems, as well as by Elaine's belief that Gig was drinking too much.

Between his marriage to Elaine, in September 1963, and September 1964, Gig made only three appearances: on *Kraft Suspense Theater*'s "The End of the World, Baby," with Nina Foch, Katherine Crawford, and Peter Lorre; on ABC's

Hollywood Palace; and in Universal's lackluster theatrical release *Strange Bedfellows,* starring Gina Lollobrigida and Rock Hudson. But if work was scarce, money apparently would not be. Averaging an annual income in the low six figures, Gig was nonetheless counting heavily on a new television series, *The Rogues,* co-starring Charles Boyer and David Niven, to catch on in the fall and make him a multimillionaire.

In it, he, Boyer, and Niven played civilized partners in crime. Sophisticated in concept for those days of stringent network censorship, the series concerned the exploits of three con men who assumed various disguises to swindle the greedy, the decadent, the social climbing, and the dishonest. Speaking of *The Rogues,* Gig explained, "It's really quite a moral show. We never cheat anyone who doesn't deserve it."

Gig welcomed the heavy schedule, even though it meant being at Studio Center by seven-thirty five mornings a week. Given this new opportunity, he concentrated on presenting himself to every advantage. Firmly on the wagon now, he dieted to eliminate any hint of a paunch. To make himself feel more at ease, he acquired two "toupettes" to cover his receding hairline. He was filled with optimism about the series' chances and looked forward to becoming financially secure.

On those high hopes, the Young family upgraded their lifestyle. Feeling that he had at last made it, Gig purchased a Rolls-Royce to complement his polished thirty-four-foot cabin cruiser, *Unicorn.* He hadn't "gone Hollywood," he explained to friends; he was just fulfilling a lifelong ambition to enjoy the best while he still had the spunk to do so. That same year, his longtime buddy Robert Webber took Gig to a party at 919 North Rexford Drive in Beverly Hills. Gig took one look at the grounds and said to Webber, "God, I'm just crazy about this house." Host Ronald Alexander overheard the remark and laughingly told Gig, "It's for sale. But I must warn you," added the man, who was in the throes of a divorce, "it's not a good house for marriages."

Nevertheless, the next thing Webber heard, Gig and Elaine were owners of the seven-bedroom, Spanish-style mansion with patio and pool. Decorating the house with Spanish antiques accented by modern design, Gig and Elaine haunted Ebell's Auction House for additional treasures. They bought so many that Gig—betraying for a moment a typical anxiety that at any time everything might go up in smoke—ordered a trailer hitch installed on the rear of his Rolls to economize on the cost of home delivery.

His money fears were well founded. *The Rogues* fell victim to weak ratings and a network power play that brought on its cancellation after one season in the spring of 1965, cheating Gig out of his chance to become rich and to establish himself as a full-fledged leading man and television superstar. Later, he told a reporter how, while on tour with his first musical-in-the-round, he was blocked from completing his exit by teenage fans who had seen *The Rogues* and were determined to have his autograph. "But I guess to television a few million fans just don't count," he commented somewhat bitterly.

Around this time, Gig's agent Marty Baum moved from General Artists Corporation to Ashley-Famous and invited Gig to accompany him. While getting oriented at his new agency, Baum arranged for Gig to play Harold Hill in a nine-week summer tour of *The Music Man*. Gig had worked on this part over a period of years with his voice coach, Bert Knapp. The role of Harold Hill was long known among musical comedy performers as a "ball-breaker." In urging Gig to try *The Music Man*, Knapp said audiences and critics would know what to expect, and Gig would either deliver or fall flat on his face. It was a formidable challenge. "It's like saying to myself, 'Put up or shut up," Gig explained to friends.

After the tour—a success—closed, Gig returned to a very troubled marriage. With *The Rogues* aborted, he worried about economizing, beginning with such minor frugalities as urging Elaine to purchase household staples at markets outside the expensive Beverly Hills area. Treating the requests as temporary aberrations, she ignored them, which only provoked her husband's anger.

On a more traumatic level for Elaine, Gig finally decided that until he signed for another television series or major movie, they could no longer afford the upkeep of the Rexford Drive house. Brushing aside her protests, he listed it for rental with a realtor, who had an immediate tenant. In an eerie foreshadowing of Gig's own end, Mickey Rooney's fifth wife, Barbara, had been gunned down in the Rooneys' Brentwood home by a young Yugoslavian actor, who then shot and killed himself. Mickey, desperate to find a new home, was ready to move into the Rexford Drive house at once. Suddenly in need of new quarters themselves, the Youngs moved into a smaller house, on the 1600 block of Doheny, a house that Elaine had been remodeling to occupy her time and in hopes of selling for a profit. Gig brushed aside her protests that the house was unsafe for a toddler because the swimming pool was unfenced. He assured Elaine they would be out of the house long before the baby walked. "In fact, we'll be out as soon as Marty gets me a job," he promised.

Once settled on Doheny, Gig grew increasingly secretive and vague. Elaine became suspicious that he was drinking again. She accused, he denied. Then, on the anniversary of his first year of sobriety, he announced that since he had gone into the AA program to please her rather than for his own benefit, there was no reason for him not to drink in moderation.

The couple's bickering increased—and so did their suspicions. Gig heard rumors that Elaine was complaining about his drinking. He tormented himself with increasingly lurid fantasies about what exactly his wife was up to. After all, she was a very attractive younger woman who he well knew enjoyed the sensual side of life. Over fifty, it was hard for him to keep up—socially or sexually. One day, he ran into a private detective who worked for one of the big studios. Gig knew this fellow utilized electronic bugging on occasion. He asked the detective's advice about how to find out what Elaine was up to and was referred to "Ears," an electronic genius who had devised what were relatively small, voice-activated recorders. "Ears" installed two of these—one for each telephone line—in a box that was surreptitiously placed in the Youngs' garage. All that was required of Gig was to replace the tape on each recorder frequently.

After picking up the used tapes, Gig would take them out on the *Unicorn,* drop anchor, and spend hours listening intently to Elaine's conversation. He would toss aside material of no interest and mark whatever seemed incriminating, for transfer onto a master tape. Unable to edit the tapes himself, he would take them to a technician "Ears" had recommended. The master tapes might be useful in convincing Elaine to seek psychiatric help—or in divorce proceedings, which he was beginning to think were all but inevitable.

After a while, Gig surprised Elaine by casually bringing up private remarks she had made to her friends during phone conversations. "I thought, Can these friends of mine be calling and telling him what I said?" Elaine remembers. "I thought, No, I'm losing my mind—because I didn't know about the tapes. Then came the day a mutual friend called me and said, 'Elaine, I want to prepare you. Gig is on his way home with a box of tapes. He's taped you for a month, and he's drunk.' And Gig came home and he sat with his tapes, and I heard them. And you know, being edited, and hearing what you said—it was like—I was screaming. I said, 'I didn't say it that way. I didn't.' He said, 'That's you.' "

Elaine maintains that the editing distorted her remarks. Sure, she was telling people around town that he was drinking, but it was only because she wanted to enlist the help of friends in getting him back into AA. The other edits, she says, made it look as if she were being disloyal. "We were at a party at John Foreman's house," she recalls. "I saw Bob Wagner. Afterward I said on the phone, 'Oh my God, Bob Wagner is so wonderful. I just love him. But my husband is much more gorgeous.' That became on the edited tape, 'Oh my God, Bob Wagner is so wonderful. I just love him.' "

To friends, Gig claimed he had transferred only the disloyal comments, and only to convince Elaine that they needed psychiatric counseling. Shaken by his divorce from Liz and further rocked by the realization that the new marriage was in deep trouble, he insisted that they both seek help. Several friends and business associates who had been under the care of Westwood psychiatrist Dr. Albert Duvall recommended him. Dr. Duvall was an unorthodox practitioner, who still relied heavily on Wilhelm Reich's orgone therapy. Gig embraced the treatment enthusiastically. Elaine insisted she needed no therapy, but went anyway. For her the treatment was a failure. For Gig it was the latest step in his lifelong search for a psychological and spiritual guide.

A disavowed protégé of Sigmund Freud, Wilhelm Reich arrived in the U.S. in 1939 and spent two years as an associate professor at the New School for Social Research. Simultaneously, he founded the controversial Orgone Institute in Forest Hills, New York. The aim was to treat patients with "orgone," a substance Reich had difficulty defining. To capture this elusive energy, he brought out the Orgone Energy Accumulator, popularly known as the Orgone Box. About the size of a small telephone booth, the first boxes were nothing more than plain sheet iron encased in ordinary wood. The patients, scantily clad, sat in the box during sessions and were, according to Reich, "bombarded" by orgone. The aim was to turn neurotics into "orgasmically potent individuals." How this bombardment was accomplished was never established to the satisfaction of nonbelievers; Reich was enjoined by the federal government from selling orgone boxes and was imprisoned in 1956 for ignoring the enjoinment. He died in the Lewisburg (Pennsylvania) Penitentiary in 1957. This, however, did not discourage some of his followers, including, apparently, Dr. Albert Duvall.

Since Dr. Duvall is deceased, we must rely on Elaine's report of what occurred during the time she spent under his "care." According to her, a struggle developed on her first of five visits, which quickly turned into a sex farce. "Dr. Duvall was really obsessive because he couldn't get my clothes off," she recalls. "I had a bra and pants on. He got me to that state of undress. He said, 'Everybody who has ever come here has taken their clothes off, except you.' He said, 'If you take your brassiere off, I can ask you a question and your nipple will get lavender-colored or you'll tense up and I'll know.' " (Skin color was purportedly an indication of orgone—blue was good.)

Elaine was convinced that Duvall was a charlatan who employed false and destructive techniques. "I came in there one day. He said, 'Lie down. . . . I am so sorry about your mother and father.' I said, 'What do you mean?' He said, 'You don't know' . . . like they'd had an accident. He did it just to get my reaction. Then—this was later—I came in . . . and he said, 'Elaine, how come you never told me about your mother and father?' I said, 'I don't know what you're talking about.' He said, 'That you were adopted. You were left on your parents' doorstep in a basket.' It was so sick. . . . And then the time he put his hand in my pants. I said, 'Why are you doing that?' He said, 'I've got to get a reaction. Why are you not naked? Why do you have to be so different from anybody else that I can't look at it?' I said, 'You just can't.'"

Elaine stopped going. Gig continued until at Dr. Duvall's suggestion he arranged to place himself under the care of Dr. Al Hubbard, a Canadian psychologist who practiced LSD therapy. It was a rather drastic move, but Gig acceded to the then-trendy treatment, having heard Cary Grant rave about the miracles his psychiatrist had accomplished for him with LSD. It is likely, also, that the suggestion appealed to the side of Gig that was all but obscured by the fancy cars, boats, and sexy blonds—his relentless search for spiritual meaning, which women like Doris Rich had recognized in him. In early 1966, Gig checked into the Hollywood Hospital in Vancouver, Canada, for a month of hallucinogenic therapy.

When Cary Grant underwent his now-famous LSD sessions, the drug had not yet been outlawed in the United States. The hallucinogen, lysergic acid diethylamide, had been around since Dr. Albert Hoffman discovered it in his Swiss laboratory on April 19, 1943. Since then, LSD's ability to trigger intense and powerful out-of-body experiences (later dubbed "trips") had been useful in medical experiments with mental patients. Hoffman himself had written about the feelings of fear, mysticism, and cosmic unity he experienced under the drug. "The memory of this experience of mystic oneness has stayed with me ever since," he wrote.

Later, doctors at Palo Alto, California, where a mind-expansion center was founded once the drug found its way to the United States, identified three states induced by LSD: (1) evasion; (2) a stage of symbolic perception; and (3) a stage of immediate perception, in which the patient experiences himself or herself in a totally new way. Fantasies and long-repressed feelings come speeding to the surface, eliciting emotional responses that can be ecstatic, fearful, religious, or terrifying—sometimes all at once. Proselytizers of the drug, like Dr. Timothy Leary, saw it as a useful tool in opening up the world to a cosmic communal awareness. Others found it dangerous and explosive and urged its prohibition as it began to proliferate as a street drug. On October 16, 1966, LSD was banned in California.

Gig told friends that the LSD therapy process at Hollywood Hospital in Vancouver entailed lengthy sessions during the month he was there. As preparation, patients were encouraged to write out an autobiographical account and were then submitted to a battery of psychological tests. They were told to bring to the sessions photos they considered especially meaningful. Gig would appear at the clinic, strip nude, and be given LSD. He told friends that he would don a ski mask and lie on the carpet, waiting for the drug to take effect. Dr. Hubbard monitored proceedings to assure that Gig did not hurt himself as he writhed, shouted, cried, laughed, and attempted to assault the doctor. Hubbard made detailed notes of Gig's muscular responses. When the chemically induced emotions became too threatening (what would later be termed "bad trips" or "bummers"), Gig could partly regain control by removing the mask. After a brief recess, under the therapist's guidance, he would replace the mask and once again slip back to the intense outer edges of the mind-expanding state.

One can easily imagine the stunning, potentially harmful effect such a "mind-blowing" agent might have had on a fifty-two-year-old man like Gig, who kept a tight lid on his subconscious feelings. The dead, in particular, are known to have an iron grip on the subconscious fantasies stirred up by the hallucinogen. No doubt, photos of Sophie and his mother were among those Gig brought to his sessions. It isn't farfetched to speculate that the screaming and moaning that accompanied Gig's sessions included a litany of pleas to these two women who so haunted his life, as well as to his beloved sister and his current wife. Transported to a world that resembled a Salvador Dalí painting, Gig confronted the ruptured feelings of the past and present with a mix of religious ecstasy, paralyzing insecurity, and whimpering child-like terror.

Vulnerable as he was to easy solutions to his increasingly conflicted life, Gig felt as though the hallucinogen offered an answer, especially to the immediate problem of the wife and the child he'd left behind in California. At one point, Gig and the psychologist placed a call to Elaine, urging her to come to Vancouver for similar treatment. She refused.

Still, Gig believed the prospects of rescuing his marriage were so improved that he cancelled a much-anticipated visit with Gen in Minneapolis to rush back to Elaine and take steps to repair their relationship. His first move was to escape the acrimonious atmosphere of the Doheny house by purchasing a new home on San Ysidro. Then, since he was committed to leave for England to begin filming *The Shuttered Room* with Carol Lynley, Oliver Reed, and Flora Robson, he suggested that Elaine come too, on a second honeymoon. When he expressed uneasiness about taking Jennifer, Elaine declined. So despite his reservations about traveling with a small child, Gig hired a nanny, and the four of them set out for London. His goal was to make a fresh start in his relationship with Elaine, to emerge from the trip with her as freshly optimistic as he had from his trips with LSD.

Sadly, neither the film nor the attempt at restoring marital harmony was successful. The script, adapted from a story by H. P. Lovecraft, abounded in exotic characters, gothic settings, and such trappings as ancestral curses, but in execution, these turned out to be more laughable than menacing. Nor did the change of locale diminish Gig and Elaine's discord. He accused her of extravagances, and she claimed he was keeping her a virtual prisoner, forbidding her to leave Jennifer alone with the nanny even while she went out to lunch. Whatever epiphanies Gig may have had up in Canada were of no use when it came to his relationship with Elaine or, for that matter, Jennifer. His estrangement from his wife was making the very sight of her an ironic reminder of the dreams he'd once rhapsodized about to writer Marilyn Beck. Elaine and Jennifer had become for Gig, in the parlance of the day, a "bad trip," a "bummer."

Back in California, the penultimate marital confrontation occurred when Gig and a friend with whom he had been out sailing and drinking appeared at the San Ysidro house. Elaine was afraid the boisterous men would awaken Jennifer. She lashed out at Gig for being such a weakling about alcohol. Gig took umbrage at her attitude. He slapped her. Elaine screamed at him. "Get out! Get out of this house, or I'll call the police." Both men took off.

It was obvious that there was no salvaging the marriage. Yet when Gig packed to leave, Elaine called and arranged for him to stay at his press agent Jay Bernstein's digs. It was at this low ebb in his life that Gig made an appearance on *The Andy Williams Show* to sing "Ya Got Trouble" (from *The Music Man*), followed by the mindlessly happy ditty "Sunshine, Lollipops and Rainbows," sung with Williams and guest Nanette Fabray. Gig was hoping some alert Broadway or Hollywood producer would spot him for a leading role in a musical comedy.

Film acting assignments for Gig had virtually dried up, and he inexplicably turned down the TV series *It Takes a Thief,* which eventually revived Robert Wagner's career. He worried about facing a camera of any kind, fearful it would detect flaws in his face. Already lopping five years off his age by claiming still to be in his forties, he was concerned that the puffy face that stared back at him in the mirror would give him away and finish him off in film for good.

In mid-July 1967, just before the Santa Monica Superior Court granted Elaine a divorce from Gig, he pulled himself together and embarked on a nine-week tour of *The Odd Couple.* Leslie Cutler, who directed the production for its stand with the Kenley Players in Ohio, found him easy to work with but extremely unhappy. "He didn't mingle," says Cutler. "He just disappeared after rehearsal. We were worried to hear that on a couple of occasions he'd been in a bar at seven in the morning, but he was conscientious about rehearsals and always on top of everything in making it a good show."

During the run in Ohio, an impressionable fifteen-year-old girl delivered to Gig a newspaper announcement of his impending divorce. Before the show one evening, the same girl—who had already seen the play—approached Gig at the stage door and requested an autograph. As he reached out for her memory book, she snapped a handcuff around his wrist and hers, delaying the curtain for the next hour and a half, until her policeman father arrived with a duplicate key to free the star. When some skeptics accused Gig of staging a publicity stunt, he referred them to his marital record and reminded his accusers, "Listen, I can get into enough embarrassing situations in my life without manufacturing more to get my name in the paper."

Time would add still more validity to that wisecrack.

· 8 ·

Giggles, Skysie, and Rocky Gravo

The picture of Gig handcuffed to the fanatic teenage fan from Ohio was as ludicrous as it was symbolic. In one way or another—spiritually, emotionally, professionally, and financially—women had always managed to manacle themselves to him, in grips that some were reluctant to loosen. Sophie haunted him, Elizabeth Montgomery constantly made discreet inquiries about her ex-husband, and Elaine Young had no sooner accepted the divorce settlement than she began maneuvering legally to gain more child support. The detritus of his marriages hung on him like so many trampled party streamers.

In spite of past troubles, Gig needed women, but he kept choosing the wrong ones. And as he grew older, they invariably turned out to be younger. After Sophie, who was six years his senior, Gig became involved with or married to women who were a decade or two—and sometimes three—younger than he was. In 1967, fleeing to New York to escape bitter wrangles with Elaine, he met a woman who would stretch the age gap even further: Skye Aubrey. Over the course of their brief but romantic affair, they had pet names for each other: "Skysie" and "Giggles." Giggles was fifty-three; Skysie, twenty-two. What do you call a fifty-three-year-old man who has affairs with women in their early twenties? Lucky. But you might also call him sexually insecure, emotionally immature, and in the throes of a full-scale midlife crisis. In the summer of 1967, Gig was all of the above. While America itself was in the grip of a youthful tie-dyed, pot-scented revolution, the actor was still steeped in the martini-drinking, blue-blazer, gray-flannel elegance of a fast-vanishing era. He was silent about the LSD therapy—his one brush with the trendy habits of the decade—which led friends to believe that he thought he had failed to profit from it. Like many his age, he felt in danger of being left behind in the giddy rush to celebrate the prevailing zeitgeist of the sixties.

The mirror did little to assuage his anxiety. Reflecting the effects of decades of drink, his face was puffy, his eyes watery, and his hair an unflattering gray—an impaired image of the youthful, dazzlingly handsome Gig who occasionally appeared on late-show movies. He had been contemplating plastic surgery for some time now. In fact, back in Los Angeles, he had got as far as the parking lot of a Beverly Hills surgeon but then panicked and sped away. Fretting over dental problems, back pains, and aching feet, he felt as though he were physically falling apart. What better way to forget one's disintegration than in the arms of a ripe, luscious woman? And there were few women riper than Skye Aubrey.

Gig met the actress when he appeared in the Broadway production of an English sex farce, *There's a Girl in My Soup,* produced by Arnold Saint-Subber. In the slight story, Gig played a lecherous older man who woos an English girl away from her hippie lover through his culinary expertise. In the end she returns to her boyfriend, which caused Gig to quip to a reporter, "I used to lose the girl to Gable or Flynn. I never thought I'd lose her to a hippie."

Gig had overcome his reservations about the part because Neil Simon was a major backer, practically a co-producer, and he hoped to ingratiate himself with the popular playwright for future projects. Still, on opening night, October 18, 1967, at the Music Box Theater, Gig was so overcome with stage fright that the audience could notice his trembling hands. However, once the laughs began coming, he rediscovered his light-comedy legs. The production proved a crowd-pleaser. No less an authority in the field than David Niven came backstage to compliment Gig: "The only other American stage actor who could have made your part work is a man named Donald Cook—and he's long dead."

There's a Girl in My Soup was playing across the street from *Cactus Flower,* which featured Skye Aubrey as the pert ingenue. With her short bob, freckled nose, and shapely legs, properly showcased by her miniskirt, she looked all of fifteen, a real-life Lolita. Skye was the daughter of Phyllis Thaxter (Gig's screen wife in *Come Fill the Cup*) and James Aubrey, Hollywood producer and onetime president of CBS Television. Much like Elizabeth Montgomery before her, Skye had had a teenage crush on Gig. Now she was determined to meet him. "It's the only time in my life I went in pursuit," she says. "I was determined to go out with him, and if I went out with him, he was going to fall in love with me—and that was all there was to it."

Since the curtain for *Cactus Flower* came down fifteen

minutes before that of *There's a Girl in My Soup,* Skye took to walking her poodle near the stage door of the Music Box, hoping to encounter Gig. After three weeks without success, she approached the stage doorman and informed him that she was appearing in the play across the street and had promised to get Gig's autograph for a friend. She went to his dressing room, and he signed his name. They started talking. It was Easter weekend and he was going away, but he said he would call her. "I thought, Oh, God, just my luck. He'll never phone," she remembers. "But like three days later, he rang and asked me out to dinner."

Their romance developed rapidly. After a couple of suppers, bingo! Every night Gig's dresser would appear at her stage door to escort her to his boss's dressing room. "We had fallen madly in love," says Skye. "Everyone around us knew it. Giggles was fifty-six, I believe, but I was always attracted to older men anyway. So I didn't care about the age difference. But my mother was horrified."

Gig, on the other hand, was flattered, almost grateful that Skye should be so attracted as to pursue him. But true to form, he was concerned about his public image, afraid that people might accuse him of "robbing the cradle." He often asked his friend Bob Webber to come along when he took Skye out for after-theater supper. Not only was Webber delightful company, he served as a "beard," making it appear they were just three friends who had got together after work. Those evenings were lighted by Gig's fey sense of humor and renewed zest for life. But there was another side. He was fretting because the play had not turned out to be a blockbuster and movie offers were not materializing. Forever the insecure actor, he was haunted by the possibility of never being able to get another job; forever the insecure child, he was desperately afraid of growing old alone.

"Whenever his career was not on an upward swing, he'd go into self-search," Skye says. "Around this time he got interested in dream therapy. I don't recall what the dreams were, but he spent a lot of time analyzing them. He also worried about getting older and did a lot of self-improvement. He got heavily into speed walking. It was supposed to keep him from getting arthritis. He even wanted me to inform him if he grew hair in his ears, like old people do. He worried that he was going to live to a ripe old age, because he said his family had a heritage of that. That frightened him. He didn't want to be alone—and old. But all of this came out gradually, and it wasn't the kind of conversation you got from fellows my age. I was fascinated."

The affair with Skye salved Gig's fear of loneliness. She had an apartment on Fifty-eighth Street just east of Avenue of the Americas. He occupied a penthouse at the Hotel Maurice, a couple of blocks away. "I literally stayed with him, but I had my clothes and my dog at my apartment so it wouldn't look as if we were living together, because at the time there were all these legal skirmishes with Elaine Young going on," Skye says. "Even though it was the permissive 1960s, Gig didn't want to provide her with any possible ammunition. The two of them were really going after one another."

Skye was so much in love that she would gladly have married Gig, had he asked her. No matter what her mother and the others felt, she was truly happy during this period. "It was an interesting relationship because in the beginning it was highly sexual," she says, "but the minute he felt comfortable with me, it wasn't. I guess because of his drinking. But he loved to cuddle, loved to kiss, loved holding—and that was fine with me. It was as much as I needed at twenty-two."

Part of Gig's problems with impotence, of course, had to do with his intemperate consumption of alcohol, which was the only negative in Gig's character as far as Skye was concerned. At first she told herself that his drinking was all right since he never drank during the day. He loved the theater too much. On matinee days, when they would go out for a snack following the afternoon performance, he would forgo any kind of pick-me-up. Indeed, work always was the only effective curb on Gig's drinking, a temporary purge of his demons. Yet the moment the evening show was over, they would head for Sardi's, Danny's Hideaway, or one of their other favorite spots, and Gig would begin his serious drinking.

A child of the 1960s, Skye preferred marijuana, and she and Webber—also a dope-smoker—devised a campaign to wean Gig away from alcohol by turning him on to grass, which they thought would be far less destructive. Webber recalled that at first Gig was a bit frightened at the suggestion that he switch from booze to pot, but then he agreed.

"I brought joints with me to his penthouse, and we proceeded to light up," said Webber. "It didn't do a thing for him. He smoked a couple of joints and then said, 'I want a drink.' I urged him to try another joint instead. But by the time Skye got home, he was drunk. And I said to her, 'Skye, he had three joints. They just didn't work.' Grass was a total failure with him."

Gig's alcoholism was becoming bizarre and out of hand. One night at Joe Allen's restaurant, Gig and Skye were dining with some new acquaintances. Skye was impressed at how graciously Gig was behaving with people he didn't know well, particularly since earlier he had not been feeling up to par. He was doing some pretty heavy drinking, but as usual, he held his liquor well. Then he suddenly excused himself and headed for the men's room. Ten minutes elapsed, and Skye became concerned. She says she knew the men's loo was hardly large enough to turn around in. She approached the bouncer and asked him to see if Gig had become ill or passed out in there. He came back and reported that the room was empty.

"Now I began to get worried," Skye recalls. "I finally

called Gig's penthouse. The phone rang and rang, and finally he picked up. In the background, I could hear the portable Jacuzzi we'd put in the tub. I said, 'Giggles, it's Skysie. What are you doing home?' He said, 'Skysie, where are you? Aren't you here? I thought you were in the bathroom.' He'd totally forgotten he had left me at Joe Allen's. Somehow he'd managed to hail a cab and gotten home, turned on the Jacuzzi, and passed out.

"That was Gig," she continues. "But he was also so sensitive, funny, and loving, you forgave him. He seldom hurt anyone except himself. He was a man of contradictions because he was an alcoholic, and an alcoholic is a mass of contradictions."

Skye viewed Gig as "a big teddy bear of a man" who needed to be taken care of. "I was a twenty-two-year-old mother to a fifty-six [*sic*]-year-old man," she says, smiling. "I was dying to marry him, and he refused to consider the idea. So we broke up slowly. I told him I had somebody else—which I didn't. We went back together a couple of times, but it couldn't work. There was no future to it." The affair lasted less than a year, but Gig and Skye's friendship endured until his death.

With or without Skye, there seemed little future for Gig during 1968. The violent and divisive images broadcast on the nightly news reflected Gig's own conflicts and contradictions as he hurled drunkenly down to a social and professional nadir. While he may well have blanked out during the social gathering at Joe Allen's, it's also quite possible that he left the restaurant intentionally, incapable of putting on that charming facade for one more minute. He could barely do it for longtime friends, much less new acquaintances. In fact, alcoholism and his real or imagined illnesses were turning him into something of a recluse.

When his pal Helena Sterling came backstage to congratulate him on his performance in *Soup,* he greeted her warmly but apologized for not being able to spend time with her, because he had made previous arrangements to meet Bette Davis. (Apparently this was during one of his and Skye's separations.) "I offered him a lift to the Plaza or wherever he was meeting Bette," Helena says. "And during the ride, on impulse I said I might never see him again, so before we died I wanted him to know what a wonderful friend he'd been. He looked at me in alarm, and I reassured him I wasn't ill or thinking of killing myself, that I just wanted to be sure I'd told him. In the light of what eventually happened, it was a spooky conversation. And it *was* the last time I ever saw him." The countdown had begun.

During the short but respectable run of *Soup,* Gig had been spending hours studying with Bert Knapp in order to get in shape vocally for a road production of *On a Clear Day You Can See Forever* during the summer. The tour turned out to be a commercial and critical failure. On top of that, *The Shuttered Room,* the thriller Gig had made in England two years before, was finally released and quickly bombed. Worst of all, Marty Baum resigned from the agency business to become vice-president of the American Broadcasting Company's motion picture division, leaving Gig without his leading cheerleader.

Not since his return from World War II did the actor's prospects look quite so bleak. Nor could he take refuge in a relationship. Looking back on the ruins of a once-promising career and four marriages, he must have been reminded of that time two summers before when he had sailed a new sloop from Fort Lauderdale to Los Angeles with several cronies. Somewhere in the Carribbean, the boat had been slammed with heavy storm gales, which threw it off course. After the winds subsided, Gig took over at the wheel and, half joking, half serious, announced: "This is your captain speaking. Where in the hell are we?"

The answer? On the brink of the greatest achievement of

his life. For on the dark horizon, there was indeed a band of light. In this case, the incarnation came in the form of Marty Baum, whose first project for ABC feature films was to be based on an obscure American novel by Horace McCoy from the thirties, which French writers had hailed after World War II as one of the first existentialist novels. Set in the Depression, it was about contestants in a dance marathon that goes on for months, presided over by a bombastic, whiskey-soaked emcee-promoter named Rocky Gravo. The title: *They Shoot Horses, Don't They?*

When Baum came on board, he insisted on a number of changes in cast and crew. Among them was that Gig play Rocky (a role that had originally been set for Lionel Stander) and that Sydney Pollack replace Jim Poe as director. "Sydney had never done any successful theatrical film," says Baum, "but I admired his work in television." It is generally believed that Pollack fought against Gig's casting, because he thought the actor was too lightweight for the part. Baum disputes this, saying that he was the boss and that he told Pollack if he wanted the job, he had to take Gig.

Baum knew that Gig could be trouble. He had already noted that on top of drinking excessively, his former client had begun to take sedatives. Gig approached every job tremulously, unsure that the writing was right or the director was right, and he was slow to learn lines. Yet Baum was willing to take the chance. He told Pollack, "Gig was born to play this role. It might take him longer, but the end result will be inspiring." When he gave Gig the script, he said, "You better deliver, pal, or we'll both end up behind some lunch counter flipping hamburgers."

Typically, Gig had reservations about the part, but he slowly grew to believe that this would be his best, and perhaps last, chance to grab the commercial and artistic success he'd lusted after since hitching to Culver City over thirty years and nearly fifty films before. The film brought

back Gig's own youthful memories of the endurance contests he attended in Washington, D.C. Baum and Pollack had
assembled an exceptional cast—Jane Fonda, Susannah
York, Michael Sarrazin, Red Buttons—but Gig's role was the
flashiest of all.

As written, Rocky Gravo is a relentless small-time hus-
tler in a world that compares the exhausted dancers to a
horse that is shot to take it out of its misery, as at the beginning of the film. Yet in Gig's hands, Rocky would assume
greater depth, seeming to suffer almost as much pain as
pleasure, more frustration than fulfillment, in his role as the
greedy manipulator. By just raising his eyebrow, he could
register cynicism, sympathy, and, ultimately, ruthlessness
in his obsessive pursuit of the American dream. "Those kids
have been pounding the boards, fighting fatigue, exhaustion, and depression in their determination to win the big
prize," the gross, puffy-eyed emcee in a white dinner jacket
tells the audience of the 1931 Monster Marathon on a Santa
Monica pier. "And isn't that the great American way? Yowzah! Yowzah! Yowzah!"

Fifty-five years had taught Gig just how brutal life could
be, and in this nihilistic allegory, he would gild that brutal-
ity with dripping sentiment and fairy tales that he himself
had once believed in. It was indeed, as Baum said, a role that
he was born to play.

As the production progressed, Gig's confidence grew. He
began to offer suggestions that would make his character
ever more complicated and emotionally rich. Although most
of Gig's ideas were either rewritten or ignored, he contributed to one of Rocky's more memorable exchanges, in which
he tries to convince Jane Fonda and Michael Sarrazin that
their getting married ("Boy meets girl, boy loses girl, boy
wins girl") would be a fairy tale ending to melt the hearts of
an audience that has come to witness not just pain and despair but joy. When they refuse to collude in the phony

setup, he stares balefully at them and says caustically, "I've seen a lot of winners in my day in this business, but I've also seen a lot of losers. And, baby, you've got the look of a loser."

On the other hand, the movie, and particularly his role in it, began to take on the look of a winner. He urged Jay Bernstein, his press agent, to spend more time on the set and to devise a slow-building campaign to draw attention to his performance. As he completed additional scenes and felt the character coming together, he became more insistent, saying he had been nominated for an Oscar twice before but had never been anywhere near as good as this. "I really believe that this time I could win," he said to Bernstein, then amended it to "No. I'm going to win."

The agent responded by informing Gig that after undertaking a premature campaign for Nick Adams, with disastrous results, he had made it a policy to not even consider setting up a drive for an Oscar nomination until he had seen the completed picture. Gig persisted, and Bernstein resisted. Then an early screening of *They Shoot Horses, Don't They?* was scheduled at the Directors Guild. Gig invited the agent; they would view the film together.

Bernstein had anticipated that Gig would be good, but he was astonished by the intensity of the performance. Others were too, and they crowded around to enthuse about the power and range of Gig's work. When Gig and his press agent finally made it outside and away from the crowd, Gig demanded, "No crap now—what did you really think?"

"You're right. You're just sensational," Bernstein said. "I not only believe you'll be nominated, I think you'll win."

Gig nodded in agreement and said, "I've waited six months to hear you say that." Then, in measured tones, he added, "Now that you've said it, I have something to tell you."

"What's that?"

"You're fired."

"Fired?"

"Fired. Don't try to make me change my mind. I've already hired another press agent," he said coldly. "You didn't believe me when I told you I was doing a good job. That hurt. You shouldn't have let your experience with Nick Adams influence you. Because I'd never bragged about my work before. So now you're fired." He turned and climbed into his car, ending their long-term business relationship—and friendship.

"That same sensitivity that had made us work so well together for so long made him draw the curtain over our friendship," Bernstein says. "That strain of sensitivity really ruled the man's life. It also probably had a lot to do with how he ended."

With the help of a new press agent, Gig's vigorous campaign for the nomination paid off. When the nominees were announced for supporting actor, he was included along with Rupert Crosse, Elliott Gould, Jack Nicholson, and Anthony Quayle.

On April 7, 1970, at the Dorothy Chandler Pavilion in Los Angeles, Gig was seated next to Dennis Hopper—who showed up in a white cowboy hat. He was so nervous that he avoided looking Hopper's way lest he inadvertently glance at the program and learn when his category was scheduled. "I concentrated all my being on not jumping up and rushing forward even if they didn't call my name," he told the press later. "I wanted this award that badly."

Indeed he did. Few actors had been quite as faithful in their allegiance to the business as had Gig, heart and soul. Broadway had been a kind mistress, but Hollywood had been his wife, and he'd been more faithful to her than to any of his real spouses or lovers. All the publicity-conscious years, the slights and humiliations of missed opportunities, the supportive relationships, the fair-weather friends, came down to the moment when Fred Astaire and Raquel Welch announced the award. "And the winner is," they intoned, "Gig Young."

It was a popular choice. Like the people filling the bleachers in *Horses,* the Academy audience loved a comeback story, one filled with heartbreak, divorce, career skids, and rumors of excess.

To a roar of approval, Gig rushed forward to accept the Oscar, his features flushed with excitement, his voice quivering with gratitude. "This is the greatest moment of my life," he told the crowd, and few could doubt the sincerity of that effusive greeting. He thanked the Academy and especially the man whose unwavering faith was responsible for his standing before them—Marty Baum. Swelling with pride, he walked off with the golden statuette, no longer the insecure little boy of St. Cloud who could do nothing right.

During Gig's stint in the pressroom afterward, he summed up the highlights of his career. In over fifty roles, he told reporters, only three or four were worth remembering: the artist in *The Gay Sisters,* because it gave him a sendoff and his name; the youthful alcoholic in *Come Fill the Cup,* which provided a chance to prove he could act; the college professor in *Teacher's Pet,* which offered an opportunity to firmly establish himself in light comedy; and the advertising man in Rod Serling's "Walking Distance" segment of *Twilight Zone.* Beaming, accepting congratulations, and expressing his thanks, Gig bypassed the official Academy Governor's Ball and headed for a gathering of his old chums from "the group" at Sue and Robert Douglas's house.

On his arm at the ceremony and the party afterward was "the girl of the moment." No one can even remember her name, except that she might have been called Ruth and that she was stunning-looking. When he was first nominated for an Oscar, Gig had sat proudly in the audience with Sophie;

the second time, with Elizabeth Montgomery. But on this all-important occasion, when he finally answered the taunts of those who said he couldn't cut the mustard, he had been with someone who, while undoubtedly pleasant enough, had not been, nor would ever be, a significant part of his life.

Walking into the Douglases' with one arm around his Oscar and the other around his beautiful date, Gig looked like a kid who had just knocked the ball out of the park as a substitute hitter in the ninth inning of the deciding game of the World Series. "He was ecstatic," Sue recalls, "and it was so Gig to want to be with old friends rather than promoting himself at some fancy do."

A month after winning the Oscar, Gig flew with Baum to the Cannes Film Festival, where *Horses* was shown and where the actor and Candice Bergen were to present awards.

"By this time he had no tolerance for alcohol," says Baum. "He had two drinks and was unconscious the entire trip. Yet when it came time to meet the reporters in Cannes, it was marvelous to see him. Like turning on an electric light. He shone. Emanated positiveness. And he was a wonderful advertisement for the film."

Indeed, Gig Young and Rocky Gravo had fused in their devotion to the American dream and what it could bring. For the moment at least, Gig had co-opted his demons—and he'd done it by playing a man who was symbolic of all the people who had ever browbeaten or bullied him. The honor conferred on him an identity at last—a royal title that would grace practically every subsequent press item ("Oscar-winner Gig Young . . .").

But even the glow of winning couldn't dispel the darker edges hovering around Gig's personality. The next morning, the joy of Oscar night was shadowed by the suspicion that his success could not last. He confided to Harriette Vine Douglas his fear that something would spoil it. This was soon to become a self-fulfilling prophecy. Less than two years later, he would be crawling around a soundstage, gasping and incoherent, while a camera crew looked on, incredulous that this could be the same man who had recently stood so proudly on the pinnacle of success.

·9·

The Oscar Curse

It's called the "Oscar Curse"—that inability to build on the momentum of winning the industry's highest honor. One might well ask whatever happened to Rod Steiger *(In the Heat of the Night),* or Louise Fletcher *(One Flew Over the Cuckoo's Nest),* or Ben Johnson *(The Last Picture Show).* Contrary to popular expectations, winning the Academy Award doesn't automatically guarantee that one's career will surge to new heights.

True, some Oscar winners indulge in self-destructive behavior, becoming more temperamental than talented, and soon cease to be tolerated. Often their asking price rockets into the stratosphere. Blinded by a false sense of self-importance, they escalate their standards to the point where a screenplay by Shakespeare with additional dialogue by T. S. Eliot is the only script that would please them.

But none of the above applied to Gig. Nor did he remain inactive so long that his triumph was forgotten. After finishing *Horses,* he'd gone straight into the light comedy *Lovers and Other Strangers.* ("Sure I play a grandfather," Gig told a reporter, "but an adulterous one!") And while *Horses* and *Lovers* were still in release, Gig defied conventional wisdom by choosing to accept a role in a television movie, *The Neon Ceiling.*

On the face of it, it was not the smartest career move. He was replacing an actor who had walked out on the project, and the film featured a scene-stealing child as its focal point. But he loved the part of Jones, a loner who operates a filling station and lunch counter on the edge of the Mojave Desert, and he wanted to appear opposite the brilliant actress Lee Grant. His instincts, in this case at least, proved unerring. The film won an award as the best TV movie of the year at the San Francisco International Film Festival, and Gig received an Emmy nomination for his performance.

So why didn't the Oscar bring a certain peace and fulfillment to the man who had chased after it for so long? Quite simply, because the glittering statuette had no magical powers. It couldn't erase the insecurity, the fears, the loneliness, and the relentless physical disintegration. On the contrary, it was almost as if the need to win acceptance from his peers had kept him from falling apart all these years. Now, having realized that ambition, he could recklessly yield to the pressures, perhaps believing—mistakenly— that the honor would serve as a safety net.

This false sense of security may well have contributed to three devastating crises that dominated Gig's life between 1970 and 1973: the court battle he and Elaine Young engaged in from 1970 throughout much of 1972; the professional brouhaha that erupted during his 1971 tour in *Harvey;* and his brutal firing from *Blazing Saddles* in 1973. All three would give new and tragic currency to the proverbial "Oscar Curse."

At a preview party celebrating the *The Neon Ceiling,* Gig had discreetly fobbed off reporters' questions about his on-going domestic turmoil with Elaine Young, which would eventually escalate into a full-scale Armageddon for him. When the Los Angeles *Herald-Examiner'*s gossip columnist Dorothy Manners cornered him, he admitted that he was keeping a low profile. "The important thing is to get my personal life straightened out," he explained, adding, when Ms. Manners pressed for details, "What is to be said should be said in court."

Despite his many personal problems, Gig had always managed to handle the press deftly. Years in the business had taught him that even if he couldn't control what was written or said about him in the public arena, at least he could help to shape it. His surface charm worked well, especially with female reporters, and the actor had enjoyed what is commonly termed "good press." That is, until his war with Elaine heated up.

The opening salvos had been fired in 1966. In July of that year, Gig and Elaine separated, and in November she had been granted an interlocutory divorce (citing irreconcilable differences) from Gig. She had accepted a financial settlement that gave her the San Ysidro house (valued at $98,000), $3,000 in cash, $1,650 monthly alimony for four years, and $200 monthly child support. And she had done so at the encouragement of her old friends Robert and Harriette Vine Douglas,* whom she had introduced to Gig early in their marriage. By the time the property settlement was being

---

*Not to be confused with Robert and Sue Douglas.

drawn up, the Douglases had shifted their loyalty to Gig, but they obviously still had influence with Elaine.

No sooner had Gig's ex-wife accepted the terms than she began having second thoughts. In July 1967, she petitioned to have the agreement set aside on the grounds that she had been "deceived, misled and taken advantage of in the property settlement": the Douglases, she felt, had exerted undue influence on her when she made the decision. She began to press insistently for more child support, and Gig believed she had directed her lawyer to dog him mercilessly through the court whenever he worked. As his resentment festered, he refused any personal contact with the child. An attempt by Elaine to maneuver Gig into accepting parental responsibility by persuading him to get together with Jennifer turned out disastrously. Claiming he had been manipulated by Elaine, Gig ended the reunion by stomping out of the house in a fury.

By 1970, the love affair that Gig had once described to Marilyn Beck as offering his "last, best chance for marital happiness" had become a rancorous battle that might have sprung from the imagination of August Strindberg. In that playwright's *The Father,* the title character begins to question whether indeed he is the natural parent of his twenty-year-old offspring. These paranoid doubts cause an escalation of marital warfare between husband and wife, in which she seizes on his paranoia to torment him, eventually leading to his demise.

Sadly for Jennifer, Gig had never really become a true father to her, except in the first few months, when she had served the useful function of establishing him in his new role as a family man ("She's mine—all mine," trumpeted the headline of one article about Jennifer's arrival). Despising the child in himself—the boy he had discarded—he was uneasy with children in general. And as his marriage to

Elaine curdled into disgust, Jennifer became a living symbol of the unhappiest period of his life, a period that had been marked with deep suspicions, however unjustified, of Elaine's fidelity during their courtship.

Those suspicions deepened further as Elaine pressed for more and more child support.

Although Gig initially assumed he'd fathered Jennifer through the "medical miracle" of his reversed vasectomy, he now became obsessed with the belief that Elaine had tricked him into marriage when she told him that he had impregnated her. He considered it a Machiavellian plot to get a famous father for Elaine's child. "She planned to divorce me even before we exchanged marriage vows," he bitterly told Bob Webber.

"I was never unfaithful to him, so of course he had to be Jennifer's father," says Elaine Young. "Medically speaking, vasectomies, well, there have been more malpractice suits because men, even having had them, still impregnated women. And when Gig had his, they hadn't even perfected them.

"No," continues Elaine, "all this was about something else. Gig delighted in making women suffer. He was cruel, sadistic. Beneath that charming facade, he hated women."

One thing was certain: Gig hated Elaine—hated her so much that he was willing to risk his considerable reputation and recently won cachet to attempt to humiliate her publicly. After submitting to three medical tests, which he claimed proved that his vasectomy was still effective, he hired Irving Apple to file a nonpaternity suit. The lawyer had misgivings. Early in their discussions, Apple advised his client, "You know, Gig, you won't win on the basis of nonpaternity. You've already acknowledged the child in court when you signed the property settlement. The maximum you'll achieve is to embarrass your ex-wife." But Gig was adamant. He'd have his day in court. He'd punish Elaine. The suit would be the weapon. Unfortunately, the weapon pointed at her ended up turned on himself.

On August 17, 1972, after a series of legal skirmishes, the state Court of Appeals upheld a ruling handed down two years earlier by Santa Monica Superior Court Judge Edward Brand, in which Gig had been adjudged the father. As Apple had foreseen, Gig had undercut his case back in 1966 by signing the property settlement in which he acknowledged that he and Elaine had one offspring, a two-year-old child. The court ruled that in pursuing his case he could not dole out additional information, presumably known to him earlier, simply because it became advantageous for him to do so. It turned out to be an expensive exercise for Gig. On top of legal costs and court fees, he was ordered not only to pay child support but also to underwrite medical treatments for Jennifer, totaling $450 a month.

Ultimately Gig lost not only in the California courts but also in the court of public opinion. Previously, friends had always been able to claim that he had never hurt anyone except himself by his behavior. He earned widespread criticism by waiting until Jennifer had reached the age of six before he entered his denial of fatherhood. While some partisans believed, as he did, that the child was not his, they nevertheless were aghast at his move.

"He rejected the child, had no interest in the child," says Marty Baum. "Whether he was the natural father or not, he became the father because of the physical proximity. He was paying for her housing and food. If he had given the child some support, some love, he would have gotten some substance in his life. It would have given him something to be interested in besides acting.

"I had a talk with him," he continues. " 'How dare you walk away from this relationship? Jennifer's innocent.

You're the only father she's known. What difference does it make if you are or aren't her natural father? You married her mother while she was pregnant. You took upon yourself the obligation not only to marry but also to be a father.'"

Years later, recalling the conversation, Baum says, "Gig lived many fantasies, many fantasies. There was very little reality to him. There was very little to get hold of as a person. It was a facade. He never wanted anyone to get too close to him. ... When you knew him, he was charming and gracious and witty. You'd say, 'Well, what's his problem?' But you didn't see what was going on underneath."

What was going on underneath was a hatred that would fester until it resulted in a denouement eerily similar to the outcome in Strindberg's violent duel of the sexes.

Gig's second post-Oscar crisis erupted in the summer of 1971. Producers T. Edward Hambleton and Norris Houghton were assembling a company for a national tour of Mary Chase's twenty-seven-year-old Pulitzer Prize–winning drama, *Harvey*. Having secured Shirley Booth for the Josephine Hull part, the producers were searching for someone to portray Elwood P. Dowd, the benign alcoholic eccentric whose best friend is a six-foot-tall white rabbit named Harvey, invisible to everyone except Elwood. This friendship alarms the "realists," who almost succeed in getting Elwood incarcerated in a mental institution.

Jesse White, who had played the asylum attendant in both the Broadway production and the film (and who is perhaps best known as the Maytag repairman in a TV commercial), was repeating the role in the touring company. As something of an authority on the play, he urged the producers to sign Gig. They were reluctant, having heard rumors of his drinking. However, when White took it upon himself to secure assurances from Gig's doctor and his friend Harriette Vine Douglas that the gossip was exaggerated, the producers tapped Gig for the lead.

White immediately approached Gig and volunteered to cue him so that he would have his lines mastered before rehearsals were called. Gig rejected the offer, telling him that Harriette would help him. He confided to friends that he had his own conception of the role and did not want White trying to turn him into a road company version of Frank Fay, who had originated the role on Broadway, or Jimmy Stewart, who'd played it in the film.

During the rehearsal period, it became evident that Gig was going to stress the pathos of Elwood's life while de-emphasizing Mrs. Chase's jokes. White was displeased. Then, in Gig's struggle to create the character, he temporarily changed some of the playwright's lines. White, who had appeared in 2,300 performances of the script, was driven berserk by what he considered a desecration of a modern classic. When his protests to Gig went unheeded, he approached the producers, said he felt responsible for what looked to him like impending disaster, and suggested they replace Gig with Eddie Albert. They refused.

The dissension between the two actors grew. Gig accused White of sabotaging his performance, and White argued that Gig was ruining the play. By opening night, at the Central City Festival in Colorado, battle lines had been drawn. Gig's partisans, while admitting the performance was still in need of polishing, insisted that his offbeat attack had brought a new depth to the script. White's sympathizers were vocal in proclaiming Gig's interpretation a disaster and spread the rumor backstage that Mary Chase had stalked out in disgust after the first act.

During the Central City run, Gig became convinced that White was stepping on his laughs. Heated exchanges between the two became commonplace nightly after the curtain fell. The confrontations culminated in a shoving match that, among gossips, quickly became exaggerated into a "fistfight" and a "brawl." Word spread that Gig had been hurt. There was speculation that he would not appear during the San Francisco stand. Gig did play the premiere there, after which understudy Edgar Meyer stepped in for the remainder of the engagement.

Before the company's September 20 opening at the Huntington Hartford Theater in Hollywood, Gig got his revenge. White was replaced by Dana Elcar, and Gig returned to the play. Theater critic Dan Sullivan assured Los Angeles *Times* readers that all the laughs were there on opening night. *Variety* hailed the show as one of the best buys in town. And Winifred Blevins of the *Herald-Examiner* found Gig giving "one of his strongest performances."

Despite the good reviews and excellent word of mouth, rumors spread that Gig had become extremely difficult. It was whispered that violent outbursts had begun to crop up. Work that should have burnished his professional reputation was eclipsed by the destructive gossip that circulated throughout Hollywood. Potential roles were lost on the assumption that Gig had become too much trouble. He was heartsick over the situation but helpless to do anything about it. To confront the rumors in the press or on TV would only bring them to the attention of people who might otherwise never hear them.

While Gig presented the public with a smiling, devil-may-care image, he was privately complaining to Harriette that the carping of his enemies was making it increasingly difficult for him to give his best performance. His emotional distress exploded into neurodermatitis, a skin condition that left his face covered with angry red blotches. Cortisone helped relieve the physical condition but could do nothing about his sorrow over what he felt was unfair treatment.

Crisis number three was Gig's most crushing professional setback. The enterprise began on a promising note.
Mel Brooks, who is known to be stubborn, vitriolic, and
tough despite his jovial public persona, had been signed by
Warner Brothers to write and direct *Black Bart,* later retitled *Blazing Saddles.* Through some complicated studio
maneuvering, Gig, without Brooks's consent, had been assigned the role of the Waco Kid. Brooks, who had other ideas
about casting, objected vehemently. The director believed
the rumors about Gig's drinking and felt that the actor
might drag down the picture. A full-scale donnybrook developed. The director summarily fired Gig and then, at the studio's insistence, reluctantly rehired him. The actor was told
to await a call from Brooks about how to proceed on the
picture.

Gig, who taped his recollections of the entire Brooks debacle shortly after it occurred, for possible legal use, had
this to say about the director's overture:

> The call finally came, and it went like this: he [Brooks]
> said, "You're back in the picture, Gig. Now, you were
> out for your interview [with me], all juiced up . . ." I
> started to protest, but he wouldn't let me. He said,
> "Don't give me that crap. You were all juiced up. Now,
> I want you to report Monday with every line learned,
> so we can go through every scene completely from
> beginning to end without stopping. I want to be able
> to change it, or you can change it, or anyone can
> change it. But I want those scenes learned word for
> word." In the middle there somewhere, he said, "I
> don't want any hrumping and hrumping and hrump-
> ing." The whole thing was devastating, to say the

least. It was a very abrupt conversation, but zing. Okay, over and out.

The conversation would have made any actor very tense. It sent Gig into a panic. He might well have thought of opting out at that point (which is probably what Brooks wanted him to do), but he loved the script and thought the role of the sheriff's eccentric sidekick was an extraordinary challenge. He wanted the job badly—it would give him the opportunity to counter the negative rumors going around town. He would show Brooks and everybody else in Hollywood that *Horses* had not been a fluke.

In order to have every line memorized by the time he reported to the set on Monday morning, as Brooks had requested, Gig borrowed one of Baum's secretaries to cue him. By Saturday night, he no longer felt he needed help. He studied silently on Sunday and then spent the night at a hotel near the studio so that he could report bright and early the next morning. Gig told his version of the events on the tape:

Now, during Friday, Saturday, and Sunday nights I didn't sleep at all because of the embarrassment and pressure that Mel Brooks had put upon me during that phone conversation. I felt more or less as though I was on trial.

I reported to the studio about 7:15 A.M. and went inside, knowing that he had said that I was juiced up on the last two Johnny Carson shows, knowing I was walking a tightrope. Someone pointed out my dressing room, but it was small, dark, and full of all kinds of wardrobe. So I went out and sat in my car and waited until some of the crew began to arrive. Then I went in at about 7:30 or so. Finally, the makeup man came in, and I went in and put on my scrubby makeup. After the makeup, the wardrobe man came in. I put on my long underwear, my gun belt, my boots, etc. . . . Mel Brooks came in finally, looked at my wardrobe, and we fooled around with that a bit. He said, "Later, I'll come back and we'll kind of rehearse the scene in your room." Which we did. He would come back from time to time. We would rehearse, come up with ideas. It progressed beautifully. I was sure Mr. Brooks was pleased. At least, that's what I thought. I had no idea of what was to come.

What was to come, according to Gig, was an invitation by Brooks to come onto the set and watch the shooting from behind the cameras for a while. By that time, the company had already been filming for some time, and the director wanted Gig to get a feel for the production.

I followed him in front of the camera through what seemed to be a maze of low lights, and I stooped down to avoid hitting any of them. I got as far as the camera, when my head began to feel dizzy. I quickly and purposely got on the floor, hands-and-knees style, with my head down, and began to breathe as hard as I could. That didn't seem to be working. So within seconds, I said, "Push on my head. Push on my head." They finally pushed, and I kept saying, "Push harder." And finally, when I was so tired I could not continue on with that action, I either said, "Okay" or I didn't say "Okay" but I went down kind of with my head on the floor and tried to relax. Which I did. I stayed in that position until I was relaxed enough. Then I finally said, "Okay. I'll crawl out of your way so you can shoot the shot." I crawled ten or twenty feet away, feeling everything would be fine. Though my head was still slightly faint, I stayed in that position. After a short time, I got to my knees, slowly, and stayed there.

Just before Brooks had arrived with Gig in tow, the set, as usual, had been a beehive of activity. Grips were wheeling machinery into place, assistant directors were shouting instructions, makeup and wardrobe personnel were standing by to make adjustments. But with Gig's collapse, everything had ground to a halt, with everyone transfixed by the sight of Gig panting and writhing on the floor. Some thought he was having a heart attack, some thought he was suffering from nervous prostration, still others guessed that he was hyperventilating—which is how Gig's doctor would later characterize the episode.

After the symptoms had subsided, Gig was helped to a comfortable spot on the sidelines and told that a first-aid man was on the way, to check him out. Activity on the set revved up once again. As Gig felt more and more himself, he sat up and followed the action of the scene with interest. Apparently noting the actor's recovery, Brooks came over to where he was seated and suggested, "If you feel okay, why don't you come over and watch the shot."

I got to my feet slowly, making sure my head was okay. I walked over, and the same thing happened in the same spot. Only this time more quickly, it seemed, and I got down on all fours, quickly, knowing what I was doing. The same action as above, asking them to push my head, which they did. Now I began to shake, which frightened me. I looked down, and I realized my elbows were bent, which would make the strain that much more. So with all my might, I straightened my elbows, but by this time my whole body was shaking. When I got that straightened out, I said, "Push on my head. Push harder, harder, harder." And the man who was pushing on my head, I heard him say, "I'm afraid I'll break his neck if I push harder."

I was completely exhausted, and I went down to the more comfortable position, though I seemed to be still having trouble with my breathing. So I said loud and clear so they would understand, "I'm going to do something. Don't be alarmed." Now, I don't know whether this was the proper thing to do, but I knew something was better than what I was doing. So I yelled three or four times like this: *"Ahhhhh . . . Ahhhhh."* So then I did something which a doctor had told me to do. I put my finger down my throat until I gagged myself, which expelled all the air and put me back into proper breathing. It brought me peace, and I began to settle down, and when I was settled enough, I said, "Okay, I'll crawl back over to my spot so you can shoot your shot."

By now the cast and crew were riveted by the increasingly bizarre scene. Some tried to be helpful. A man came over with a blanket to place under the head of the prostrate actor on the sidelines, but Gig, thinking his head should remain low, pushed it away "two or three times." Finally, he grudgingly accepted the blanket. Someone whom Gig identifies on the tape as "a first-aid man" then came to take his blood pressure. He said it was 190. Gig became alarmed, since 128 was normal for him. An angry argument ensued over whether the reading was accurate. He began shouting loudly for someone to call his doctor. The response to the request was too slow for him, and he became "infuriated."

I really yelled out, "God damn it, will somebody call my doctor. Dr. Rudner. RE 1904 [*sic*]. And stay on the line and say it's Gig Young calling, and Dr. Rudner will come to the phone." I said, "God damn it, will you do it!" . . . Finally, Mel Brooks, followed by Michael Hertzberg [the producer], arrived. . . . One of them said, "Well, we all have opening-night jitters in different ways. Some throw up. I throw up." And the other one said he did something, and then he said, "You"— meaning me, Gig Young—"you tried to faint."

Even in the state he was in, Gig says on the tape, he realized that Brooks and Hertzberg might want to use the incident as an excuse to throw him off the picture. To show them that he was in command of his faculties and aware of his surroundings, he began to do routines that sounded as though they'd been excerpted from old vaudeville turns or were rewrites of the spiels he had done as Professor Harold Hill in *The Music Man.*

Whatever the filmmakers thought of Gig's rap, Brooks broke in to say, " 'I know, instead of beginning at the last half of the scene, why don't we start at the beginning? With you hanging by your heels, dangling in the air like a dead chicken.' Only he didn't use the word dead *chicken.* 'You know, hanging will take the blood out of your stomach and put it into your head, which would really be a good thing. I happen to know a little about medicine.' He was quite sincere. I said, 'I don't think, perhaps, it is a good idea.' "

At that time, according to Gig, Hertzberg summoned him to a dressing room phone, on which the producer was talking to the actor's doctor. When Gig got on the phone and told Rudner that he had had a rough go but was now feeling fine, the doctor informed him that he'd told Hertzberg that the incident had occurred because of the pressures that had been placed on him. After he hung up, Gig retired to his dressing room to rest. When Mel Brooks came into the room, the actor suggested scenes they could shoot other than the one that had him hanging upside down.

Brooks, according to Gig, responded, "Naw, naw, naw,

Gig, why kill yourself over this whole thing? I have a couple of days' shooting. I can shoot around you. Go home and get a good night's sleep. We have been putting pressure on you. Don't worry about a thing."

Obviously, Brooks and Hertzberg were more concerned than they let on. Instead of sending the actor home, they insisted on sending him to his doctor's office—in an ambulance.

> The gentleman sitting with me in the back part of the ambulance seemed to be interested in pictures. He asked me a few questions. I really wasn't in the mood for that, so after a while I discouraged it by closing my eyes, pretending to be asleep. I would say that the ride over to Dr. Rudner's, that twenty-five miles, was the roughest ride ever. That ambulance must have been fifty years old—I'm kidding. I didn't really look at it that well, but it was really rough.

After his doctor examined him (Gig's blood pressure had dropped to 145), a nurse drove him home and put him in the elevator to his apartment. He felt fine about the future. "I had no suspicion I was really off the picture," he recalls. A couple of days later, he was officially sacked.

When word of his firing got out, various people intervened on Gig's behalf. Naturally, his agent, Tom Korman, tried to reverse it. Marty Baum spoke with both Brooks and Warner Brothers. Director Sydney Pollack called to assure Brooks that while it might take a little longer to get the performance he wanted, the results would justify the wait. Brooks refused to budge. The part was offered to another Korman client, Dan Dailey, who accepted it and then withdrew at four o'clock in the morning on the day he was to work. Gene Wilder would play the role—to great acclaim.

On April 25, *Variety* reported that Gig had filed a

$100,000 damage suit against Warners in Los Angeles Superior Court, charging that the studio had breached their contract with him to appear in *Black Bart.* He claimed that the studio's decision not to use him was made after he had qualified for production insurance, been fitted for wardrobe, and learned his lines. He had been ready and willing to perform when the studio notified him and his agent that he had been replaced. Warners contended that as he had appeared unfit for work, they were not obligated to pay him the $75,000 base or the $25,000 deferred bonus, which was to come from profits.

Eventually Gig collected fifty percent on the contract. However, in the opinion of many friends and associates, no amount of money could have recompensed him for the lasting psychological damage he suffered.

"I don't think he ever recovered from that firing," Baum says. "It was especially humiliating to be dropped from a major picture after having recently won an Academy Award. It did something to his self-esteem, and he began seriously deteriorating at that point."

·10·

Lady Goddamn

To Gig, the *Blazing Saddles* episode was an unfortunate embarrassment, a simple case of hyperventilation brought on by too many pressures. To others, however, it was another messy incident that reinforced Gig's growing reputation of being unreliable. More often than not, the scripts he was now offered featured a character who was an alcoholic. But on screen or off, there was no longer any hint of the insouciant martini-drinking playboy of the Doris Day films. His roles, like the burned-out correspondent he played in the television movie *The Turning Point of Jim Malloy,* were becoming as intractable and bitter as he was. Art was beginning to imitate life.

Licking his wounds following the *Blazing Saddles* disaster, Gig was becoming more and more dependent on people who turned a blind eye to his erratic behavior and ministered to his deteriorating physical and emotional health. Some were astute professionals, like psychologist Dr. Eugene Landy, who temporarily helped him overcome his increasingly desperate line-memorizing problems. Others were sympathetic listeners, like Skye Aubrey, with whom he always enjoyed having lunch when she was in town. Still others were dubious mentors, like vocal instructor Bert Knapp, who began to exert an insidious influence over his pliant student. Then there were what might be termed the "nursemaids"—the women who, like Mrs. Harry Kaines and Sophie, soothed his ego, bound his wounds, and selected his neckties. One, Doris Rich, was content to be a rather eccentric cheerleader: through mystical letters, she urged him on to greater artistic achievement. Another woman, however, was far more influential. In the actor's waning years, there wasn't a more faithful and determined nursemaid than Harriette Vine Douglas, who, following Gig's death, would describe herself to police and press alike as "the lady in Gig's life."

That description came as news to some of Gig's closest friends. Guy Vincent became aware of her only after Gig's death. Bob and Marilynn Horton met her briefly, on a single occasion. Bob Webber encountered Harriette for the first time when she was making arrangements for Gig's memorial service. Yet she was so conspicuously at his side during the later court skirmishes over his daughter, Jennifer, that when someone at the hearings inquired who she was, Elaine Young sniped, "His maid." Harriette was referred to in Gig's circles as the "phantom lady" because, though Gig spoke of her and quoted her often, he rarely escorted her to public functions. They wondered if he wasn't in some way embarrassed about the relationship.

On the surface, at least, there was nothing at all embarrassing about her. Unlike her predecessors, Harriette was within five years of Gig's age, and through the magic of cosmetic surgery, she possessed the ageless countenance of a classic Beverly Hills matron. Her hair was tinted a flattering blond, her bold theatrical features—a fluty speaking voice and large, expressive eyes—caught people's attention, and her ex-dancer's movements made her appear at least a decade younger than she was. Like Sheila, Gig's first wife, Harriette would have turned heads anywhere except in Hollywood. But even in Hollywood, she was clever enough to capture Gig's eye and still manage to remain friendly with the husband she had divorced.

Part of her charm stemmed from a colorful past. Harriette Vine came from a show business family. Her father, Dave, was a "big comedy talent" plagued by bad timing. Her mother had made a name for herself in burlesque as Sliding Billy Watson's leading lady, before marrying and teaming up with Vine in a vaudeville act. The Vines' success was somewhat impeded by the unplanned appearances of Harriette and her brother, Billy, who eventually developed into a popular borscht belt and nightclub comedian.

Harriette's childhood playground was Broadway. By the time she was sixteen, she was a songstress on WINS radio; by eighteen, she was a dancer at the Swing Club in Los Angeles. While there, she auditioned for club impresario Nils T. Grauland: she danced onto the stage, twirled, paused, moved, and twirled again. "Halfway across, I stumbled and fell on my duff," she recalls. "Surprised, I said, 'God damn!' and I picked myself up and stalked into the wings, sure I'd blown my chances of getting picked. But when Grauland chose his girls, he said, 'I want the tall doll in blue, the redhead in polka dots, and—where is the elegant Lady Goddamn?' All the time I worked for him and Earl Carroll, everybody called me 'Lady Goddamn.' Then I caught the eye of a Paramount scout. I had a stock contract for two years. Never did anything great. Right after that I married Bob Douglas and was with him—even though it wasn't much of a marriage—until I got involved with Gig."

In the beginning, Harriette and Bob, Elaine and Gig, were the perfect Hollywood foursome. But later, during Gig's separation from Elaine, the actor and the Douglases spent a weekend together at Lake Arrowhead. Bob, who was a "gun nut," wanted to teach Gig how to shoot (he later persuaded Gig to purchase his first pistol).

It was on this trip that Harriette and Gig first "got into trouble," as she puts it. Bob would go into one of the rooms of their suite to clean and polish his guns, leaving Gig and Harriette alone in the sitting room. Says Harriette: "Gig and I really enjoyed each other, talking. And I warned Bob not to leave us alone so much. I told him, 'Bob, times are changing,'" but Bob paid little heed to her warning.

"One day, Bob was again polishing his guns, and Gig and I were alone in the living room," as Harriette recalls it. "I had on a pretty negligee, and he was in his robe. And I didn't expect it, but suddenly he reached over and kissed me. I felt nothing. And the next day the same thing happened. Except this time I felt it."

That was the beginning of a complicated and strange relationship, which Harriette herself found perplexing. "If I don't understand it, how can I expect to explain it to anyone else?" she asks. "I can only tell you, we lived inside each other's heads."

And, on occasion, in each other's arms. Whatever the dynamics of the relationship were, they were strong enough to cause Harriette to secure an amicable divorce from her husband. Early on, according to her, she often shared Gig's bed, but their sexual encounters were infrequent. To rectify this, she prepared a "surprise," which, she says, turned out to be "a big mistake." She visited a plastic surgeon and had breast implants. Gig was offended, outraged. He never would touch her enlarged bosom again.

While Gig insisted to friends that his relationship with Harriette was platonic—they always maintained separate apartments—he confessed making love to her on his auto-biographical tapes. "I believe he fucked her a few times," said Bob Webber. "I didn't know her until after he died. She's a very nice, wishful-thinking dreamer, but I try not to talk to her too often because she rambles on. She's a nervous, neurotic woman." Gig's sister, Gen, would only politely say about her and some of the others who she felt inveigled their way into Gig's life, "My brother seemed to have strange taste in women."

For whatever reasons, the relationship clicked. But it was more of a special friendship—a *folie à deux* or shared madness—than a blazing romance. This was not surprising, given their ages. Gig was physically and emotionally spent. Harriette, who was in her fifties, was willing to accept the relationship for whatever it turned out to be, even after she'd divorced Robert Douglas to devote her energies to her new obsession. "I don't know whether I loved Gig or was in love with him," she says. "Let's just say we loved with an open hand. He was free to go, but I was sure he wouldn't." Yet it was more than that. The knowledge of her power over him made up for any negative feelings that might arise. "No matter where else he laid his head, I was always secure that he'd come back to me, because I was the person he was most comfortable with," she says.

They developed an exchange called Bitter Truths, which allowed them, under the guise of bantering, to delve into real feelings they wouldn't otherwise expose. They explored their fears, fantasies, resentments, and hopes. Through these sessions, Harriette came to know Gig as a mercurially complex man—"lovable, temperamental, humble, funny, arrogant, suspicious, sweet, and sometimes a real bastard."

Gig needed her, but he dictated the terms of the relationship. Though his behavior toward her bordered on the sadistic, she accepted whatever he doled out. She feigned indifference, for example, when Gig left her to squire young beauties around town on publicity dates, despite, as her friends put it, "all Harriette did for him." Instead, she looked forward to their quiet get-togethers at restaurants like the Tail of the Cock, where the maître d' always found a secluded table for them. "It was my choice to be with him," she says. "Nothing was holding me except that he wanted me there."

No matter what people whispered about them, it was okay with Harriette. She saw no need to be a part of his earlier friendships. She knew that he had concentric circles of friends, each of whom thought of themselves as "closest" to him. He often told her that he could never give a cocktail party. There were too many "closest" friends. Harriette was under no such illusion. She was certain she knew where she stood with him. What she didn't see, ironically, was that all those "closest" friends believed the same thing.

To Harriette, Gig was endlessly fascinating. To Gig, Harriette represented a woman with whom he could be himself. She was no threat to him. He could behave unreasonably with her, order her to go home—and she would go. Then he could call her a couple of hours later to tell her he wanted a sandwich, and she would ask, "What kind?" He talked with her about his love affairs and other intimate details of his life. While she may have had her own agenda beneath her slavish devotion, she presented a warm and sympathetic facade. Explaining her behavior, she says, "He was the most loving man and a pain in the ass, but I didn't mind, because I understood his terrible frustrations."

On simply a practical level, Harriette was quite handy to have around. And it was through her helpfulness that she was able to insinuate herself into a central position in his life. During their friendship, Gig moved frequently—buying a home from Rona Barrett, taking a suite at the Beverly Comstock Hotel, purchasing a small condominium in the Century Towers, then a larger one in the same complex, and finally a place on Spaulding. All of this moving around necessitated the frequent acquiring and disposing of furniture. Gig, who had no inclination or aptitude for such transactions, was dazzled by Harriette's wheeling and dealing.

She also proved indispensable in helping to make Gig's life run smoother on a daily basis. Just as important as soothing his fears or managing his moves was the way she oversaw his day-to-day existence, tidying his apartment, picking up the clothes he flung around, washing dishes that would have piled up in the sink, dusting and cleaning. Sometimes Harriette went beyond what was prudent in attempting to smooth Gig's path. For instance, when the rumor spread that he was pressuring his doctors to write a lot of prescriptions for pills, she said, "Tell people they're for me. Am I making a picture? Are they going to cancel me next week?"

He appreciated her candor as well. She was one of the few who challenged his obsessive concern with his appearance. Aware that he was self-conscious about his thinning hair, for instance, she warned him that no matter how he combed those four long strands, they were not going to hide his loss. When he asked what she would suggest, she took him to Little Joe's shop and supervised the cut. After that, he insisted she always go with him.

Harriette was able to be with Gig during times when, for vanity's sake, he had shut the rest of the world out. When the "mod comedy" that Disney studios had promised Gig he would star in failed to materialize, Gig blamed the cancellation on the fact that he was aging. He attempted to turn back the physiological clock by secretly undergoing plastic surgery to remove the bags under his eyes. Something went askew and the membranes of his lower lids gaped, making him look like Frankenstein's monster. He wouldn't let anyone but Harriette see him without his dark glasses until remedial sugery could be performed.

What Harriette provided best, though, was mothering, and for reasons of health, Gig was especially in need of such nurturing. In 1968, serious dental problems had begun to plague him. Just before he went on tour with *On a Clear Day You Can See Forever,* he had all his teeth recapped, resulting in an occlusion that tortured him throughout the summer tour. In desperation, he visited dentists in several cities to have "hot spots" ground down so he could chew soft foods without flinching. Eventually his dental crisis became so painful that during the filming of *Lovers and Other Strangers,* he could eat nothing but mashed potatoes and purees. "I couldn't even chew lettuce," he said, noting that in two and a half years of "malnutrition," his weight dropped from 185 to 145. To escape the pain, he upped his dosages of sedatives, and finally he had his teeth recapped again.

Then, in early 1972, he went to New York to do *The Tonight Show.* When he got off the plane, he discovered a new ailment: his feet were numb. He initially assumed the problem was caused by sitting for so long, but when walking to the terminal failed to restore feeling, he became alarmed. He was forced to watch the floor in order not to stagger. With Mel Brooks's accusation that he had been "juiced" during earlier appearances on the Carson program still ringing in his ears, he canceled and returned to California at once.

The moment Harriette heard of his deteriorating physical condition, she suggested he check into a hospital, and in the latter part of March 1972, he entered St. John's Hospital in Santa Monica for extensive testing. Always having been something of a hypochondriac (he'd once checked into the Mayo Clinic, convinced that he had a terminal illness, only to be given a clean bill of health), he became terrified when the nurse routinely raised the sides of his bed. It stirred nightmarish memories of the only other time he had seen it done—when his brother was dying.

Gig became obsessed with the fear of death. He began to feel that he would never leave the hospital alive. To make matters worse, during his first night in the hospital, Southern California was rocked by an earthquake. Frightened, he rode out the tremors alone, remembering an earlier quake, in the San Fernando Valley, when Sophie was gravely ill. At that time he had protected her by placing his body over hers, supporting himself on his hands and knees.

By the time Harriette and Dr. Rudner arrived at St. John's the next morning, Gig was in a state of panic. He had begun hyperventilating and was convinced that he was in the throes of a heart attack. Rudner calmed him, and a series of tests was ordered. Gig, prepared for the worst, learned that he was suffering from circulatory problems and gallstones. He underwent surgery to remove his gallbladder, and by April 2, 1972, he was back home recuperating, with Harriette at his side.

His illness was the perfect excuse for living the kind of reclusive existence they both enjoyed. Self-conscious about his thinning hair, thickening jawline, and startling weight loss, Gig felt no desire to see or be seen. He lay low for the better part of a year. Harriette was delighted to have his undivided attention and spent long hours making him comfortable. In their conversations, Gig would sometimes make plans for the future, but frequently he reminisced about the past, examining all the reasons for his many failures. More and more he regretted squandering his talent on inferior projects. Harriette tried to focus on his achievements and the pride he could take in them. He responded with a litany of all the films he had wasted his time on "merely for money."

Gig's weakened state gave Harriette the opportunity to assert a fierce protectiveness that alienated some of his friends. They felt that she was stirring up his resentment over slights—real and imagined. Her biggest battles were with Bert Knapp, the vocal teacher–guru in New York, who was equally insistent about his prerogatives when it came to Gig. He repeatedly urged Gig to dump Harriette, derisively calling her the "Encyclopaedia Britannica," for what he considered her "know-it-all" attitude. When she began her annexation of Gig, he protested.

"Harriette used to take care of him when he was drunk and full of Valium, but he paid a big price for that," Knapp would say of her later. "What she was in his life was a police warden. I told her what she was."

He told her more. Once, calling from New York, Knapp became angry when she refused to put Gig on the phone, and he dressed her down, saying, "I didn't know Gig needed a keeper west of the Mississippi." Harriette shot back, "That's all you know about him. He needs a keeper on any side of the Mississippi." Then she slammed down the phone. Gig and Harriette collapsed in laughter.

Nursed back to health, Gig faced the daunting task of revving up an ailing career. He had done it many times before. When people were counting him out, he managed to show them that he could still do it and do it well. But it was becoming progressively harder to summon up the strength for another go-round. Despite his lament to Harriette that he'd sold out, he appeared in five productions between 1974 and 1975, largely for the money. He accepted the films *Bring Me the Head of Alfredo Garcia* and *The Hindenburg* because he wanted to work with directors Sam Peckinpah (with whom he'd later make *The Killer Elite*) and Robert Wise. He was surprisingly charming as a debonair holdup man in the television movie *The Great Ice Ripoff* but was a washout as a French foreign minister in *The Ambassadors.* Finally, he flew to Rome to replace José Ferrer in *A Ribbon for Deborah* without first reading the script, because he thought a change of scenery would revive his spirits.

He was in a downbeat mood again when he was approached to star in *The Turning Point of Jim Malloy,* a ninety-minute NBC television movie, based on John O'Hara's widely admired Gibbsville short stories and fashioned into a teleplay by Pulitzer Prize–winning playwright James D. Gilroy. The script examined the relationship between a young reporter named Jim Malloy, played by John Savage, and a burned-out war correspondent named Whitehead, the part Gig was offered. The movie was planned as a pilot, which could be spun off into a series.

Gig expressed his doubts about the project to the ever-supportive Doris Rich. Rich, a devout Christian Scientist, warned against negativism and embarked on a campaign to restore her old friend's confidence in the project and himself. She reminded him of the story about the great Laurette Taylor, who rolled into the theater in Chicago at 8:45 one evening to be met by the frantic cast of *The Glass Menagerie* on its pre-Broadway tryout. Once the worried actors got the tipsy star into her dressing room, she brushed them aside and grandly issued the command: "Take up the rag—and I'll make with the magic."

"You see, Gig, Laurette trusted her own divine gift," Miss Rich said. "She knew she didn't do it. It was her gift straight from God—divine love. And nothing could stop it."

Gig got the point. He went on the wagon and firmly resolved to stay there. However, he began to rely more heavily on Valium and Placidyl to anesthetize his persistent demons—age, health, rejection, career, and finances. Nonetheless, the response to *Jim Malloy* proved that Gig was an exceptional actor, who could still deliver when he had a good script and director. The reviews were good enough all around for the network to commit to placing *Gibbsville,* as it was retitled, on its fall schedule.

After recharging himself with a revival of *Harvey* in Edmonton, Canada (a favorite spot for Gig because of the fishing, swimming, and friendly locals), he returned to Harriette and Hollywood to prepare for the series. No sooner had he arrived than he was revisited by his old nemesis—his inability to remember lines. The sedatives didn't help, but that was the only way he could allay his anxiety—that and complaining about the scripts to his friends, including Doris Rich in New York.

She responded to Gig with an effusive letter extolling the "old, quickening Gig-spirit" and advising him to "Just pour on the oil of gladness, the oil of joy, the oil of gratitude, boy—does that fill the emptiness!" Then she proceeded to tell a story about actor John Barrymore, the alcoholic genius whose last years were marked by an impressive and tragic dissipation. "I saw him act in all stages of drunkenness," she wrote. "In a wheelchair when his legs were so swollen they had to cut the boots, and once when his teeth had to be wired! But nothing stopped him. And I had been complaining about bad radio scripts! What I learned from John Barrymore! Have always been grateful."

Gig could well relate to both Laurette Taylor and Barrymore, but that didn't stop the producers of *Gibbsville* from threatening to fire him because of his line-retention problems. As usual, when facing a crisis, he turned to Marty Baum, who had a suggestion. Baum and members of his family had been patients of a psychologist named Eugene Landy and had observed him doing miraculous things. Baum felt that Landy's treatment was unorthodox but highly effective. He called Dr. Landy and told him there was an emergency: if Gig didn't find a way to master his lines, he was going to be fired—and if he got fired, he would go to pieces emotionally.

Dr. Landy met and talked with Gig. Then he called Baum to report: "Look, I can't cure anybody in a few days. All I can do is to get him to learn the lines, but he needs—badly needs—psychological help. And he needs it on a constant basis, because his problems go far deeper than learning lines."

Gig agreed to immediate therapy and promised to consider in-depth treatment. Daily, Dr. Landy accompanied him to Warner Brothers in Burbank. He had no specific task to perform for Gig. His presence was sufficient to reassure the shaken actor. "Just having a guy in his corner whom he could count on to understand his problem was an enormous help," the doctor points out.

Privately, Dr. Landy conferred with John Savage, Gig's co-star, and secured his cooperation. Savage agreed to press on in a scene, so long as Gig managed to convey the right thought. Dr. Landy also spoke with the director, explaining that Gig was apprehensive and needed all the reassurance he could get.

He kept reminding Gig that no one demanded the script be followed word for word. Knowing that he had a certain amount of freedom removed a great deal of the pressure Gig had been under about blowing lines. As long as the scene flowed, Landy assured him, nobody cared if he was word perfect.

Initially, the doctor made it a point to have lunch with Gig daily. Once his client started getting into his scenes, Dr. Landy made various excuses to wean himself away; and within a week, Gig was doing fine.

"I served as the ego strength he'd lost. Ego strength means deciding you're going to undertake a task and it will have a beginning, a middle, and an end, and then it will be over," Dr. Landy explains. "A healthy person with ego strength is confident he'll complete it no matter what the difficulties or how long it takes. A person without ego strength doesn't know whether he can complete it. He has lost the strength he once had—or never had. Gig had it once but lost it."

The series premiere on September 29 was eagerly anticipated, but the concept proved too meandering and gentle to survive for long in the tightly plotted world of mid-seventies television. Yet for all Gig's problems during production, his gifts couldn't be hidden, especially the talent to bring ironic overtones to his scenes. The *Los Angeles Times* asserted: "Gig Young is, of course, what every newspaperman visualizes himself to be, a charming erudite rascal who drinks too much and chases too many chorus girls, but who when he gets hold of a story, can make a typewriter sing."

After the series ended, Dr. Landy began tackling the underlying causes of Gig's problems as manifested in bouts of hallucinatory paranoia and sexual impotence. Since the initial couplings with Skye Aubrey, Gig's lovemaking powers, to his distress, had diminished considerably through an overindulgence in tranquilizers and alcohol. But once Dr. Landy began delving too deeply, Gig abruptly quit therapy. Landy urged him to reconsider, but Gig was having none of it. The doctor gave him his private number and urged him to use it in case of emergency. He felt that Gig was in such trouble that he might do harm to himself—or someone else.

Instead, Gig attempted to handle his inner conflicts through external improvements. He had his teeth redone for the third time and lifted his chin and drooping eyelids. He thought it made him look younger and more handsome, but in fact his face began to look like a mask.

"He became a shell of what he had been," says Marty Baum, who had returned to agenting. "He'd had a great quality of character in his face when he did *They Shoot*

Horses, Don't They? and it was all going because of repeated plastic surgery and dental jobs."

Then, just when Gig's prospects looked especially bleak, an inquiry from New York set him dreaming. Robert Whitehead, who with Roger Stevens was co-producing Arthur Miller's new play *The Archbishop's Ceiling,* thought Gig was right for one of the roles. Gig rushed to Manhattan, where he met with Miller and director Arvin Brown. Everyone seemed pleased, and without much ado, Gig found himself cast in a play by one of the world's leading playwrights, under the auspices of a prestigious producing company.

"Everyone was pleased for him," says the distinguished Whitehead. "There was something simpatico about him. Although he had a kind of cocktail charm that he could easily turn on, he was a serious actor. There was a subjective quality about him, something not acknowledged, that made him interesting in a strange way. I felt a lot of people were in for a surprise when they saw his performance."

While Gig was still carrying the script, everything progressed smoothly. But once he relied on memory, the old bugaboo with lines began plaguing him. Intimidated by Miller's renown, Gig projected the despair he felt on the playwright. He complained to Bert Knapp (who was assuming an increasingly influential position as a friend and adviser) that the playwright was displeased with his performance and wanted him fired. Knapp, instead of reinforcing Gig's ego, as Dr. Landy had done, took the complaints at face value and intensified Gig's panic.

Finally, the production team concluded that the situation was so difficult for everyone involved that action had to be taken. Whitehead asked Gig to come to his office. "Dismissing an actor is always painful, but this was particularly hard to do because he was a complex man, at once vulnerable and tough," Whitehead observes. "Those conflicts made him interesting. One felt he was both pathetic and yet capable of a kind of violence. There was something in his personality that embraced both those qualities. Actually, most successful, gifted actors have that mix."

Gig and the producer had a long heart-to-heart talk and Whitehead explained that Gig's performance just wasn't happening. Gig understood, but the meeting was painful and awkward nonetheless. "I think a part of him wanted me to say, 'Come on. Keep the part. Let's take a chance,' and the other part of him was grateful that I'd confronted him and he was out of his dilemma," Whitehead says. As Gig left, the two men embraced.

Asked, years later, what he recalled about his artistic disagreement with Gig, Arthur Miller replied, "There was nothing to disagree about—he couldn't remember his lines. It was very sad."

Though *The Archbishop's Ceiling* turned out to be a commercial and critical flop after all, Gig was still humiliated by his dismissal. It was the last thing that his battered career and ego needed. Broadway, his reliable refuge, had pulled in its welcome mat. Confronted with failure, he followed a pattern established early in his boyhood: he fled.

He returned to Harriette and the West Coast, where he hid out, driving thirty or forty miles for breakfast to avoid running into anyone connected with the entertainment field. The "Gig-spirit" celebrated by Doris Rich was in a tailspin. "The oil of gladness, the oil of joy" had turned rancid and been replaced with a paranoid fantasy.

Gig became convinced that he was being stalked by a tall, slim, dark-haired man. Object: murder. When he called Bert Knapp to confide his suspicions, the vocal teacher suggested that "the tall, dark, slim man" sounded like a description of Gig himself. Insulted by the implication that he was imagining the threat, Gig slammed down the phone. He began sticking close to his apartment, arranging for Harriette to come over and ride in the car with him when it was necessary to leave home.

Desperate, Gig continued running beyond Los Angeles—all the way to Hong Kong. To the astonishment of many friends and associates, he signed to do a kung fu movie—and, in the process, severed a most loyal and fruitful working relationship with Marty Baum. "We'd had a seventeen-year association," says Baum. "Then one day another agent called him with a job in this picture to be shot in Hong Kong. And as casually as saying, 'I'm going for a cup of tea,' he took the offer. He just walked out. I was very hurt the way he did it—as though it was obviously the proper way of saying goodbye after seventeen years." Nevertheless, for the rest of Gig's life, Baum continued to be available as a friend when Gig needed him.

During September and October of 1977, Gig worked in Hong Kong on his fifty-fifth and last film, called, appropriately enough, *The Game of Death.* It was on this trip that he would meet Kim Schmidt, the woman who would die with him at the Osborne.

In a curious way, Gig was correct to take umbrage at the implication that his story of the tall, slim, dark-haired man was an imaginary one. In this, the last year of his life, the specter of death had begun to stalk him. And the stalker, indeed, was Gig himself.

·11·

Rat Feet

The filming of *The Game of Death* had been suspended in 1973, when its star, Bruce Lee, dropped dead from a heart attack attributed to drug abuse. The fans of the kung fu box-office champ were clamoring for the release of their idol's last movie, so Golden Harvest scrapped most of the footage, with the exception of Lee's scenes, and proceeded to devise a new story around them. Gig was cast as a hard-drinking, tough reporter who was Lee's best friend. "What I had to do was act out my part as if I were talking to Lee, and then they spliced him in," he explained. "It certainly was eerie."

Providing relief from the morbid atmosphere was the frizzy-blond script girl who sat beside the director to remind

Gig, Colleen Camp, Hugh O'Brian, Dean Jagger, Chuck Norris, Kareem Abdul-Jabbar, and the rest of the cast about any changes in position, clothing, or props from matching scenes. "Rat Feet," as she was nicknamed because of her long, red-painted finger- and toenails, was efficient, quick-witted, and gregarious. Meticulous about detail, she was a Germanic taskmaster on the set. Yet after hours, she became an easygoing companion, with a vital spirit and an open smile.

She was on friendly terms with all the actors, but with Gig there was a special current. Cynics at once marked down Kim Schmidt as one of Gig's potential one-night stands. After all, she was a sensuous blond, not that different from some of the other women in Gig's past. They were astounded, therefore, when a deeper friendship began to develop between the blond and the badly burned survivor of four matrimonial disasters.

When one of Kim's longtime male confidants dismissed Gig's flowers, candy, and telephone calls as part of the "corny old Hollywood rush," her temper flared. She was touched by the sweet romantic gestures. Observing Gig on the set, she was thrilled to be working with one of her all-time favorite actors, especially since he seemed so vulnerable and lonely. He might drink too much; but then so had her father. She was used to men like that. There would be times during their stormy courtship when Kim felt that all of her thirty years had been merely a prelude to prepare her for loving a man like Gig Young.

Christened Ruth Hanalore Schmidt, Kim was born in Schwalmstadt, Germany. When she was six, she and her baby sister, Irmi, were taken to Australia by their parents. The family settled in Eildon, a tiny resort town, and grew to include twin boys and another girl. Kim, always extremely independent, later said that even when she was a tiny tyke, a power war had been waged between her and her mother.

She also sadly admitted that her love for her father had been tempered by his fondness for strong drink.

From age ten, Kim became obsessed with getting away and making her mark in the world. An avid movie magazine reader, the girl dreamed of going to Hollywood and meeting the stars. She graduated from school at sixteen and high-tailed it to Melbourne, where she secured office employment. The only other junior office worker at the firm was a young beauty named Judy Washington. Soon they were best friends, sharing an apartment and plotting to escape becoming Australian housewives. At eighteen, Judy struck out for Hong Kong. Eight months later, Kim turned up—whether in pursuit of or pursued by a lover isn't clear. She always seemed to have one; they never seemed to last.

The bustling international port city of Hong Kong was made for a woman like Kim. It was almost as if there were a large neon "Opportunity" sign hanging from the sleek steel-and-glass bank buildings. Ferryboats and Chinese junks plied the harbors, and ambitious young men and women worked the bars. "You can do anything there," Kim later told a reporter. "Just print up a card."

Ruth Hanalore could reinvent herself—and she did. Sometime after her arrival, she adopted the first name of her new lover, Kim Richardson, thinking that Kim sounded mellifluous and Oriental. She bleached her hair, acquired a perpetual tan, and dieted strenuously to shed baby fat. Fun-loving and vivacious, she spent her spare time at the Foreign Correspondents Club (although it was private, attractive women found it easy to acquire a guest card), where her uninhibited Australian laughter was an amusing contrast to the muted conversation of other young women, especially the Orientals.

"Young as she was, she had a cosmopolitan approach to life," says Russell Jones, an advertising executive who gave Kim her first job in Hong Kong and became a lifelong friend.

"She had the advantage of another language. And her basic attitude toward men was very Australian: frank and open."

When her second love affair went up in smoke a year later, Kim decided to leave for a while and see the rest of the world. She toured Europe, taking jobs as a cocktail waitress and an English teacher in Germany, and then moved to Spain, where she worked as a disc jockey and nightclub manager. In London, after employment as a receptionist with Young and Rubicam Advertising, she became a tour guide for Thompson Holidays, a travel agency that sent her on far-flung trips to the Italian and French Rivieras, Majorca, and Moscow.

Kim soon became enamored of one of Thompson's regional managers, named Gianni, for whom she worked as an assistant in Florence. The relationship became serious enough for the handsome Italian to invite her home to meet his family, who were aghast that their son wished to marry not only a foreigner but also someone outside their faith. When the family's blessing was not forthcoming, the romance eventually petered out, but not before the couple returned to Hong Kong to visit Judy, who was ill. Soon Gianni returned to Italy, promising to send for Kim. But her letters went unanswered, and she wasn't able to reach him by phone. Kim took refuge with her good friend Russell Jones and his wife, Hai-Tien. She was devastated that this love affair had gone sour. "She could really go into a funk," says Jones. "Her lows were very black. It was scary."

Hai-Tien took a special interest in the occult, and Kim often went to her for advice. She was simply told that when these sorts of problems occurred, she was living under "dim stars" and had to lie low for a while and regroup. She followed Hai-Tien's advice, and in time, a vivacious Kim resurfaced at the Correspondents Club. She rented a first-floor apartment at 12 Kennedy Terrace and took a part-time job

Gig with Phyllis Thaxter (Skye Aubrey's mother) and James Cagney in the 1951 film (for which Gig received his first Oscar nomination), Come Fill the Cup.

Gig and Joan Crawford in Torch Song, *1953.*

Stripper and actress Sherry Britton.

(courtesy of Elaine Stritch)

Gig and Elaine Stritch.

Gig's third wife, **Bewitched** *star Elizabeth Montgomery.*

(courtesy of Genevieve Barr Merry)

Gig and Elizabeth during happier days.

(photo by Doris Nieh, courtesy of Elaine Young)

At home with his fourth wife, Elaine Young.

Gig and Jennifer.

(courtesy of Elaine Young)

Skye Aubrey.

An evening with Harriette Vine Douglas.

Gig's Oscar-winning role as master of ceremonies, Rocky Gravo, in the 1969 feature
They Shoot Horses, Don't They?

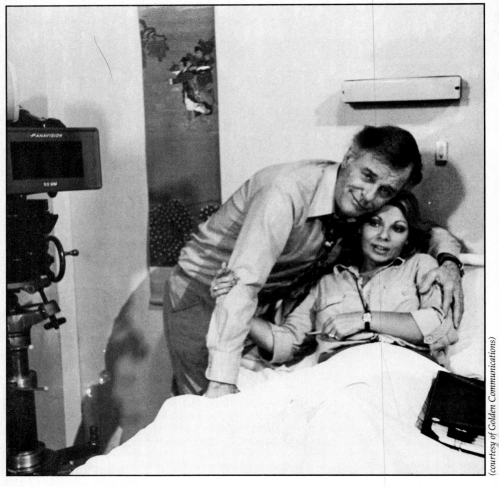

Gig and Kim in 1973 on the set of his final picture, **The Game of Death.**

as an assistant at Couldrey, Jones, Lindberg Associates, an advertising agency in which Russell Jones had become a partner.

Reconciled to the fact that she was unlucky in love, she set out to become a successful independent woman. Through Hai-Tien, who was a painter, she got a job managing an artists' cooperative gallery called The Quorum. Before long she was writing and publishing a four-page newsletter, also called "The Quorum." She used the newsletter to promote Hong Kong's art scene in general and the gallery and herself in particular. The publication was a success, giving her high visibility on the social circuit. She grew to love the limelight. She was often seen at parties, champagne glass in hand, her throaty laugh rising above the cocktail chatter. She was constantly on the move, socially and professionally. She bounced from advertising, to the art gallery, to a travel agency, to the Hong Kong Trade Development Council, and then to writing features and movie reviews for a local rag. And through all these changes, she continued publishing her art newsletter.

Hong Kongers remember Kim as quite a mover and shaker, a good-time gal who was a lot more complicated than she seemed. Andrew Simpson, who worked with her for a spell at the advertising agency, says that beneath Kim's vivacious exterior was a fiercely ambitious adversary who could get on colleagues' nerves with her nonstop go-go-go. "If you said to her, 'Piss off, Kim. It's a terrible idea,' you wouldn't get a word out of her for the next week. I never met another woman with a personality like that, before or since," Simpson reflects. "She wouldn't attack, but she'd make life very difficult. When she was in that mood, doors would slam. She'd throw the presentation book around. She'd freeze you out. She could be very irritating."

Ted Thomas, one of her early romantic interests in Hong

Kong, knew her as a woman who was quite concerned with her public image and who was not averse to faking it if that's what the occasion called for. What a casual onlooker saw did not always accurately reflect Kim's real feelings, he maintains. "She was a tie straightener, and she'd give you a kiss on the ear—even when you were having a row with her," he says. "As far as the public was concerned, Kim would come on very strong. And she could make you feel like a million dollars, but she could also be a pain in the ass if she didn't get her way." She was, in his opinion, a tough adversary. And a persuasive one.

Just how persuasive she could be was illustrated when an intruder gained entrance to her apartment, robbed her, and started undoing his pants. Keeping her cool in the face of threatened rape, Kim used a combination of sweet talk, reasoning, and intimidation to talk the man out of it. All the while she was mentally making notes on his appearance. The moment he fled, she called the police, giving them such an on-the-nose description that within forty-five minutes officers arrived with the suspect in tow for her identification. While terror-stricken, she had managed to observe and recall his clothing and appearance in minute detail—down to the brand of sneakers he was wearing. So impressive was the feat that it was later written up in a police magazine.

Dynamic as she was, it isn't surprising that she became bored when her job at the Trade Development Council turned out to consist more of doing office work than of staging fashion shows at Ready-to-Wear Festivals. So in the mid-seventies, when film producer Patrick Kelly (her lover at the time) asked if she'd be interested in becoming a "script girl," she accepted on the spot. She prudently arranged to take a leave of absence from the Council and went to Bali with the film company. She loved the work and decided that this was the life for her.

She wrote to her parents about her thrilling new career:

When I got back from Bali, the day I got back to the office at the TDC, I quit. I can't work 9-to-5 in an office—it's insane. After I resigned, I realized I was so broke, so I sat around chewing my nails, worried—but I've always been lucky, and I was again. The next day, someone asked me if I'd like to be a continuity girl on a couple of movies at $6,000 HK a month—double what I was getting at the TDC. Three months, all expenses paid, in Manila (love that place). I've rented my flat at a profit to a French lady for three months, and I'm off next week. First, there's another holiday (Chinese New Year). So things are *great.*

Cause for more cheer was that Kim was in love. Rangy Patrick Kelly was an English-born entrepreneur. Arriving in Hong Kong with no money but plenty of determination, he quickly landed a spot as headwaiter at the Excelsior, acquired a Chinese model for a wife, and set about cultivating people who could help him rise in the world. Using his inexhaustible supply of *chutzpah* to promote himself, more "by accident than good management" he soon began working for film companies on location in Spain, Germany, and France, "doing anything from financing to catering."

Having snagged the catering account for Francis Ford Coppola's marathon location shooting of *Apocalypse Now,* Kelly lined his pockets with American dollars and adopted a high-flying, Hollywood-style act, complete with gold chains, a Rolls-Royce, suites in world-class hotels, and endless flights from the Orient to wherever films were made. Kelly's obvious success was an aphrodisiac for the ambitious Kim, and soon she was deeply involved with him. But it quickly became apparent that he was not a man in whom one ought to make any serious emotional investment. After a brief hot affair, Kelly lost interest in romance and returned to his wife, but he suggested continuing their friendship and business association.

While Kim put on a cheery "just-one-of-the-boys" face, she was distraught at her failure to exact a lasting commitment from any of the men she fell in love with. When she bemoaned her bad fortune to friends, they told her that she should consider herself lucky to have found this out before marriage. She agreed. But in poems denying that her attachment to Kelly was anything but lust, she gave voice to a darker side and toyed with the attraction of suicide.

In "The Stranger Within," written in June 1977, she expressed her confusion:

> *Oh what a waste.*
> *Taking pills, drinking anything that's here—with ice.*
> *These are the best years of my life.*
> *I never looked better, never made more sense.*
> *Never understood my situation more.*
> *Never . . . why am I crying?*
> *What am I scared of?*
> *Nobody loves me, that's all.*
>
> *Just like a little kid, crying, nobody loves me.*
> *Take a handful of sleeping pills, and in 20 minutes,*
> *It's all a dream. You sleep, guaranteed, until*
>   *tomorrow. . . .*
> *He said it would hurt and it does. But is this all?*
> *What about dying, the final solution?*
> *But if I die now, what a waste, what a shame. . . .*
> *I'm never lonely, I say. What lies we tell ourselves.*
> *Growing older without growing wiser.*
> *Running in the direction of death, acting my life with*
>   *bravado.*
> *And who can I talk to, after all?*

The same month, she wrote "When Digby Died," in which her depression deepened at the death of another lover and her thoughts again turned to self-destruction:

Look at my face in the mirror.
I am 30 years old. In six months I'll be 31.
What have I gained?
Tonight, I got drunk deliberately because I had
  nothing
Better to do. Now I'm thinking about death.
Consumed by self-pity. . . .
I would kill myself, but I don't want pain.
Anyway, that's too easy.
Living is masochistic, so I punish myself by going on,
Not knowing why. . . .

While these bitter interior monologues smack of romantic self-dramatization, they also clearly reveal a woman in crisis. Who, she questions, is wise enough to perceive her worth? To discount her bravado, her mask of happiness? Who is strong and sensitive enough to bolster her flagging spirit and help her get through the night, the day, the week, the years? Gig Young, a man hardly on speaking terms with the stranger within himself, was Kim's unlikely choice. Perhaps what she really wanted was someone who would not pull off the mask, one whose delusions would collude with her own. If so, that is exactly what she got.

What initially piqued Gig's interest in Kim was her resemblance to Elizabeth Montgomery. Seeing Kim working at the director's side or socializing after hours reminded him of Liz moving effortlessly among New York and Los Angeles celebrities and socialites, helping him to feel temporarily less of an outsider. At the same time, his physical attraction to Kim—her blond hair, provocative eyes, big breasts, and hearty laughter—was immediate and reckless. Momentarily, he seemed to forget his age and ailments, to pursue the thirty-year-old as if he were a young man again, like a character in one of Somerset Maugham's exotic tales of the East.

For Kim, given her recent heartbreak and crisis of confidence, the flurry of phone calls, flowers, and love notes would have been flattering even if Gig had not been the sender. But with her lifelong addiction to movie magazines and her ranking of Gig among her top-five favorite actors, the rush was dizzying. If age and hard living had tarnished his youthful elegance and dimmed the luster of his career, he was still a well-known, well-turned-out older man, somebody far beyond any other man she had met. He was the passport she had been looking for to the great world of celebrity.

Each appeared—if not flawless—eminently desirable to the other. The bonds between them grew, and for the first time in several years, Gig was able to sustain a physical relationship. That Kim had a healthy sexual appetite seems evident. Her early Hong Kong flame, Ted Thomas, notes that when he met her, the vibes between them were so strong that he told himself, "I'm going to fuck her tonight." And he did.

Kim and Gig began dating steadily. Despite her youth, Kim exhibited a motherly side toward Gig—like so many of the other women in his life. Casually she started trying to help him with his lines. When cueing didn't work, she suggested cutting down on the pills. He stopped them, but soon after began drinking again. She attempted to persuade him that liquor was more destructive than Placidyl. He promised to give it up.

As always, when anything momentous occurred in her

life, Kim wrote to her best friend, Judy Washington. Then, unable to wait for a reply by post, she called her friend to say she couldn't believe her good fortune in meeting this man "who is just wonderful except that he drinks too much." She was working on that. "He needs looking after," she wrote. "And I am just the person to do it."

He, in turn, Oscar-winner and famous film star, gave her a social cachet that elevated her beyond script girl status. On the set of *Game,* she confided to leading lady Colleen Camp and Ann Clouse, the director's wife, how "madly in love" she was with Gig. She showed him off to her Hong Kong friends. Jovey Couldrey recalls that she and her husband were invited to dine with Kim and Gig. The evening was pleasant, but Jovey was struck by Gig's reserve. She later inquired whether he was always that quiet. "Oh no, he was so nervous meeting you guys," Kim informed her. "Nervous? It was no big deal," Jovey remembers responding. "To him it was," Kim said. "He worries that my younger friends will think he's too old for me."

To a man almost sixty-four, that was an understandable concern. As Kim became increasingly maternal in her care, Gig began to experience sexual difficulties. He worried, as any man might, about satisfying her. Fame and success might be aphrodisiacs, but past experience had taught Gig that they weren't enduring ones.

Then another complication arose. Patrick Kelly was back in Kim's life. "Not romantically," she claimed, but as a friend. She told Gig that he was interested in employing her on *Opium,* a film to be shot in Manila. Gig brooded over the association, falling into dark moods whenever Kelly called or was mentioned. Yet, ultimately, the tenuousness of his hold over Kim made her more attractive to him.

Feeling on the defensive, Gig flattered Kim. He told her how much he needed her, how her encouragement allowed him to overcome his dependency on pills and liquor. He praised her for helping him get off tranquilizers entirely and for making it possible for him to drink nothing except an occasional glass of wine with dinner. The ploy worked. To a woman like Kim, whose father had been an alcoholic, there was nothing quite so irresistible as Gig's admission that she had helped him curb his drinking.

She boasted to her friends of her success, until one day a crisis developed. Kim was alone in Gig's hotel suite when the room boy came to replenish some little bottles of vodka. She informed him he was in the wrong room, but he insisted he had been restocking the supply daily. When Gig returned, Kim confronted him hysterically, and he sheepishly admitted that he had been sneaking vodka into his orange juice. The exchange between them escalated into vicious baiting, and Gig ordered Kim out. Separately, each got dead drunk that night.

During the "dim star" period that followed, Gig ordered the hotel telephone operators to hold all his messages so that he could return only those calls that interested him. When, after a few days, Gig failed to call, Kim went on a blind date with an American garment importer named Elliot Bass. They spent the evening dining and dancing; and when Kim learned Bass was interested in seeing paintings by Gerard d'Henderson, she arranged a visit to the artist's studio.

Bass bought some paintings, but the one thing he remembers about the evening was that Kim spoke longingly of going to America. "She wanted to become a celebrity and felt the U.S. was the only place to do it," he recalls. "She *had* to get to America." When Bass later heard of her involvement with Gig, he assumed that was a major attraction for her in the relationship.

Kim's friends felt Gig had treated her badly and were almost unanimously opposed to any reconciliation. Kim agreed, spelling out reasons why the relationship could never lead anywhere. He was too old, he was alcoholic, his best years were behind him, he was too blocked. She avoided Gig at the studio and generally fled to the apartment of Russell and Hai-Tien Jones at the close of the workday. Yet when Gig finally called, saying he was depressed, lonely, and missing her, she eagerly accepted his invitation to talk over their problems. Kim ignored the objections about him she'd voiced earlier, and the couple reconciled. She told her friends that she couldn't help it. "He needs me," she said.

If, as some cynics suggested, Gig merely represented a passport to the United States for Kim, he came through. One day, while going through the unopened mail that Gig had left at the hotel, Kim came across a copy of Eugene O'Neill's *Long Day's Journey into Night,* which had been sent by Archer King, his New York agent. Accompanying the script was an offer for Gig to appear as guest artist in the play at the University of Memphis. Kim, taking charge, read the play and contacted the agent to say she'd see that Gig gave him a decision directly.

Gig, who liked take-charge women, was delighted at the opportunity to involve Kim in his career. With encouragement from her, he agreed to play the part of James Tyrone on the condition that she come to Memphis to help him master his lines. This created a dilemma, since Patrick Kelly was pressing her to accompany him on location in the Philippines, promising her $7,500 HK a month as unit publicist on *Opium.* Before deciding, Kim consulted Hai-Tien, who, looking over astrological charts, advised her to forgo the trip to the Philippines. Something bad was going to happen there. When Kim had dinner with Kelly to tell him of her decision, he expressed disapproval of her getting further involved with Gig and said that if things went wrong she was to cable his partner, Leon Choluck, in Los Angeles for whatever she needed. He also claimed he was in love with her.

"God, life is strange," Kim wrote Judy Washington.

"Where was he when I was in love with him? Thank God, I got over that!"

(That was the last time she ever saw Kelly. A year later, while he was scouting locations in the Philippines, his helicopter hit an electrical wire and crashed, killing everyone aboard.)

In October 1977, Kim realized her lifelong dream to reach American shores. New York City! She came prepared. Discovered after her death were notebooks that contained a glossary of famous places along with brief descriptions. "Sardi's: a theatrical hangout for Broadway actors, Italian food." "Joe Allen's: young people, not expensive." "Russian Tea Room: Hipper, more eclectic crowd, expensive."

While in New York, Gig and Kim stayed at the Elysée Hotel, and he introduced her to Bert and Bernice Knapp, Archer King, and other close associates. Knapp was especially taken with Kim, proclaiming, "I've waited twenty years to be able to say to a woman in Gig's life that she's the best thing that ever happened to him. Now I can."

With the Knapp stamp of approval, Gig felt confident showing Kim off at brunches at the Stage and dinners at "21." After seeing a big Broadway show, which she had no hesitation in proclaiming "lousy," he took her to Sardi's for supper and amazed friends by spreading the word that he was undertaking to play James Tyrone in *Long Day's Journey*. Anybody in show business knew that *Long Day's Journey* was a ball-buster when it came to sheer volume of lines and the kind of repetition that tended to throw an actor off. The *Archbishop's Ceiling* debacle was in everybody's mind, since it had spread like wildfire that he'd been fired because of memory problems. Yet he appeared recharged, and one of the main reasons was the woman who was there at his side.

While Gig was attending to business, Kim "did Saks" and went on a spree at Bloomingdale's, all at Gig's expense. "Do you believe what's happening?" she wrote somewhat naively to Judy Washington. "He wants me to move to New York permanently, and he has movies slotted for Europe after this, and I know he's getting so he doesn't want to be without me because I can help him with his acting. I love it because it makes me feel useful, necessary and creative. He's proud of me, but not as proud as I am of him. We have fun together and enjoy being alone when they let us. It's nice." Yet she harbored some unexpressed reservations, adding: "Cross your fingers that it lasts which will mean that you have a home in New York, if nothing else, and we must keep our flat in Hong Kong, mustn't we?" (The Hong Kong flat had been sublet.)

Having shown off his young mistress and, he hoped, countered rumors about his failing memory, Gig flew off with Kim to the University of Memphis in high spirits. He was nervous about the project, but he had to prove to himself that he still had it. Time and again, people had counted him out—he had counted himself out—but he'd always been able to bounce back with a good role. And the role of James Tyrone was a doozer. So many of the lines in this play about a family hemorrhaging from regret resonated in his own life. The patriarch was a boozy, guilt-ridden actor who'd made a Faustian bargain. Instead of fulfilling his potential as one of the greatest actors of his generation, he became one of the richest—choosing to tour endlessly in an old warhorse (not unlike the playwright's father, James O'Neill, who starred in *The Count of Monte Cristo*). James Tyrone's reflexive parsimony contributes to the morphine addiction of his wife and earns the contempt of his sons, one tubercular, the other terminally alcoholic. Desperately fighting to keep from drowning from all the lies and delusions,

James Tyrone ultimately yields to his tragic destiny of facing up to the artistic and emotional bankruptcy that has engulfed him.

Although Gig had promised the director to have his role memorized by the time he arrived, he had spent so much time talking about the role that he hadn't had time to learn it. Arrangements had been made for him and Kim to stay at the Alumni House, and he was thrilled with its twenty-foot ceilings, blue velvet drapes, Oriental rugs, and general opulence. Gig told an interviewer, "It's the height of luxury. Richard Burton and Liz never had it any better."

"Fantasy, fantasy," Kim wrote Judy Washington. "Who'd have thunk it? I find myself completely at home in my role which consists of making sure Gig doesn't forget his glasses, making sure he remembers to wear clothes that match—he's the original absent-minded professor type. At night, when we study lines, from midnight to 3 A.M., we sit in two beautiful armchairs facing each other and I make him learn the words, and explain the story to him so he gets into it more."

The rehearsal period was strenuous, beginning after lunch, with an hour dinner break, and then back to work until midnight. Initially, Gig beguiled the director, cast, and crew with anecdotes about Broadway and Hollywood. But as the days passed without his seeming to master the dialogue, apprehension spread. Joanna Helming, who taught acting at the university and was playing Mary Tyrone, began to suspect that the theatrical anecdotes were a ploy Gig was using to avoid coming to grips with the part. "It's a barbaric role," she says. "Just awful. I had trouble with lines myself. The play is written in short, direct sentences, and it's very repetitive. It will make you crazy."

Director Henry Swanson secretly conferred with Ms. Helming and the students about ways to help Gig. A kind of crisis mentality gripped the cast and production staff. Perhaps because she was totally inexperienced in theater, Kim didn't realize that the injection of her ideas was contributing to the problem. "I'm directing his performance more, I realize, than the director of this play," she wrote to Judy, oblivious to how destructive her meddling could be. "Gig says in thirty years of acting no one has ever made a role come so alive for him before, and no one has ever given him more tricks to learn and remember pages of dialogue."

This kind of manipulation of Kim by Gig also clearly extended to everyone else concerned, but as pressure mounted, his affability all but vanished. At rehearsals, Joanna Helming noted he was becoming more and more tense. His inability to retain lines unnerved him and everyone else. "He was not mean, and he was not ugly," Ms. Helming says. "He was just—he was pretty direct. He'd pop off. And you could tell he was real nervous. He stumbled a couple of times, and everyone wondered whether he was drinking, but I never smelled anything on his breath. If he was taking anything, it was medication."

Kim refused to recognize impending disaster, focusing instead on their personal relationship. In her letters, she confided to Judy that Gig was pressing her to cut her Hong Kong ties and come to New York to live. "He's not asking me to marry him, thank God. That would scare the hell out of me," she wrote, perhaps disingenuously. "But he's like no one I've ever met before and I could get very used to this life." She then added matter-of-factly, "I'm not in love with anyone. Hence, my air of cool detachment. So far anyway." But was she fooling just Judy, or herself as well?

As it became increasingly clear that Gig was not going to conquer his memory problem without intervention, Henry Swanson asked Kim to step aside and began privately cueing Gig. Kim threw a tantrum. Abandoning flattery, Gig informed her he needed professional help. Mutual hostility escalated, and he moved out of the room they had been occupying. Kim then placed a secret phone call to Bert Knapp to report Gig's behavior toward her. They discussed whether she should leave Memphis. Knapp discouraged such a move, telling her actors often behaved irrationally under pressure. Eventually she decided to stay, blaming their problems on stress.

On Friday morning after Thanksgiving, at the final dress rehearsal prior to the premiere that evening, Gig was frequently going up on his lines. Grasping at straws, Swanson recalled an occasion when an actor had mastered his part during the first performance, and he told everyone to pray for a miracle.

Their prayers went unanswered. At the premiere, the final curtain, which was scheduled to fall at 11:25, came down at 10:40. Gig had simply excised hunks of the play. The students in the cast were outraged. "I must admit for a long time afterward when I tried to remember the title of our play I had to say *Look Back in Anger* before I could get the right one," says Ms. Helming. "It was an awful evening for everyone, but the audience stayed. Gig's agent had come down from New York but fled the same night. Gig was very down. Yet by the time we played our last performance we'd added forty-five minutes to the running time, and Gig was charming. In fact, by the end of the run, it was my opinion that if we had another two weeks, he would have been magnificent in the role. He had moments as it was. He had that magnificent voice, and when he turned on the charm, he'd just melt people in their socks.

"At the end of the fourth act, there is a scene where Mary Tyrone comes out dragging her wedding dress, and he takes it. On opening night and closing night, Gig had tears in his eyes, and I don't think it was within the moment particularly. I just think that opening night those tears came from the realization of the general awfulness of it. He was an intelligent man. He knew the students were just dismayed.

They were not appreciative of his problems and they were disappointed after putting in so much time and energy, the payoff should have been so little in terms of rewarding experience.

"Those closing-night tears in his eyes undoubtedly were because he could have been good and wasn't," Ms. Helming speculates. "That's exactly what James Tyrone talks about through the fourth act—squandered resources. And I believe it hurt Gig to think about it. It hurt his feelings. Sidewalk psychology being what it is, the more he understood, the more he got into the role, the harder it was for him to do. Because it was a version of the truth about himself."

Indeed, in Tyrone's summation of his professional downfall, he might have been composing the epitaph for Gig's career as well as his own: "Well, no matter. It's a late day for regrets." However, Gig's regrets were not the kind to roll over and play dead. The Oscar-winning actor was reduced to kung fu pictures and college productions that he dragged down with his lack of preparation. Such regrets would pursue him like Furies, until he silenced them in the only way he knew how.

·12·

Albatross

Following their Memphis skirmish, Gig and Kim's relationship became increasingly volatile. Gig needed a woman
in his life, but he wasn't sure that Kim was the one. She was
formidable and, he thought, devious. He could never be sure
what she was up to. What was she after? Money? A green
card? While Bert Knapp always insisted that Kim loved Gig
for himself, other people thought that she was using him to
accomplish her own agenda. Years later, Joanna Helming,
who worked so closely with Gig in Memphis, said she had
come to the conclusion that although Kim was fond of him,
for her their relationship was a means to an end. "Not that
it was my business," she added. "Because I felt Gig was
canny enough to have figured it all out. At least one part of

him understood, and that part just decided, well, the hell with it. I'll go forward and do what I'm doing."

Certainly Gig was experienced enough to realize that there are trade-offs in most relationships. But he had always impetuously followed his heart, not his head, and he was not about to change now. Even though three of his four marriages had been personal disasters, he still argued that if a couple wanted to be together, they should wed. He called friends with whom he'd stayed close—Skye Aubrey and Bob Webber—to talk about Kim. And above all, he discussed it with Gen, who suggested he consider the differences in their ages, only to be told that Kim was unusually mature since her mother (actually alive in Australia) had died when Kim was nine and she had taken the responsibility of rearing the family.

Back in New York from Memphis, Gig and Kim quarreled, made up, split up, and reconciled. He promised to get rid of his Beverly Hills place and buy an apartment in New York. He proposed, but Kim insisted that it would be more sensible for them just to live together. When they battled again, Gig threatened to send her back to Hong Kong, and she retaliated by threatening to become a unit publicist on Patrick Kelly's long-delayed feature film.

In an attempt to save the relationship, Bert Knapp, with Gig's blessing, stepped in to give Kim some informal counseling. Portraying himself as an objective adviser, Knapp urged her to stick with Gig whether or not they married, build his ego, make him feel important, as only a woman could. Like most of the other women who had been part of Gig's life, Kim easily assumed the role of mother and cheerleader—and things began to look up.

In a dizzying mood swing, Gig convinced himself that the relationship could work out after all, and on December 18, 1977, the couple flew from New York to Hong Kong. The purpose of the trip, aside from celebrating the holidays, was for Kim to pack her belongings, "close shop," and move to New York with Gig. He was confident they would soon wed, while she clung to her idea of simply living together—at least for a time.

On New Year's Eve, the couple hobnobbed at the raucous bar of Hong Kong's Foreign Correspondents Club, where hard-nosed old hands bought them drink after drink and toasted a relationship that seemed warm and loving. It was a standing maxim at the FCC that an evening was not a complete success unless everyone was rip-roaringly smashed. They were happy to oblige.

Being ten thousand miles away wasn't sufficient to escape the sting of failure he felt from the Memphis fiasco. True, his humiliation had been far from the spotlight of either Hollywood or Broadway, but word traveled. And he knew that since the *Blazing Saddles* dismissal, rumors had flown on both coasts that he was unreliable. At least here in Hong Kong, he wouldn't have to stand around at parties and spin bar lies when people asked him what he was going to do next. All he had to do was get blissfully drunk and let Kim take care of everything.

Kim was good at exploiting the public side of their relationship. She was a valuable partner to him at this tenuous stage in his career, someone who actively colluded with him in presenting the best possible public face of Gig Young. He could rely on her to go along with deft evasions of past troubles and to hype possibilities for the future almost as if they were *faits accomplis*. Being with Kim was tantamount to having a personal press representative on hand to run interference.

The day before they were to leave Hong Kong, all the tensions and difficulties came to a head. Once again he proposed marriage, and once again she expressed her reluctance. "If two people want to be together, they marry," he told her. He interpreted her preference for simply living

together as signifying that she wanted to be free to walk out
if problems arose. That, he said, was not what their relationship was all about. "There will be tough times," he told her,
"but it will never work if you're not prepared to commit
yourself to a permanent relationship."

When she held out for retaining her freedom, he gave her
an ultimatum—either marry him or forget about New York.
He said he was too old to waste time on another mistake.
Mention of age, Kim later wrote, led him to a discussion of
the difference in their ages and the possibility that he would
live on as a shell of his former self when she was just reach-
ing her prime.

"Couldn't argue with any of that, and I suppose he took
my silence to mean I agreed to end the relationship," she
wrote her parents. "I was too numb to think about it. I mean
my suitcase was packed, and standing there in the corner.
Mentally, I was already living in the States."

Gig and Kim went out to dinner, calmly talked over their
problems "like sophisticated adults in control of the situation," and torpedoed their plans for the rest of their lives.
That neither was behaving rationally seems never to have
occurred to them.

The next morning, Kim stood in her doorway and waved
a smiling goodbye to Gig as a friend drove him to the airport
to catch his plane for New York. Once Gig was gone, Kim
retreated to her bedroom. "I went to bed and didn't get up for
four days," she wrote her parents. "Every time I woke up, I
took another sleeping pill. Good way not to think. How's that
for drama?"

Whatever else Kim expected from the relationship, she
got plenty of drama. From the beginning of their courtship
there had been emotional fireworks between the long
stretches of ponderous silence. They both had grown ad-
dicted to the game. So naturally it wasn't long after their
split in Hong Kong that Gig called in the middle of the night

to apologize for the inconvenience of having caused her to close out her Hong Kong life and the embarrassment of her having to explain his abrupt departure. In the next four days he called six times—often enough to repair the damage. "It's all on again," Kim informed her parents. Whatever their age difference, whatever the insecurities, they would get through them. Kim was triumphant since, with or without Gig, the States was where she had to be to make it big.

"All his years of experience haven't made him cynical or 'old.' I'm older than he is," she boasted to her parents. (Although her family seems never to have interfered in her personal affairs, Kim took great pains to explain to them what was happening at different periods of her life.) "I feel more tired, more cynical, more worn out by the weight of the world than he ever will. I'm more cautious, smarter at business, have read more books, been to more countries, speak more languages, had more love affairs than he has. How about that? If you count it that way I'm old enough to be his mother, and sometimes I feel as though I am. . . .

"Now that everything's ok, it's almost like an anticlimax," she continued in the letter. "If there's a lesson to be learned from the trials and errors, it's that nothing is certain, the mystery grows year by year, and the answers get further and further out of reach. . . . One thing is for sure. I'll always be all right." By early February, Kim was in New York.

Among the reasons for Gig's reappraisal of his precipitous split with Kim was his relationship with Bert Knapp. Their friendship would later be revealed (through secret tapes Gig made of their sessions) to be the strangest and most destructive in the actor's life. Upon his return to New York, Gig began spending a great deal of time with Knapp, who by this time was far more than a vocal coach to his

impressionable student. Knapp had become even more of a
Kim partisan after he'd begun to counsel her. She was firmly
in his corner as well, praising him to Gig as someone who
cared about him and could help him. He in turn touted her
to Gig as the only woman aside from Sophie Rosenstein and
Elaine Stritch who truly loved him. Now the vocal teacher
worried that the split between Gig and Kim might lead his
favorite student to resume his friendship with Knapp's
nemesis, Harriette Vine Douglas.

He mercilessly goaded Gig, taunting him to leave Kim for
good, knowing that this would inevitably lead to his desired
aim to effect a reconciliation. It worked. Once Gig had
agreed to call Kim in Hong Kong, asking her to join him,
Bert Knapp gave his blessing, on tapes that Gig played over
and over for guidance in conducting his daily life.

"I hope Kim is going to be the catalyst and that dear little
lady will keep you from making false friendships. I beg you
on this tape, when you're with her that you won't run to
mama. I'm not mama. I'm a friend of you both. I'm very
neutral, as you know goddamn well."

While one could call Knapp many things, "neutral"
wasn't one of them. Elaine Stritch had introduced Gig to the
voice coach in 1955, shortly after *Oh Men! Oh Women!*, and
Gig had begun working on musical comedy technique with
him. Gig was captivated by the man—and he was not the
only one. Knapp's ability to solve vocal problems had earned
him a number of passionate devotees, including Stritch,
Peter Falk, Robert Shaw, Mama Cass, Walter Matthau, and
Sergio Franchi.

Knapp had started out in show business, as an orchestra
leader at the Astor Hotel in the twenties. Later, he composed
music for the Ringling Brothers and Barnum & Bailey Cir-
cus, but it was in the late 1940s that he finally found his
niche, as a vocal coach. In his studio on Seventh Avenue, he
held forth not only as maestro but also as a spiritual director

who demanded fealty from those who placed themselves in his hands.

Soon after beginning his lessons, Gig became a disciple, encouraging his friends to check out Knapp's system. Not all of them were enthusiastic. "We all see different things in people, don't we?" Robert Webber asked twenty-nine years later. "Gawd! Bert Knapp struck me as the most arrogant man I'd ever met. He almost drove me nuts with that inbred arrogance of his. But Gig idolized him. Knapp told me, 'Open your mouth.' I wasn't quite fast enough. 'Open your mouth!' Gig barked. I did, and Bert popped a cork between my teeth. He had all kinds of corks and waxes and gadgets he worked with. The idea was to straighten out my tongue or something. He told me to do these exercises for a couple of days. It sounded foolish, but I did. And by God, I was better. Even I had to admit that. Gig wanted me to sign up to study with Knapp, but I couldn't deal with the man. I thought he was dangerous."

Over the years, Gig often referred to Knapp as his closest friend, and the voice coach encouraged this view, pointing out that everyone—family, professional associates, and friends—had failed Gig: everyone except Knapp and, later, Kim. Off and on during 1977 and 1978, Knapp foolhardily attempted to analyze Gig's life experiences. This no-holds-barred wrestling with past traumas, triumphs, and fantasies represented a misguided attempt on Gig and Knapp's part to grapple with problems that required a bona fide psychiatrist. Knapp did not hesitate to browbeat, cajole, ridicule, encourage, or challenge Gig in an effort to get this troubled man to face his demons.

Skipping back and forth in time, as recorded on tape, Gig covered his exploitation by and resentment of his family, schoolteachers, former wives, ex-girlfriends, lawyers, business managers, drama school classmates, and studio associ-

ates, among others. He settled old scores and searched his
and others' actions for hidden motivations. For the most
part, he reserved praise for people long dead—the only exceptions being Gen, Kim, and Knapp.

Gradually, Knapp virtually assumed control of the
actor's life. Aside from control, what did he get out of it? "I
was paid," he once said. "Well paid."

Knapp devised a regimen that required Gig to spend at
least half an hour each night writing up traumatic events
and suppressed fears for examination during their frequent
taping sessions. These sessions ranged over Gig's home life,
sexual exploitation in childhood, humiliating experiences
in Washington, and struggles in Hollywood.

At various points, Knapp would interrupt to touch upon
various emotions without actually analyzing or dealing with
them. For example, he lectured Gig on his potential for violence (seemingly confusing boxing and wrestling):

> We'll talk about your boxing, right? You don't want to
> hurt anybody, but if you get up against a wall, you'll
> get desperate and you might kill somebody. Those are
> your words. "I got a scissor lock on him, and nobody's
> going to get away from me if he's fifty-five feet tall."
> Isn't that on your tape? Good. "I know I knocked him
> on his ass. I don't know how I didn't kill him." Now,
> yet again, if the guy said, "What did you do it for?"
> you'd say, "Oh, God, please forgive me. I didn't mean
> to hurt you." The anger would have left you com-
> pletely.

On another occasion, Knapp browbeat Gig:

> You are brave on one hand and yellow on the other,
> did you hear me? Now, where does your yellow streak

come from? Hiding behind women's skirts until they
go to hit you or you get up against the wall. Now, are
you going to follow me?

Accepting this abuse, Gig said meekly, "I follow." Later,
Knapp continued with what seems like gobbledygook but
apparently made sense to Gig:

> And then you get a footlock, not particularly that way,
> but you get a footlock and you kill, and you destroy or
> you become destroyed. So you do two things—instead
> of killing, not in a wild-man sense but in a legal sense,
> you run away. Like one day you called me here. "I'm
> coming in tomorrow." Next day: "Can't see you." No-
> body knew where you were—in Canada someplace,
> fishing. You ran away. So the pattern of running away
> is like you did when you were a kid. Yes or no?

Gig rather sullenly replied, "Correct." Throughout their
relationship, Knapp urged the actor to sever his other business associations, while Gig's dependency on him increased.
Gig complied, throwing over agent Marty Baum and, later,
Archer King with Knapp's encouragement. While Knapp
had many student-disciples, none of the others allowed him
the amount of control Gig granted. That is, not until Patrick
Shields signed up for vocal instruction.

Shields managed the prestigious Le Club on East Fifty-
eighth Street, whose patrons included such members of the
power elite as Lee Iococca, George Steinbrenner, and the
up-and-coming Donald Trump. As generous as he was well-
connected, Shields began frequently inviting Bert and Bernice Knapp, Gig and Kim, to Le Club to dine. "Bert was a
very giving man, and his wife was divine," Shields once
said. "They were almost storybook mother and father fig-

ures. Gig and Kim were wonderful too. I would have liked to have a brother like Gig."

It was not long before Shields began to occupy a place rivaling Gig's in Knapp's entourage. Shields, although he was aware that Knapp "was very into controlling," played Knapp's game in hopes of furthering his singing career. After he had been studying voice with Knapp for about six months, something happened that he shied away from discussing for many years. It began more or less as a joke. At opening day of the 1978 baseball season at Yankee Stadium, after Robert Merrill sang the national anthem, Shields turned to Yankee owner George Steinbrenner and demanded, "George, why wasn't I up there singing that for you?" Steinbrenner deadpanned that Yankee Stadium was not a grand enough setting for Shields. He must be heard in a concert hall. The upshot of their bantering was that as a birthday gift, Steinbrenner rented Town Hall to present "An Evening with Patrick Shields" for charity.

Before agreeing to the stunt, Shields consulted Knapp, who assured him that vocally he was up to the challenge. "That was Bert's dream," says Joanne Jacobson, a friend of Shields's and another of Knapp's students. "Bert was going to be the conductor, he was going to select Pat's songs and mastermind the whole show. It was his ego trip."

Plans went forward. Suddenly, two days before the concert, Shields realized he had no one to introduce him. In a panic, he asked Knapp to sound out Gig. Gig accepted. Then Shields began worrying that Gig would ramble on too long. He again went to Knapp, telling him how fond he was of Gig but reminding him that the power brokers from Le Club would have a short attention span, so Gig must keep his introduction brief. "They're coming to hear me," he said. "As an example, Donald Trump just told me, 'You know, Patrick, I wouldn't pay twenty dollars to go across the street to see Sinatra, but I'm donating a hundred dollars for this charity to come and see you.' So make sure Gig keeps his introduction short." Knapp assured Shields he would, but he never got around to mentioning it to Gig.

On the evening of May 16, Shields, who had had little opportunity to rehearse with the band, was edgy. He had never sung in public before and was insecure about some of the songs. Then he got a message from Kim that he had better keep an eye on Gig, because he had been drinking. He went backstage and into shock. "There was Gig shuffling pages of notes he'd prepared," Shields remembered. "Not only that: he was still drinking. When he got in the spotlight, he rambled on until the audience began shouting, 'Get on with the show!' "

Joanne Jacobson, who was in the audience, later recalled: "Poor Gig. Poor Patrick. He was charming but not a singer. His voice was quavering, drowned out by the orchestra. It was just horrendous. I quit studying with Bert. Patrick quit. So did some others. And here's the kicker: Bert cut Gig dead."

Everyone lost. Ten years later, Shields remembered: "Bert used to tell people what to do, and if they didn't do it, he'd cut them off. That night he cut Gig off. Which was very irresponsible, because you do not take somebody and give him that much support and then turn on him because he goofs."

At first it was assumed that Knapp's anger would quickly pass. Not so. Knapp ignored Gig when he dropped by the studio, and he refused to take his calls. Gig was devastated. He'd come to believe that Knapp was his *only* friend, the only one who'd never failed him. Whenever things had started to go out of control, whenever the tunnels of his inner psyche had become too dark and threatening, Knapp had been there to advise and to coax, to bully but—so it appeared—to care. Knapp's rejection was not only humiliating, it was emotionally terrifying. The only recourse was what Gig had always chosen in the face of difficult circumstances: flight.

By June 26, 1978, Gig and Kim were ensconced at the Mayfield Inn in Edmonton, Canada. The natives were friendly, the fishing was good, and the pressures of New York and Hollywood seemed light-years away. Edmonton's Stage West, a dinner theater where Gig had done *Harvey,* was glad to mount a production of Ronald Alexander's *Nobody Loves an Albatross* for six weeks. After shaking out the kinks, Gig envisioned attracting a producer who would mount a full-scale national tour as far west as Hollywood before bringing the production back across the U.S. for a gala Broadway revival.

Some people thought his grandiose plans were pipe dreams. In fact, he and Archer King had fallen out over the revival. When Gig first broached the idea to his New York agent, offering him $1,000 a week to put together a summer touring package, King had vociferously refused. He reminded Gig that when he had returned from Hong Kong after the New Year, he had promised that he would "learn to be out of work" in order to wait for the first-class Broadway production that could reinject some badly needed momentum into his flagging career.

Gig wanted to heed his agent's advice in order to repair the damage that the kung fu film and the Memphis fiasco had done to their relationship. But he panicked when he considered the financial burden of building a life together with Kim in New York: the new apartment King had found them at the Osborne, the moving expenses from Hong Kong and Beverly Hills, even the daily expenses, which loomed large when the till wasn't being fed. Gig had not worked since the previous fall in Memphis, and that was for peanuts. He needed to make some money quick. *Albatross* seemed to him like a sound commercial prospect.

The agent not only disagreed but told Gig that if he insisted on going out in yet another revival, King would have no enthusiasm in representing him. A confrontation took place; neither man budged. Gig stomped out of the grim meeting and the next day hand-delivered to King's office a two-page diatribe, discharging him. They never saw each other again.

With King and Knapp, two of his most trusted advisers, severed from his life, Gig seemed to be pursuing an erratic scorched-earth policy both personally and professionally. The partings served to strengthen Kim's hand in the relationship, and when they left for Canada, she wrote Judy Washington, she was introduced as his fiancée. She added that it was assumed they would marry eventually, but she was in no hurry.

In her letters home to friends and family, Kim tended to paint a calm and happy picture of unfolding events. Writing to her parents in late June, she said she and Gig would be at the inn until September 12, spoke of everyone commenting that Gig looked younger, slimmer, more elegant than ever, and of course, it was all because of her. She was busy taking driving and tennis lessons, swimming and reading two books a week. "I have no excuse not to," she admitted. "Do you realize that I haven't worked since September?"

Then she continued in a somewhat more mercenary tone:

> Gig made out a new will a month ago, leaving half of everything to me, the other half to his sister, who is 70 [*sic*]. When she goes, I get what's left. I own half the apartment in New York. I found it all rather depressing, but Gig said, "If I stepped under a truck tomorrow

you'd be in an awful mess, stranded and broke." He insisted. He didn't have to, but to me that's more secure than getting married. I'm still scared getting married will change the happy atmosphere.

One of his ex-wives was Elizabeth Montgomery from "Bewitched." The day we got here we turned on the TV and there she was. I waited for a reaction. All he said was, "She's as phony an actress as she is a woman." So much for that. Enclosing a leaflet for this play—photo of Gig is about 15 years old—they're not with it here.

For all Gig's hopes, *Nobody Loves an Albatross* was getting off to a rocky start, living up to the reputation of the bird of the title—an unlucky omen for sailors. In fact, the play had nothing to do with sailors. It was about Nat Bentley, an esteemed television writer-producer who had clawed—and slept—his way to the top, exploiting talented ghostwriters and compliant secretaries. Set in the living room of Bentley's posh Beverly Hills pad, the light comedy ricochets with the hero's misadventures when he hires the wrong ghostwriter for a new series and tries to seduce a secretary with principles, who is aware of his reputation.

On the face of it, *Albatross* seemed like typical Gig Young fare, and the playwright, an old friend who himself was an actor, was glad to grant him the rights. But Alexander suggested that if Gig was serious about the national tour, he should find an experienced producer and director to guide the project. Gig agreed about the producer but brushed aside the advice about hiring a director. Wanting to keep as much of the financial reward as possible, he proposed to direct the play himself.

No sooner had rehearsals begun than Gig started to fret that the cast of local actors provided by Stage West was devoid of an instinct for comedy. When the Chicago-based actor Edgar Meyer, who had worked with him several times before, arrived, he found Gig in an agitated state. "I hate to say Gig was paranoid, but I did feel that he was a little overconcerned about people moving or doing things during his dialogue," Meyer says.

Gig would blow up and stalk off the stage, abandoning rehearsals. After a cooling-off period, he would summon Meyer, explain what offenses were being committed, and send him back to eliminate the problems. "I felt like sort of a go-between," Meyer says.

The management at Stage West attempted to reassure Gig, but he was convinced that another fiasco was brewing and placed a frantic call to Ronnie Alexander. In early July, Alexander and his girlfriend, Panda Hoffman, came to Edmonton. Both knew Gig well. He and Alexander had been young actors together, and Panda had grown close to Gig when he was married to her cousin Liz Montgomery.

Panda and Alexander arrived at the airport and were picked up by Gig and Kim. Both visitors were surprised to find Gig in such good spirits in view of the agitated tone that had marked his phone call. They immediately liked Kim, although she struck Panda as somewhat ingenuous when she repeatedly described Gig, in their confidential chats, not as thoughtful, or kind, or even attractive, but as "a movie star."

When Alexander broached the subject that had brought them to Canada, Gig tensed up and said he didn't want to discuss the production until after the visitors had seen a performance. That night, Panda, Alexander, and Kim occupied a front table at the dinner theater. After the play, they picked up Gig and started back to the Mayfield Inn. Panda and Alexander had regarded the performance as a fiasco, but Gig plunged into a diatribe against the cast without giving his guests a chance to express their opinions pro or con. He claimed that the actors were feeding him his cues incorrectly, making it impossible for him to get his laughs. The only real pro other than himself, he said, was Edgar Meyer.

They arrived at Gig's suite, and he ordered food and a bottle of red wine. The visitors relaxed. Then, gradually, Gig's mood altered. He grew visibly agitated. "Is it possible this is my fault?" he demanded. "Is it possible I'm not remembering your lines? That's why I got you up here. I wanted you to hear the show." Yet he kept on babbling, making it impossible for Panda or Alexander to offer any feedback.

The next night followed more or less the same scenario. This time when Gig inquired whether it was his fault, Alexander responded that there was nothing wrong with the show that a strong director couldn't remedy. That remark sent Gig into a sudden fury. He leaped to his feet and moved toward Alexander, shouting that he totally disagreed. To which Alexander replied, "Well, the show is not working as it is, so why not see what a top comedy director could do with it?"

"I don't remember exactly what was said, but Gig became angry to an extent I'd never seen in all the years I'd known him," Panda recalls. "There was an awful tension as he moved toward Ronnie in a threatening way. Ronnie said something that turned it into a joke, and we all went on talking. After Ronnie and I left, I said, 'Am I crazy, or was Gig going to try to hit you?' Ronnie said, 'No. He meant to.' "

The incident troubled Panda, since it seemed so out of character. She had always regarded Gig as the gentlest of men. She was now convinced that something in him was seriously askew. "When Ronnie and I were alone, I said I thought Gig ought to be institutionalized. To be treated for a sort of nervous breakdown. I said I thought he should have medical care. I don't believe in shrinks, but there are all kinds of drugs: lithium—who knows?"

Before Panda and Alexander returned to New York, the

playwright arranged a private conference with Gig in which he reiterated the need to find an experienced producer and a Broadway-caliber director. Gig heard him out, promised to give his recommendations serious consideration, but refused to commit himself to any given course of action. "I didn't know what he was going to do," Alexander says. "He wanted marvelous actors who would set him off like a jewel. And he wanted a big director and a well-known producer. And then he wanted all the money as well."

After pondering alternatives for several days, Gig hit upon the idea of persuading Bob Douglas to take over the direction. He called at once, only to be told that his old pal had a commitment to direct a television drama. But Gig was so obviously disappointed that Douglas agreed to come to Canada for a couple of days to look over the production.

On the morning of August 10, the day Douglas was to arrive, Gig awoke with feet so swollen that he was unable to get them into anything other than bedroom scuffs. Sensitive that Douglas would think he was in no condition to work, he began soaking his feet in ice water, hoping the swelling would go down. Finally, at noon, he phoned Edgar Meyer to ask him to go to the airport and pick up Douglas, explaining that he didn't want their potential director to see him hobbling around. Meantime, he said, he was going to a chiropractor to try to get some relief.

Douglas was taken aback, after coming all the way from California, that Gig was not on hand to meet the plane. But presently Meyer identified himself and they retrieved the luggage and set out for the inn. During the drive, Douglas inquired how Gig was and was told "Fine, just fine," although he detected something ambiguous in the reply.

When he arrived at the inn, the director asked the desk clerk to ring Mr. Young and was informed that he was not in. Douglas left a message.

"I waited until after five o'clock, and I was getting a little pissed off," he says. Finally, the phone rang. Gig greeted his guest without explanation or apology. Douglas said, "Gig, I've been waiting two hours. Where are you?" Gig said, "I had to have a massage, and I had a few things to do. Anyway, come down and have a drink."

In the room, Gig puttered around rather vaguely, offering his guest some red wine. When Douglas asked for a Scotch, the actor seemed put out. "I'll have to order room service," he said. "Well, why don't you do that?" Douglas snapped. "And while you're at it, order a double."

After putting in the order, Gig suddenly remembered the woman he'd left waiting in her bedroom. "Oh, you haven't met Kim! Of course, you haven't met Kim," he said. "I'll get her." He went down the hall and banged on another door in their suite and shouted, "Come out. I want you to meet Bob."

"A few minutes later, Kim walked in. A cute little thing. Awfully sweet," Douglas recalls. "Gig poured her a glass of wine, and we sat around talking about nothing. Finally, I said, 'Gig, what is the purpose of my being here?' He said, 'I want you to see the play. The cast is not very good, but if we can have a really good cast, I'd like to do it in Hollywood. You can recast and redirect it, and we'll take it to Broadway.' I told him we'd better wait until I'd seen it to talk about that."

At that point, Kim sent Gig to the theater, saying she and Douglas would follow. Douglas took the opportunity to inquire how Gig was, and Kim assured him that her fiancé was fine. At the dinner theater, Kim and Douglas were ushered front and center to her table, where she ordered "the usual," which turned out to be a bottle of expensive red wine. The play began. Several actors performed bits and pieces. Then Gig made his entrance. Impeccably dressed and groomed, he cut a dashing figure. He sat down and crossed his legs. A rustle went through the audience as people began to whisper. Some giggled. Gig was barefoot.

"He played the entire play without shoes or socks," says

Douglas, "and Kim never blinked. The cast was terrible, simply terrible, and Gig gave a pretty bad performance. There were times when he looked quite vague and he really didn't seem to know what was going on."

After the final curtain, Kim and Douglas went backstage, and Douglas asked, "Gig, what on earth was that thing without shoes and socks?"

"Oh," he said, "my feet were hurting me tonight."

"Oh, really, that bad?"

"Yes, really," Gig said. "I couldn't walk around in shoes and socks." With that he put on a pair of old sneakers, stood up, and led Douglas and Kim to a restaurant several blocks away.

It was an unpretentious little place, to which Gig obviously came often, because automatically a bottle of red wine arrived at their table. Douglas ordered a beer. Then he attempted to broach the subject of the production, but Gig said they would discuss it later. When the bill came, Gig said to Kim, "Have you got my wallet?"

"Gig, you had it."

Gig was fairly certain he had given it to Kim, and an argument ensued. To avoid a scene, Douglas paid for the dinner. Gig insisted on searching the floor to see whether the billfold might have fallen out of his pocket, but he finally concluded he had been robbed. Back at Gig's suite, speculation over the disappearance of the wallet provided Gig with an excuse to avoid hearing what Douglas thought of his work and the cast's. But as they were talking, Kim, sitting on the sofa, ran her hand between the cushions, pulled out an object, and asked, "Is this what you lost?"

Gig took the wallet and two large pills she had also found and disappeared into the bathroom. When he came back, Douglas again suggested talking about the play. Gig begged off. "Let's think about that tomorrow," he said.

The following morning, the Youngs and Douglas did almost everything but talk about the play. First there was a "holistic" massage for Gig (Douglas refused), then lunch, then another brouhaha over Gig's wallet, which again he'd left back at the hotel room. Douglas lost his patience. He told Gig the production was not worth the worry of recasting and redirecting. He had no interest in producing or directing it. "If you want to go on tour, do *Private Lives.* Small cast. You'd be wonderful. You'd make yourself a fortune. But don't consider coming to Hollywood in this."

Gig was annoyed. "Oh, I don't agree with you at all," Douglas remembers him saying. "I promise you with the proper cast this play will be a big hit in Hollywood and New York."

Douglas informed him that they didn't see eye to eye, and Gig suggested that the director come to see the show that night.

"I saw it last night," Douglas reminded him.

"Well, see it again tonight and reconsider."

In the interest of their friendship, Douglas saw the play again. The only difference was that Gig wore shoes and socks. After the performance, he and Gig and Kim went to the same little place and talked for a long time. Douglas pleaded with his old friend to drop the project. Gig's final words were "No. I think I've got to go on with it."

So on the third morning, Douglas exited the scene. And Gig, hurt and angered by the rebuff, pushed ahead with his plans, determined to show Hollywood and Broadway how unimaginative and wasteful they had been in their squandering of his talent.

Douglas, on the other hand, was clearly worried about his old friend. Here was a guy who had once been one of the best light-comedy actors in the business, someone who'd won an Oscar for a startling dramatic performance. Now he was in kung fu movies—taking over roles in them, for chrissakes—and starring in dinner-theater revivals. Douglas had known Gig for a long time, knew him as someone who'd loved acting, as someone who'd aspired to be the best that he could be. He couldn't believe that Gig was oblivious of the nadir to which he had sunk. But then again, Douglas thought, maybe he was actively making himself oblivious.

On his way back to Los Angeles, Douglas kept remembering an incident that had occurred after Gig had gone to the theater. He and Kim remained at the inn. He had asked to use the bathroom. What he saw there alarmed him. "I'm not exaggerating when I say he had to have had a double table to hold all the pills. All over, all over, were bottles of pills," Douglas emphasizes. "Little bottles. Big bottles. Bottles, bottles, bottles. When I came out of the bathroom, I asked Kim what on earth all the pills were doing there. She said, 'Oh, he's taking a lot of pills. One doctor says one thing, another something else.' I said, 'It's like a joke. It's like a pharmacy.' She brushed aside my remark, saying Gig didn't touch half of them."

As the summer of 1978 came to a close, Gig was obviously in pain. His once-brilliant career was in tatters, he was shuffling around with swollen feet, and he was involved in a mercurial relationship that alternately assuaged and exacerbated those hurts. Earlier that year, before his falling out with Bert Knapp, the vocal teacher was questioning him about his ailments.

"Where exactly does it hurt anyway, Gig?" asked Knapp.

"Everywhere," responded Gig disconsolately. "It hurts everywhere."

·13·

Apartment 1BB

With no role in sight beyond the nebulous national tour of *Nobody Loves an Albatross,* Gig transferred his penchant for make-believe from the stage to his home. Incongruously for a man well into his sixties, the role he chose to play was Romeo.

In a letter home to her parents in early October of 1978, Kim painted a pretty picture of the life she shared with Gig in the apartment at the Osborne: "My office is up on the balcony overlooking the living room. The apartment has 20-foot ceilings so one corner has two levels called a balcony. . . . Gig looks up here and says, 'How's my Juliet?' and I say, 'Just great, Romeo. Couldn't be better.' How romantic."

Less than two weeks later, the bodies of this aging Romeo

245

and his deluded Juliet would be discovered near the spot where, according to Kim, they'd enacted that romantic exchange. Such a gruesome scenario seemed inconceivable, however, as Gig and Kim arrived home from Edmonton on September 12, determined to talk some producer into sponsoring a tour of *Albatross,* despite the reservations of those friends who had trekked northward to see the show.

They were also preoccupied with overseeing renovations on the apartment, which had turned into a nightmare. When Gig returned from Hong Kong back in January, he'd enlisted Archer King to locate a "permanent nest" where he and Kim could settle. King had found the one-bedroom at the Osborne for the modest price of $65,000, but the premises were in extensive need of repair and refurbishing. Gig felt the deal was worthwhile, and at the time of the sale he'd laughed off the request from the former owner to please not disturb "the nice ghosts" that she believed lived there.

Ghosts or no ghosts, the place had begun to haunt him throughout the spring, as the bills mounted for electrical wiring, plumbing, and the installation of a new bathroom, which later had to be torn out and reinstalled properly. New carpeting had to be replaced because unsupervised plasterers had failed to cover it properly with a drop cloth. Costs spiraled to $24,000 for improvements on the modest apartment, and Gig mulled a lawsuit against the original contractor, with whom he'd had a series of nasty and bitter exchanges.

Before leaving for Canada, Kim had persuaded Gig that while they were gone he should lend the apartment to Russell and Hai-Tien Jones, who were spending the summer in New York. No sooner had the Joneses moved in than they began experiencing firsthand what they came to call "the curse" that hung over apartment 1BB.

A few days after taking up residence, the normally robust Jones began developing a series of respiratory and other

flu-like symptoms. Since the only two windows on the premises faced onto an air well and the air-conditioning was
malfunctioning, Jones attributed his illness to poor ventila-
tion.

"It was eerie," says Jones. "The living room had high
cathedral ceilings but no windows at all. So a stained-glass
window, lit from behind to simulate daytime, had been installed against the wall. If the lights were on, you couldn't
tell what time of day it was or what the weather might be
like. It was claustrophobic."

Then one night not long after the Joneses had settled in,
the phone rang. The caller, an old friend of Hai-Tien's, was
the respected Professor Lin Yun, a mystic and a practitioner
of *feng shui*. The ancient art of *feng shui* is controversial,
regarded by some as based on scientific principles and by
others as superstition. Followers believe a person's life is
influenced for good or bad by the layout of buildings, rooms,
and furniture in relation to wind *(feng)* and water *(shui)*.

The Joneses invited Professor Lin over. Shortly after entering the apartment, the professor detected a malevolent
influence and gave Hai-Tien ominous news. "There is very,
very bad luck in here," he said. "It is very bad for the man
of the house." Lin suggested that the bed be repositioned and
that mirrors be installed to refocus certain areas.

Since Jones was reluctant to tamper with their host's
apartment, he and Hai-Tien moved to a hotel, where he
experienced an immediate remission of his mysterious ailments. He wrote Kim and Gig, thanking them for their hos-
pitality and explaining his reason for moving. "The place
really gave me the creeps," he said years later.

Kim, who had spent years in Hong Kong, treated Professor Lin's warning seriously and wanted to follow his instructions. Gig, retaining his Midwestern skepticism, ridiculed
feng shui as hocus-pocus and forbade either changing the
furniture arrangement or installing mirrors. "The irony,"

Hai-Tien later observed, "was that if the mirror had been rearranged as Professor Lin had suggested, then Kim would have been able to see Gig as he pointed the gun at her and perhaps been able to talk him out of it, as she had once done with the rapist who'd broken into her apartment."

A ghost of another sort haunting Gig and Kim's relationship was the irrepressible Harriette Douglas. Harriette continued to believe that the actor was simply going through a phase and would soon return to his senses—and to her. Despite his deepening involvement with Kim, Gig was often on the telephone with Harriette. After purchasing the Osborne co-op earlier that year, Gig had flown back to Los Angeles to sell his Spaulding condo and break to Harriette the news of his engagement to Kim.

Throughout all the ups and downs of the last dozen years, Harriette had held firm to her belief that Gig would never find anyone with whom he was more comfortable than her. No matter what he said, she was not at all convinced that he was terminating their complicated relationship—even when he instructed her to put the condo on the market, send some of the furniture to New York, and get rid of any she didn't want. She maintains that unhappy as she was for herself, she was so certain Kim wouldn't last that she urged Gig to just live with her and "get it out of his system without another costly divorce."

Convinced of the transience of Gig and Kim's relationship, she drove him to the airport for his return to New York. "He was always like a naughty child, but he was so lovable and so lost I could forgive him anything," she later explained. "Anyway, I was sure he'd come back to me. I never dreamed it was the last time I'd ever see him. The bastard. That's what I can't forgive him for."

But Harriette appeared to have lost her composure as Gig

and Kim neared the altar. Kim wrote Judy Washington that Harriette called her constantly, warning her not to marry him. Harriette insisted she only urged Kim to keep Gig away from booze and pills. But Kim maintained that Harriette was threatening to sue to have herself declared Gig's "common-law wife," although he "never legally lived with her."

Other acquaintances claimed Harriette spread stories that Kim was a "militant," although she didn't bother to explain in just what way. "You know, guns!" she would exclaim with some exasperation when she was pressed. She also spread rumors that Kim was "bisexual." Harriette later denied ever saying any of this.

Whatever Harriette was pouring into the ears of friends was probably mixed double for Gig's consumption. Yet it seemed to have no discernible effect on his marital plans. Still, when things went wrong, he always called Harriette to pour out his complaints. As his paranoia grew stronger in later years, Gig had begun to tape conversations—with friends, tradesmen, or business associates. And according to a man who claimed he listened to a taped dialogue with Harriette, Gig appeared to be reassuring her that whether or not he married Kim, their friendship would endure.

In spite of the fact that the issue of marriage had not been resolved, Gig was introducing Kim as his fiancée, in both Edmonton and New York. Yet when a reporter from the New York *Post* inquired of Gig, "Are you still looking?" Gig quipped, "Yes, the other way." And when Kathleen Carroll of the New York *Daily News* persisted in that line of questioning, Gig said, "In view of my previous marital adventures, the only way I'd consider it is if I'm underwritten by the Ford Foundation."

Such levity aside, friends were impressed by Gig and Kim's public show of devotion to each other. Robert and Del Webber dined with the couple at the Russian Tea Room after their return from Edmonton. It was a joyous evening.

Webber remembered how Kim hung on Gig's every word. Both were ebullient. "Now, let's for the sake of argument say they were having a few problems, as some people claim," Webber said in 1987. "I didn't see any indication of it. Okay, they might have hid them during dinner. But surely they wouldn't invite us back to the Osborne for coffee. No, they'd try to end the evening as gracefully as possible. But they did invite us. And after that they walked us back to our hotel. They were ecstatically happy, as far as Del and I could see—and we both knew Gig well."

Even the Joneses, who had initially taken a dim view of Gig, came to accept that for whatever reasons, he and Kim seemed deeply committed to each other. Although there was no real warmth between the two men, Gig was agreeable to seeing the Joneses frequently because he sensed that they diminished Kim's occasional feelings of isolation in a new environment. Once when Kim and Hai-Tien were shopping together in Greenwich Village, Kim had dropped her carefully cultivated facade to admit that she was lonely in New York. "You're the only ones I have," she said. When Hai-Tien responded that she and Gig were going to these wonderful parties, she answered, "Yes, but they're his group."

One evening when Gig and Kim were having dinner with Russell and Hai-Tien, Gig was unusually aloof and moody. Apparently there had been some kind of setback in his campaign to get a producer to send *Albatross* on tour. Attempting to jar him out of his mood, Jones inquired in a jocular tone what was so great about acting anyway. In a flash, Gig leaped up, grabbed Jones by the lapels in a threatening manner, and snarled that he'd show him what was so great about acting. He seemed to have suddenly gone out of control. Everyone at the table became alarmed that Gig was going to hurt Jones. Then, just as abruptly, the actor released Jones and sank back into his chair, smiling at the effect he had created. "That," he announced with satisfaction, "is what is so great about acting."

On September 27, Gig and Kim went down to City Hall for the simplest of wedding ceremonies. Because of a newspaper strike, the event was scarcely noted by the press. Syndicated columnist Earl Wilson (who had been tipped off by a mutual friend) phoned Gig at the Hotel Elysée and found him at the center of a small wedding luncheon. For a presumably happy new bridegroom, he was remarkably subdued. "Don't make a big thing of it" was his surprising request.

Later in the day, Gig and Kim met Elaine Stritch and her husband, John Bay, at a small, out-of-the-way restaurant. The Bays were in town from London. Gig had phoned the day before to say he wanted them to meet his girlfriend. (How he discovered they were in New York, Stritch doesn't know.) Now, as they gathered convivially at a hole-in-the-wall, to avoid anyone they knew, Gig broke the news that he and Kim had married that morning.

"Now, that was cause célèbre," says Stritch. "So the next day we go to *On the Twentieth Century* on Broadway. And we go through a whole thing of Gig deciding whether or not to do a play with Hal Prince. I finally said, 'Why not, you silly asshole? He's wonderful. And he's hotter than a pistol. Do it!' But Gig was afraid. Gig was always afraid. That was Gig's problem. He was always afraid." And he found reasons not to accept the role, if it even existed.

A couple of weeks later, Stritch ran into Bill Harbach on Madison Avenue and mentioned that Gig was in town. Harbach, who hadn't seen him in years, immediately wanted his old friend's number. Stritch gave it to him and reported that Gig and his "darling new wife" had moved into the Osborne and Gig was "getting his life together."

Harbach impulsively rushed over to 205 West 57th Street, where he found Gig and Kim conferring with several workmen, trying to get an oversize refrigerator through the kitchen door. "It was 'Gigger!' and 'Willie!' Big hug," Harbach says.

Gig introduced Harbach to Kim, who, Harbach says, "was this darling German girl, who anybody could see from her adulating looks just worshiped the ground he walked on." Harbach asked the Youngs when they could come to dinner, and Gig said anytime, so Harbach called his wife and set dinner for the following Tuesday.

When Harbach left the apartment, Kim accompanied him for a few blocks, on her way to Bloomingdale's. Harbach told her how glad he was they were in town. Kim thanked him for coming by and then confessed that Gig had been through hell and was trying to get his life back together. "He still feels his career is over, but he's going to try to start on Broadway again and get it in gear," she explained. Harbach agreed, saying, "Gig needs to get back into being the old Gig again." As they parted, Harbach told Kim how pleased he was that Gig seemed to have found happiness at last.

On the appointed evening, Stritch, John Bay, and two other old friends of Gig's, Dina Merrill and Cliff Robertson, were on hand at Bill and his current wife Barbara Harbach's Park Avenue apartment when Kim and a subdued Gig arrived. It was a long-overdue reunion. Everyone seemed to have a ball except Gig. Kim impressed everybody as quiet but delightful. They all noticed how she held Gig's hand and seemed to worship him.

"Barbara cooked dinner, and Stritch was a riot with actress stories," Harbach recalls. "She had me on the floor. Cliff Robertson was screaming. But Gig wasn't his old self. He just sat there politely, giving a little chuckle once in a while."

During the evening, Gig had five or six glasses of red wine—which Harbach worried over since he had heard that Gig was in AA, but since Kim didn't object, Harbach kept his doubts to himself. Still, he kept wondering what had happened to those roars Gig used to let loose.

When Gig and Kim were leaving, Harbach remembers Gig saying, "Goodbye, Willie. It was nice seeing you again." Harbach was struck by the lack of warmth in the farewell.

Later, when Cliff Robertson and Dina Merrill were bidding their hosts good night, Robertson inquired whether Harbach knew what was bothering Gig. They agreed something was amiss but couldn't pinpoint what it was. Years later, Harbach would say, "Well, obviously there was a war going on inside him, but how would anyone know that at that time?"

Judging by his erratic behavior during the last months of his life, the war going on in Gig seemed to be a hit-and-run conflict filled with phantom targets. To Panda Hoffman he seemed in the midst of an emotional breakdown. To the Webbers, the Youngs had been an ebullient loving couple. To those gathered at the Harbachs just weeks later, they were less the picture of happy newlyweds than of a doting young woman worshiping a strangely subdued clone of the fun-loving friend they once had known.

It's not hard to imagine why Gig would have been so depressed at the Harbachs' dinner party. He was surrounded by those who so vividly recalled for him the ripe days of his younger self—his madcap courtship with Stritch, the croquet and cocktail parties when he and Elizabeth Montgomery were part of a world they thought would never end. But it had ended, and so had a career that had then been so full of promise. He was sixty-four years old, and just too tired to trot out the charming facade he'd summoned up so effortlessly for most of his life.

Kim, for her part, kept up the facade in her letters to friends in the Far East and family Down Under. On October 9, she informed her parents that as of September 27, they could refer to her as Mrs. Gig Young. But through the lines one could sense that perhaps all was not right. For a new bride who claimed to be "madly happy," she exuded in her letters an unseemly preoccupation with the "perks" of being a movie star's wife. She expressed disappointment that the newspaper strike had diffused the publicity surrounding their marriage, though the California papers had picked it up. She also hinted at what some people speculated were among the reasons she'd married Gig: "I'm not working (actually haven't even tried). I haven't been to the American Embassy to tell them to stick it up their you know what's, and that they can't throw me out because I'm married and all that now. They don't like single foreign ladies here, believe me. I had nightmares about being deported before we signed the thing."

On October 13, she wrote more ecstatically to Judy Washington that she was perched at her typewriter twenty feet above her living room, amid her baby pictures and dictionaries and behind a wrought-iron railing that stopped her from plunging down into the area below. She apologized for Gig's having refused to allow Judy to stay with them, explaining that he had never gone through the friends-sleeping-on-the-couch phase, as they had. She hoped Judy was still planning to visit New York and promised to find her a good, cheap hotel.

In the letter, Kim went on to say that Gig hadn't worked all year apart from the stint in Edmonton, which "was a drop in the bucket" in relation to what they had spent. In addition, he was depressed about being absent from Hollywood, "much as he hated it," because it made him feel cut off from those who had the power to hire him. She had arranged through Russell Jones to be introduced to people who produced television commercials and was subtly dropping the hint that "Gig Young wouldn't mind doing the 'right' commercial. Hell, everyone else does. $100,000 for one TV commercial without residuals," she wrote. "That way, he wouldn't have to be tempted to do a lousy movie he hated just because we need the money. We're not down to the last $50,000 yet (cash in the bank that is) but at the rate we go through money without even spending any officially, just living, it won't last long. I don't care, but he does."

The truth of the matter was that the money situation was a concern to both of them. With the bills on the apartment beginning to snowball, they were both aware of the tensions a financial crisis could exacerbate. Kim, at least, seemed eager to nip them in the bud so that they wouldn't turn her and Gig into "one of those couples who start yelling at one another at the drop of a hat"—unusual preoccupations for a new bride. In these paragraphs written to Judy Washington, Kim reveals that she was sensitive to the mean streaks in her personality. She had inflicted them on past lovers, but she vowed she was determined to spare Gig.

"He is so considerate and generous and understanding that it has to rub off on me. No more being the moody bitch. I find I can actually stop it and be nice and fun to be around," she wrote. "I have been very selfish in a very hard-to-live-with way with all the past live-in lovers, looking back. It's a wonder anyone stuck around."

Having unburdened herself, she apologized that this had not been a very happy letter and explained that she just wanted to fill her friend in so she could concentrate on her usual "happy rave" next time. And she ended on a note that would take on an eerie quality in retrospect:

This is great weather for walking and looking in shop windows and getting high on fresh, sweet delicious carrot juice, which I am *hooked* on. Gig hasn't had any vodka since I got here in February. We only drink wine, and he looks 10 years younger. He hasn't had a hangover or the guilts the way he always did when he was on the heavy stuff, and his eyes are clear and his skin is young and his hair is thicker and shiny and everything and he's just thrilled. Everyone says he hasn't looked this good in 10 years, and seeing photos, it's true. He says it's funny that all the other women in his life encouraged him to be a closet drinker. He didn't want to drink alone and he couldn't go out, so they had him by the balls. He says being able to drink wine in restaurants with his dinner is the first time he's felt like an adult for 25 years. He always drank only coffee in restaurants and drank when he got home if he felt like it. But he so obviously is not an alcoholic, after I've been watching him with nervous dread for a whole year, that it's a great relief. I drink more vino than he does, for christ's sake. He says what he liked most about drinking was holding the glass and feeling it go down his throat. He says he can do that just as well with wine without getting drunk and he loves it. Jesus Jude, if you knew how happy that made me feel. I love him so much. I want him to last forever. We take about 100 vitamins a day for our brains, bodies, psyches, that we just might.

Forever was six days.

·14·

Flash Point

Gig Young's final days are shrouded in mystery. According to one neighbor, there were loud and nasty arguments emanating from apartment 1BB in the mornings, while later those same days, others reported Gig and Kim to be "lovey-dovey." Could it be that Gig was now starring in a double feature: matinees of *Who's Afraid of Virginia Woolf?* followed by a rather grotesque version of *Romeo and Juliet* at night?

Whatever the couple's respective states of mind were, as their "game of death" kicked into overtime during the week of October 16, 1978, the situation had to have been even more volatile than usual. One of the most mystifying facts to emerge after the deaths was an autopsy report that revealed no barbiturates or alcohol in Gig's system. Only seven Oxazepam tablets, bottles of vitamins, and two bottles of wine were found in the apartment. To those who knew Gig as a heavy drinker and pill-taker, this came as a shock. The theory that he had killed his wife in a drunken or narcotic rage flew out the window, replaced by the more realistic view that the sudden withdrawal had induced psychosis.

Apart from these speculations, Gig's abstemiousness revealed another aspect of his mysterious, often pathetic, self: roughed up by life's vagaries as he may have felt, he intended to start anew, to try and lift himself out of the morass one more time, despite his exhaustion and paranoia. At the beginning of his marriage, he called on the last of his moral reserves to hold at bay the despair that had been so movingly telegraphed in his greatest triumph, *They Shoot Horses, Don't They?* In a tender note, which was found after the shooting and was probably written only a day or two before the tragedy, Gig pours his heart out to his bride. He begs her, challenges her, to join him in patching up a shaky start. "I'll give it all I've got, if you will," he writes pleadingly.

As part of that promise, Gig was apparently willing to throw out the booze and the pill bottles. Kim had made it a personal crusade to wean him from the alcohol that had destroyed her own father and the pills that she felt were interfering with Gig's work. It had become a point of pride to her, a symbol of the control that she'd always tried to exert on the important men in her life.

Gig got another boost of encouragement in that direction from Elaine Stritch, a woman he had never stopped loving, even long after he was *in* love with her. As joyful as it had been to see her again, first on his wedding day and then at Billy Harbach's, it had also been a painful reminder of those carefree and joyous days that now seemed eons away. He felt the loss deeply. Yet he wanted to see her once again and would even risk Kim's disgruntlement at feeling left out.

On Friday the thirteenth, Stritch and Bay received a phone call from Gig, ostensibly to say that he wanted to bid them goodbye before they sailed for England. Sensing by the tone of his voice that he was seriously troubled, Stritch suggested that the two couples have breakfast the next day. Again they met at an out-of-the-way place. Gig showed up without Kim and offered no explanation of her absence. Sensing his distress, Stritch says, she inquired, "Gig, what's the matter?" He said he didn't know. He thought he had it made now, that he loved Kim and everything was terrific, but . . .

When he didn't continue, Stritch said, "But it's not quite right, is it?" Then she told him that he didn't have to fight these feelings alone. She said, "Stop the drama. Go to AA. You're such a nice fellow. Make some friends at AA, because they're the nicest people in the world. They're your kind of people. You and Kim try having dinner two or three nights a week with some guy who's stopped drinking and his wife. Then you'll find out how nice people can be."

There was a feeling of great warmth. "Gig loves John and me," Stritch said. "We love him. Everybody's huggy-huggy. Our boat's sailing next day at six. We agree to meet at four-thirty P.M. We'll have a cup of tea and say goodbye."

Next day comes. Four-thirty comes. No Gig. Five forty-five. Still no Gig. They never saw him again.

Where was Gig on that Sunday before his suicide? No one's quite sure. Nor did Gig and Kim resurface together on Monday. Strangely, he spent part of that day—as he had spent so many days since moving into the Osborne—in the basement of the building. It was an odd place for anybody, especially a newlywed movie star, to hang out. Yet it was there that Gig had often sought out the sympathetic ear of Constas Matsoukas, the building manager. For hours on end, he would settle into a chair in Matsoukas's office and ramble on. With Bert Knapp no longer available, Gig had found a kind man who would listen to his problems without brow-beating or cajoling him.

"He'd talk to me like I was his psychiatrist," said Mat-soukas years later. "I didn't understand half the things he was telling me. I guess I'd seen him in pictures when I was a young man in Greece, but I was a perfect stranger to him, who didn't know anything about him. But he was a nice man, a very, very, very nice man."

In the course of many conversations, Gig told Matsoukas about his life and career. He spoke of his young ambitions, of his beloved sister, Gen, of his idols James Cagney, Cary Grant, and Clark Gable. He laughed at the picture he drew of himself, a hayseed hitchhiker dumped in Culver City, of Bette Davis and Joan Crawford and the thrill of it all. As he spoke, he exhibited regret for all the hopes he never ful-filled, but as James Tyrone had said, it was "a late day for regrets." He thought of the film scripts lying around the den of his apartment—"all that kung fu crap"—and wondered if he'd ever get another chance to create a memorable char-acter on stage or on screen. He reminisced about all the people who'd bucked him up—Mrs. Kaines, Doris Rich, Marty Baum, Helena Sterling—and wondered, "Where are they now?" giving little thought to the fact that it was he who'd walked away from most of them. It was obvious that Hollywood still cast a powerful spell over him, that the re-jection by a business in which he had invested no less than his soul not only hurt him but frightened him as well.

Irrationally, Gig had even become convinced that *They Shoot Horses, Don't They?* had been badly executed, that the director or writers or cast had somehow gotten something wrong. Matsoukas didn't understand what he was talking about, but Gig kept saying something about the wrong per-son being shot or the wrong person doing the shooting in the final scene in which the Jane Fonda character begs the Mi-chael Sarrazin character to put her out of her misery.

Gig also spoke to Matsoukas about his personal relationships. That Monday before he died, he seemed especially
anxious to review his marriages, as if trying to fathom what
had gone wrong between Kim and him. Matsoukas sensed
that a dark cloud was hanging over the Youngs.

Gig spoke warmly and lovingly of Sophie Rosenstein and
Elaine Stritch, the only two women whom he had ever really
loved. He stammered and his eyes filled with tears as he
recalled Sophie's untimely death. He talked endlessly of the
foolish mistakes he had made with women. Elizabeth Montgomery had been spoiled, he told Matsoukas, and Elaine
Young had used him. He had been such a patsy. The very
thought of Elaine curdled his stomach, and he refused to
talk about Jennifer at all. "You know, if a marriage is not
ideal," he told Matsoukas, "the quicker it's dissolved, the
better for all concerned."

Matsoukas wondered if he might have been talking about
his three-week-old marriage. "My gut feeling is she married
him because he was Gig Young," he says. "She was trying to
get into Hollywood, she loved the parties, the publicity. He
was trying to get out of all that. He wanted to stay home, to
do a play in New York. They were going in opposite directions."

As Matsoukas pointed out, Kim was indeed concerned
about fame, more specifically about the publicity surrounding her marriage to Gig Young. Among her set in Hong
Kong, she had been known as terrifically ambitious, as
someone who had set her sights on making it in America. In
a letter to Judy Washington shortly after the marriage, she
wrote that she had bought a movie magazine on an outing
to Central Park. "I looked at the pictures first in case I was
in it since we got married two weeks ago, but no," she confessed. It may well have been just the understandable giddi-
ness of a thirty-one-year-old woman eager to see her name
and picture in print. But her public avowals of love and

devotion to her new husband might have seemed more sincere had she written that she'd looked in the magazine "to see if *we* were in it."

The importance of publicity to Kim was driven home on Wednesday of that fateful week when she bumped into Sy Presten, a public relations man whom she'd met the night before. She hailed him with a friendly greeting and then, to his surprise, she blurted out, "I'm so disappointed that my marriage to Gig didn't make *Time*'s 'Milestones' column. Being in publicity, is there anything you can do?"

Presten was taken aback by the request. On the previous evening, Roz Starr, who clocks the comings and goings of celebrities and books them on television shows, for charity affairs, and on cruise ships, had taken the Youngs and Presten out to dinner at La Verte Galante, a Manhattan restaurant well suited to people-watching. Gig and Kim presented the image of high-spirited, happy newlyweds. A publicity break seemed the farthest thing from their minds. Presten, who had not met either previously, found them an effusive, affectionate couple given to quick little love pecks. Roz felt then and continued to feel that they seemed "all wrapped up in one another."

During dinner, Roz offered to set up a free honeymoon cruise, to originate in the port of their choice. Their only obligation would be that they mingle with the other passengers and that sometime during the holiday Gig would spend forty-five minutes entertaining the guests with tales of his Hollywood years. The accommodations would be deluxe. Gig would be paid a three-thousand-dollar fee. Kim was ecstatic about the prospective trip. She loved such perks, and as the new Mrs. Gig Young, she expected them. Gig glowed with excitement but delayed committing himself; he said he was awaiting a meeting about a play in which he hoped to star.

By the time Roz and Presten dropped Gig and Kim at the

Osborne, that instant intimacy that people in entertainment often nurture had blossomed, and plans were set to celebrate the Youngs' first monthly anniversary on the twenty-seventh. As the foursome talked, Gig and Kim snuggled close to each other. But when the car started to move away, Kim turned abruptly and entered the building while Gig waved at the departing automobile. Their body language seemed inconsequential at the time, but in the light of what was to occur, it raises doubts regarding the show of affection. Both Gig and Kim were adept players. Gig knew instinctively what the public expected from him, especially after so recent a march down the aisle. And Kim had a reputation among those who knew her as someone who, once the spotlight was on her, could jump in a second from tack-spitting shrew to cooing tie-straightener.

There now seems little doubt that once they were inside the Osborne, the facade dropped to expose a couple wondering if somehow everything had been a terrible mistake. Kim, in her last letters, remained buoyant and positive about her new life in New York. But to Judy Washington, she confided that she now had to contend with a husband who was desperately anxious about his career and their precarious finances. Moreover, he waxed more and more paranoid about aging, often asking Kim to pluck the hair from his ears and studying his ravaged face in the mirror to see if it could stand one more tuck. He also worried constantly about satisfying her sexual needs.

Gig had been intermittently impotent since his involvement with Skye Aubrey during the late sixties. Alcohol and fear of aging were part of the problem. According to Judy Washington, Kim was well aware of Gig's problems when she married him. "He was worried about the sexual aspect," says Judy, "because she mentioned it again in the letter that I received after she died. But she really convinced him that she didn't care about all that. They could love each other without the completely sexual part, to put it delicately. Sex was very secondary to Kim anyway."

Nonetheless, the police found sexually explicit magazines in the apartment and, according to Detective Richard Chartrand, Polaroid photographs of Gig and Kim in various erotic positions that were taken with an automatic timing device. The detective said he made sure they didn't fall into the wrong hands. "It wasn't something I'd never seen before," he says. "Gig probably was using the books and photos to see if he could try to get something cooking. Maybe he's impotent, but the man's got himself a new young wife, and he's trying to keep up with her. He's off booze and drugs and pounding down vitamins like they're going out of style. It's an entirely different ball game."

While the sexual problem could have been an injudicious but tempting weapon for Kim to use in the *Who's Afraid of Virginia Woolf?* games that may have heated up that week, it probably wasn't the immediate cause of the icy standoff that developed between the couple. Money was a much likelier culprit.

Kim understandably sought financial security. After all, she had given up publishing "The Quorum" and building a career as a movie publicist to take care of him and help get his career on track. She was aware that Gig was not rich, and she was prepared to live in a modest apartment, do her own housework, and even learn to cook. Nonetheless, she crowed in her letters home about the presents from her husband: a midcalf-length mink, designer clothes, and pricey jewelry. She yearned to be part of the beautiful people, and these were the accessories. And if Gig's friends took little effort to remember her name when she met them, as she complained to Bert Knapp before his and Gig's falling out, it was only because, as Knapp had told her: "You haven't earned their attention."

Indeed, Kim was anxious to prove herself a good business

partner and help generate income. She'd taken it upon herself to find Gig a commercial, and it was in connection with
those dealings, apparently, that she missed a Wednesday
lunch date. At least that is the excuse Gig gave his good
friends Don Kingman and his wife, as Kim kept them waiting at the Museum of Modern Art. The Chinese artist, who
had found Kim especially simpatico because of her interest
in painting, had invited the couple to lunch, after which he
intended to guide Kim through the museum.

At the appointed hour, Gig appeared, telling the Kingmans that his wife would be along any minute. As they
waited in the lobby, Gig chattered compulsively. Finally, at
two-thirty, it was mutually agreed that something had happened to detain Kim, and the lunch was canceled. Gig apologized profusely, saying that she must have gotten her
appointments mixed up. "Bless her, she's trying to meet people to get me a television commercial." He laughed, then he
hurried off toward the Osborne.

The Kingmans were the last friends to see Gig alive.

The next twenty-four hours were a crucible of the insecurity, sexual rage, and despair that sixty-four years of
living had funneled into the man born Byron Ellsworth
Barr. A contretemps over Gig's last will and testament—an
argument that was about to be rendered moot with tragic
irony—apparently brought matters to a head.

Just before Gig and Kim had left for Edmonton, Canada,
he'd drafted a new will, for an estate that would later be
valued at $200,000. As Kim had written to her parents, Gig
had left half of everything to her and the other half to his
sister, Gen. Gig provided further for "my friend" Harriette
Douglas, in the form of a $7,500 bequest. For Jennifer, he left
only ten dollars, a legal technicality so that the will could not
be contested. Graciously, he added: "I would be very happy
if Mr. and Mrs. Martin Baum would accept my Oscar ... that
I won because of Martin's help."

Kim's initial reaction was one of gratitude. She felt secure. But shortly after the marriage, according to Harriette Vine Douglas, Gig was disturbed by what he believed were subtle pressures Kim began applying to get him to change his will. There were sharp telephone exchanges regarding the subject between Harriette and her. Gen, whom Gig named as a major heir in all of his wills, noticed that Kim's attitude toward her had become aloof and resentful. She later said she could understand Kim's resentment at having to share Gig's estate with her.

Gig brushed aside attempts to discuss possible changes, but Kim was persistent. According to Harriette Douglas, Gig called her on the Tuesday before the fateful Thursday to complain that Kim had presented him with a revised version of his will. In it, both Harriette and his beloved sister had been cut out and the entire estate went to Kim. He had refused to sign.

Kim had retaliated with an impenetrable barrier of silence, broken only occasionally with a snappish remark that Gig referred to as a "zap." As Kim had pointed out in a letter to Judy Washington, she had used this icy reproach many times before in her relationships with men. Her resolve to no longer be the "moody bitch," as she put it, apparently went out the window at Gig's refusal to change the will.

Yet while other men had either yielded to or dumped Kim when confronted with her freeze, she made a major miscalculation in attempting to force the hand of someone in Gig's condition. Under the best of circumstances, he was a gentle but frightened man when it came to women. Under the duress of withdrawal from both sedatives and alcohol, his nerves were even more ragged than usual. Friends also concluded that he had had very little sleep during those last nights, as it had been his habit to take "five or six sleeping pills a night," according to Harriette Douglas.

By Wednesday night, Gig was a man at the end of his

tether. As Kim moved around the apartment, provoking him with the occasional "zap" or monosyllabic answer, she must have seemed more and more of a stranger to him—a hostile stranger, at that, shutting him out, ignoring his attempts at reconciliation. He apparently came to the conclusion that he had made a desperate error in marrying her. Yet he couldn't stand the idea of being ridiculed for having foolishly allowed himself to be taken again.

He once again phoned Harriette Douglas in Los Angeles, and in a taped conversation that Constas Matsoukas claims to have heard after Gig's death, he told his old friend of the power struggle between him and Kim and begged Harriette to come and take him back to Hollywood. He was apprehensive and humiliated about the break with Kim, but if he had Harriette's support, he felt he could get through it.

Egged on by her friends, who felt that Gig was simply using her, Harriette says she chose this moment to stand up for herself. She assured him that she would always be there for him, but, knowing him, she would not run the risk of coming to New York and being publicly embarrassed if he and Kim impulsively reconciled.

Before hanging up, Gig once more asked Harriette whether she wouldn't reconsider coming to get him. When she refused, he bade her goodbye. She had, she says, no inkling she would never speak to him again.

"Of all the times for me to take a stand," Harriette says. "It's too bad I didn't say to him, 'Get your ass on a plane. Don't go back for a coat. Don't go back for a cup of coffee. Don't go back for anything. I'll meet you at the airport.'"

But Harriette said none of those things. And as Gig hung up the phone on Wednesday night, he must have felt abandoned and alone. All his life, as Bert Knapp had once caustically pointed out to him, he had "run home to mommy." Gig had always been unwilling to face the darkness alone. Now they were freezing him out—Bert Knapp, Kim, Harriette. In

a way, Gig was still very much the little boy running around
in the pools of light that dispelled the dark outside his home
in St. Cloud and yelling, "Is enny-bodee home? Is enny-bodee
home?" And the answer, this late in life, was chilling.

From all outward appearances, October 19 seemed a very
ordinary day for the occupants of apartment 1BB. Early on,
as the doorman at the Osborne recalled, Gig had called and
asked about the weather. He gave the impression that he
was dressing and was about to rush out for an appointment.
Still, he never left the apartment. Some time later, Kim telephoned the Grenoble market and placed an order for $23.30
worth of groceries.

Yet at some point on this very ordinary Thursday, Gig
slid open a secret panel he had had built into a hidden cabi-
net and withdrew a .38-caliber Smith & Wesson from a
fleece-lined case. At his request, Harriette had sent this and
three other guns along with the California furniture to Gig's
New York apartment. Since his trip to Lake Arrowhead with
Harriette and her husband, he had become an aficionado of
guns, taking up target practice, keeping his firearms in spe-
cially constructed cases.

That Thursday, perhaps Gig's intention when he took out
the gun was simply to polish it. But holding it in his hands,
he must have felt some sort of empowerment after the particularly brutal drubbing he had taken both personally and
professionally. In retrospect, that *Nobody Loves an Albatross* should be the title of his last play was almost as fitting
as *The Game of Death* as the name of his last movie.

It's impossible to determine the exact flash point that
caused Gig to aim the gun at Kim and fire the fatal shot. But
the police noted that the murder had all the earmarks of an
impulsive act. Was it simply a psychotic episode brought on
by withdrawal, or was it a massive nervous breakdown? Was

Kim simply at the wrong place at the wrong time, or did she in some way provoke him into shooting her?

Soon after the investigation of the crime was completed, Lieutenant Gallagher studied the evidence and formed his own scenario of what occurred in apartment 1BB around 2:30 P.M. His theory of what had incited the final incident was manipulation. Kim had used Gig to get to America, and now she was planning to walk out on him.

"Things had been rocky since the marriage," he says, setting up the situation. "Now there's a final confrontation. She confirms what he probably has always been afraid of. She tells him something like, 'I married you. I'm Mrs. Gig Young now. I'm an American citizen. I don't need you to stay in this country. I can go back to work. My old boyfriend always wanted to hire me as a publicist. Somebody else will hire me. I'm good at it. So I don't need you financially. I certainly don't need you sexually. We've been married three weeks, and you couldn't even get up to bat.'

"And now, from his point of view," continues Gallagher, "he thinks of his having to go back to the Hollywood crowd and take the needling: 'Hey, Gig couldn't hit the curve ball, huh? Three weeks and you couldn't get up to bat!' Finally, he's had enough. She starts to take a walk. He says, 'Oh, no you don't. You're not going to do this to me, baby. You're not going to pull this crap on me. You've used me. You're not going to use me again.' Boom!"

Certainly there is a basis for Gallagher's theory. Gig had shown himself to be a timid man who repressed his rage, especially when directed against women, only for it to resurface later, disproportionately.

Indeed, it could be argued that Kim was the unfortunate scapegoat for all the crimes—real and imagined—that Gig felt women had perpetrated against him. Gig's experiences of the opposite sex had veered between the maternal tenderness he got from women like Sophie Rosenstein and what he felt was the betrayal by Elaine Young. Cut to the quick, Gig had never recovered from the ugly public spectacle of his third divorce and his nonpaternity suit, and he may well have feared another such debacle with Kim.

A man who had so often passively endured whatever life dished out to him may have finally decided to take fate into his own hands in the form of a .38 Smith & Wesson. There were other ways of "getting up to bat" for the psychologically maimed. Boom!

Having killed her, Gig then turned the gun on himself. There couldn't have been much of a conflict about it. All that he had fought to achieve in his life could not end with his being led off in handcuffs through a blizzard of popping flashbulbs, newspaper headlines, and a trial, where he would be forced to sit in court day after day to be stared at, whispered about, and pitied.

As a halo of red spread out around his wife's head, it must have been with a feeling of resignation that he placed the gun in his mouth and "sucked the metal nipple," as the police call it.

In his hand was the solution to answers that had eluded him all his life. He had tried to find salvation on the silver screen, but the euphoria of winning an Oscar had only made the subsequent decline more humiliating. Drugs and alcohol and five wives had blunted, but not dispelled, his aching loneliness. Sitting in apartment 1BB, Gig Young was old, tired, spent. He must have welcomed the oncoming dark.

Later that day, the phone rang in the stateroom of John Bay and Elaine Stritch as the *Queen Elizabeth 2* steamed toward Southampton. The line popped and crackled, but Elaine could make out Billy Harbach's voice on the other end.

"Elaine, I have something to tell you."

Stritch prepared herself for some joke. She imagined that the gang was all at P.J. Clarke's and had decided to call her. She could see them now, all soused, telling bar lies and joking around. She was sure that Gig was going to get on the phone and make up a whopper as to why he hadn't seen them off. "Yes," she said with anticipation. "You're now coming in loud and clear."

"Elaine, Gig shot himself," said Harbach.

"Well," said Elaine numbly. "How is Kim?"

"Well, he shot her too."

Elaine dropped the phone and sat on the bed, with her face in her hands, feeling as though she were in a B movie. Would somebody please yell, "Cut!" she thought, before she began to sob.

The newspaper strike kept the screaming headlines about the murder-suicide down to a minimum in New York, but ironically, Kim and Gig made *Time* magazine's "Milestones" after all:

Died: Gig Young, 60 [*sic*], handsome, smooth-tongued actor whose portrayal of a cynical, whiskey-voiced dance M.C. in "They Shoot Horses, Don't They?" earned him an Oscar in 1970; by his own hand, after apparently shooting and killing his fifth wife, Kim Schmidt, 31, three weeks after their marriage; in Manhattan. . . .

Back in Los Angeles, after persuading Gig's sister, Gen, to allow her to fly to New York to identify the body and represent the family, Harriette Douglas flung the magazine across the room. She burst into tears. At the last moment,

Gen had refused to allow her to bring Gig back to Los Angeles, insisting that his body be sent to the family plot in Waynesville, North Carolina.

Harriette's psychiatrist had asked her, "How do you like that bastard? He killed himself and he killed that little girl. Doesn't that make you angry?"

"No," she replied, "it doesn't make me angry. The man painted himself into a corner where he killed her and then turned around and killed himself. How could I get mad at that poor sick son of a bitch?"

"You know," said Detective Chartrand, who has spent a long career dealing with murders and suicides, "to this day, I avoid looking at Gig Young movies when they're on television. I don't know why. It's probably because I can still see him lying on the floor in a pool of blood. It just doesn't jibe with that smooth charmer on the screen."

Selected Filmography

1954 *Young at Heart*—Doris Day, Frank Sinatra, Ethel Barrymore

1955 *The Desperate Hours*—Martha Scott, Arthur Kennedy

1957 *Desk Set*—Spencer Tracy, Katharine Hepburn, Joan Blondell

1958 *Teacher's Pet*—Doris Day, Clark Gable (Gig's second Oscar nomination)

The Tunnel of Love—Doris Day, Richard Widmark, Elizabeth Fraser

1959 *Ask Any Girl*—Shirley MacLaine, David Niven

The Story on Page One—Rita Hayworth, Anthony Franciosa

1962 *That Touch of Mink*—Doris Day, Cary Grant, Audrey Meadows

Kid Galahad—Elvis Presley, Lola Albright, Charles Bronson

Five Miles to Midnight—Sophia Loren, Tony Perkins

1963 *For Love or Money*—Mitzi Gaynor, Kirk Douglas

1964 *Strange Bedfellows*—Rock Hudson, Gina Lollobrigida

1968 *The Shuttered Room*—Carol Lynley, Oliver Reed, Flora Robson

1969 *They Shoot Horses, Don't They?*—Jane Fonda, Michael Sarrazin (won Oscar as best supporting actor)

1970 *Lovers and Other Strangers*—Bea Arthur, Anne Jackson, Cloris Leachman

1974 *Bring Me the Head of Alfredo Garcia*

1978 *The Game of Death*—Bruce Lee

Index

275